DIGITAL GAMES AND LEARNING

In recent years, there has been growing interest in the use of digital games to enhance teaching and learning at all educational levels, from early years through to lifelong learning, in formal and informal settings. The study of games and learning, however, takes a broader view of the relationship between games and learning, and has a diverse multi-disciplinary background.

Digital Games and Learning: Research and Theory provides a clear and concise critical theoretical overview of the field of digital games and learning from a cross-disciplinary perspective. Taking into account research and theory from areas as varied as computer science, psychology, education, neuroscience, and game design, this book aims to synthesise work that is relevant to the study of games and learning. It focuses on four aspects of digital games: games as active learning environments, games as motivational tools, games as playgrounds, and games as learning technologies, and explores each of these areas in detail.

This book is an essential guide for researchers, designers, teachers, practitioners, and policy makers who want to better understand the relationship between games and learning.

Nicola Whitton works as a Senior Research Fellow at Manchester Metropolitan University. She holds a doctorate in the use of educational games for learning and her research focuses on the relationship between games, play and learning. More broadly, her research interests encompass learning and teaching innovation and the use of rich media and technology for learning.

Digital Games and Learning

Series Editors Sara de Freitas and Paul Maharg

Online Gaming and Playful Organization by Harald Warmelink

DIGITAL GAMES AND LEARNING

Research and Theory

Nicola Whitton

Routledge
Taylor & Francis Group

NEW YORK AND LONDON

First published 2014
by Routledge
711 Third Avenue, New York, NY 10017

and by Routledge
2 Park Square, Milton Park, Abingdon, Oxon OX14 4RN

Routledge is an imprint of the Taylor & Francis Group, an informa business

Library of Congress Cataloging in Publication Data
Whitton, Nicola.
Games and learning : research and theory / Nicola Whitton.
pages cm. — (Digital games and learning)
Includes bibliographical references and index.
1. Computer games—Research. 2. Learning. I. Title.
GV1469.15.W52 2014
794.8—dc23
2013032634

ISBN: 978-0-415-62938-6 (hbk)
ISBN: 978-0-415-62939-3 (pbk)
ISBN: 978-0-203-09593-5 (ebk)

Typeset in Bembo
by RefineCatch Limited, Bungay, Suffolk, UK

Printed in Great Britain by TJ International Ltd, Padstow, Cornwall

For Anne Smith, mentor and friend, sorely missed.

CONTENTS

LIST OF FIGURES

LIST OF TABLES

ACKNOWLEDGEMENTS

I would like to thank everyone who has supported me while writing this book.

In particular I would like to thank Simon Brookes, Nick Bunyan, Mark Childs, Simon Grey, Thomas Hainey, J. Tuomas Harviainen, Paul Hollins, Rosie Jones, Alex Moseley, Katie Piatt and Andrew Walsh for their feedback and insights.

Special thanks go also to Peter Whitton for his ongoing support, critical eye and artistic skills, and to Sue Beasley for her fine editorial skills.

Grateful thanks also go to Sara de Freitas, Paul Maharg and Harry Torrance for their support of this project.

SERIES EDITORS' INTRODUCTION

Sara de Freitas and Paul Maharg

While clearly the use of games for supporting education is not new, the use of digital games is comparatively recent. With the emergence of web-based services, increased broadband and the growth of online communities, the use of digital games presents us with a unique set of engaging tools and techniques, based upon game mechanics such as competition, narrative, missions and quests.

Increasingly games are being seen not as a technology but as a cultural form with its own genres, be they casual games played by everyone, serious games played to learn and engage or gamification whereby game elements are used to reach new audiences. Games offer us new toolsets that can be used effectively in activities as wide-ranging as therapy, awareness-raising or marketing as well as more conventional curricula. The versatility of digital games to be applied to any problem or challenge has gained games a new cultural status that they did not have previously. Digital educational games seek to inform, educate and motivate learners and to extend the range of our ability to learn in classrooms by making the world our classroom and by putting social interaction rather than curriculum objectives at the centre of the learner's experience.

Game science is evolving, too, and game mechanics are just beginning to transform education and how it is produced and how learning is assessed, with real potential for providing just-in-time learning and supporting hard-to-reach learner groups. However, the growth and spread of digital games in educational contexts is still relatively in its infancy and the best methods for developing, assessing and deploying these approaches are also in their earliest stages of advancement. This book series thus aims, primarily, to bring existing game theory and practices together to support the ongoing development of game science as a sub-disciplinary and cross-disciplinary academic body of evidence, as a methodology of investigation, and as a set of tools and approaches, methods and frameworks for learning.

While game science has the power to transcend normal silos of disciplines, the academic communities in different disciplines and in different continents have had too few opportunities to work as an interdiscipline, in part because the field is so new and research has been taking place in such diverse disciplinary, sectoral and international contexts. This book series therefore specifically aims to build bridges between diverse research, teaching, policy and learner communities and is inspired by the next generation of young researchers currently completing their early studies in the field. Towards this end, the series brings together leading theorists, thinkers and practitioners into a community of practice around the key themes and issues of digital games and learning. These theorists come from areas as diverse as health and well-being, business and innovation, education, computer science and engineering to name a few. Their perspectives include views from professional practice as well as from theoretical perspectives.

It is important not to underestimate the scale of the work ahead in this new field, but it is also important to recognise the power of these new tools beyond our current understanding of what they can do or will do in the future. Games will always be a central part of early-stage learning, but now the capability of games to save lives, to inform citizens and to contribute positive outcomes socially is just beginning to be understood. We have always understood the power of games to entertain: this series shows us scientifically how the power of play can be harnessed for more profound purposes, more altruistic reasons in new forms of sustainable and scalable education. *Digital Games and Learning* will explore the lineaments of the new learning, and will reveal how and in what contexts that learning will take shape.

Professor Sara de Freitas, Coventry University, Coventry, UK
Professor Paul Maharg, The Australian National University,
Canberra, Australia
June 2013

PART 1

Introduction

1

OVERVIEW

This book provides a starting point for anyone with an interest in the relationship between digital games and learning, who wants to gain an overview of the most up-to-date research and theory in the field. In this book, I aim to create a case for why computer games provide such an exciting and pedagogically robust way of learning, as well as highlighting their potential pitfalls. I am a passionate advocate of the use of games and play in learning, for all ages, in formal and informal contexts, so I apologise in advance if I come across as a little over zealous at times; I have aimed throughout to temper my enthusiasm by the research evidence that is available in the field. However, I strongly believe that games – digital and traditional – can provide a way in which to move the focus of our schools, colleges and universities to more active, experiential and student-centred models of teaching, learning and assessment. Of course, computer games are not appropriate in every situation, they will not appeal to all learners, they will not appeal to all teachers, and they certainly will not be suitable for every type of educational content, but I believe that the use of games, gaming elements and playfulness provides a different way to think about how, when and what we learn.

This book is about games and learning, and the four core parts are structured around the reasons why digital games facilitate learning – the ideas that: 1) games instigate active learning; 2) they create motivation; 3) they allow for meaningful play; and 4) they act as learning technologies. In the four central parts of this book, each of these areas is considered in turn, bringing together related research and theory from the field of game-based learning as well as associated areas such as computer science, psychology, interaction design, game design, game studies and education. As well as providing a theoretical overview, I provide a critique and synthesis based on my own knowledge and experience. Of course, in a single short book I shall, out of necessity, explain only briefly some of the detail and nuances of the theories and research that I discuss, as I hope to provide a broad overview of the field of games and learning as a whole, and I would encourage readers to explore the works cited here in more detail where they are of particular interest.

Digital Games and Learning: Theory and Research is intended for researchers, practitioners, teachers, academics, trainers and others in the fields of learning and game studies, essentially anyone who is interested in developing a broad theoretical grounding in the subject. My previous books (see Whitton, 2010a; Whitton & Moseley, 2012) have concentrated on the practical aspects of using games for learning, and this one aims to redress the balance by focusing more on the theoretical. Having made that claim, I still hope that this book will have practical value in terms of stimulating ideas and debate within the field, and will be accessible to a wide range of readers. Getting the most from this book will depend very much on the preferences and motivations of the reader. It can be read from cover to cover to get a complete overview, but it is designed so that it can be accessed as six separate parts, each covering a different perspective on games and learning, with the four core parts each containing three chapters looking at different topics within the part. My aim is that the material in this book can be accessed and understood at both a part and chapter level, so can be accessed depending on the preferences of the reader.

Scoping the Field

In this book, I have purposefully avoided using the term 'game-based learning' in preference to the phrase 'games and learning' because I feel that the second term is broader and more inclusive of the ideas that I am exploring here. In the context of this book, there are (at least) eight different ways in which the idea of games and learning can be interpreted.

1. Learning *with* entertainment games. The use and explicit re-purposing of games that were originally designed for pure entertainment, in an educational setting (e.g. school, university, workplace). This includes high-budget professional games – referred to as commercial-off-the-shelf (COTS) as well as non-commercial, hobbyist and low-budget games.
2. Learning *with* educational games. The use of games developed with the express purpose of learning in an educational setting. This can be games that were designed by commercial organisations for learning as well as bespoke games created by enthusiastic individuals or as part of development projects.
3. Learning *inspired* by games. Using games as a context for learning, but not learning about the game directly, for example, using chess as a stimulus for designing algorithms.
4. Learning *within* games. The analysis and consideration of the informal learning that happens while games are played for entertainment.

5. Learning *about* games. Taking the perspective that games are cultural artefacts and studying them as such.
6. Learning *from* games. Analysis of the design principles that are embedded within many games, and considering how these principles could be applied to learning situations.
7. Learning *through* game creation. Learning that takes place during the process of design, development and creation of games.
8. Learning *within* game communities. Understanding about the groups and communities of practice, both online and real world, which develop around games, and the collaborative and supportive learning activities that take place within these groups.

Throughout the book, I draw on this range of perspectives on games and learning to describe what I believe is a holistic overview of the field. I also intentionally do not focus on any particular area of formal education, but draw on the breadth of research into games and learning from early years, through primary and secondary schooling to further and higher education; I also include informal learning, learning that takes place at work and learning that takes place through the whole of life into retirement and throughout later life.

Background

Researchers, theorists and philosophers have spent years discussing the definition of a 'game', with whole books being devoted to creating a definition (e.g. Suits, 1978) in which definitional problems relating to the multi-faceted nature of games are explored (e.g. Wittgenstein, 1958). Therefore, to try to explore the range of definitional discussions within a short book section would be a difficult undertaking, and I am not going to attempt it here (an excellent overview can be found in Egenfeldt-Nielsen, Smith, & Tosca, 2008). In the field of games and learning, I do not believe that debating the exact definition of a 'game' is of primary importance because what is of interest is the value of an activity in the context of learning, not whether or not it adheres to a strict definition of a game. However, to enter into any meaningful exploration of an object, it is important to have an explicit understanding of the topic under study, so I propose the following definition of a 'game' for the purposes of this book (Huizinga, 1955; Salen & Zimmerman, 2004; based on the ideas of Suits, 1978).

In the context of this book, a game is:

* a *challenging activity*;
* structured with *rules, goals, progression* and *rewards*;
* *separate from the real world*;
* undertaken with a *spirit of play*.

In addition, games are:

• often played with, or against, *other people*.

By a challenging activity, I mean a task that is non-trivial and involves doing something difficult and meaningful. Rules, goals, progression and rewards (tangible, such as prizes or intangible, such as satisfaction) are the basic structural elements of games. The idea of a game being distinct from the real world, and taking place in a separate play space is an important one; games provide a safe alternate space in which 'real-world' rules and normal behaviour do not apply. This means that they can, in theory at least, provide safe spaces for experimentation and mistake-making in an environment that is stress-free and where the consequences do not matter outside of the game space. Games, in this context, are inherently playful, undertaken with a lightness of spirit, with scope for exploration and creativity and having fun. Of course, this raises the question about the appropriateness of play in the context of learning, particularly formal education, and this is discussed later on in the book (in Chapter 9). Finally, games are often – but not always – played with other people, either in real time or asynchronously, which highlights the importance of the social dynamics of games in the context of learning.

I have tried here not to dwell on the issue of 'what is a game?' but to provide a straightforward working definition that will apply to the vast majority of games applied in learning contexts. Of course, there are examples of activities that are typically described as games (for instance, simple games of chance like *Snakes and Ladders* that offer little challenge, or professional sports, which are deadly serious for many) that fall outside of this definition. A problem with any usable definition of games is that it will often exclude common, accepted everyday uses of the term, but I believe that this ambiguity is simply something that we have to accept if we are to avoid coming to a definitional standstill, or creating a definition that is so over-complex that it is meaningless in practice.

This book focuses primarily on digital games (although much of its content will be equally relevant to non-digital and traditional games). By digital games, I mean games that are played on, or use, an electronic device. This includes arcade video games, computer games played on desktop or laptop machines, video games played on consoles, or mobile devices such as phones and tablets. It includes games that are played wholly on an electronic device, as well as those that take place in the real world in additional to the digital, for example games using augmented reality, or digital treasure hunting such as geocaching. It includes 'traditional' models of digital game, such as first-person shooters or adventure games, along with more recent game developments, such as casual games and social network games. It includes games played alone by a single individual, those played online or in the real world by small groups, to massively multiplayer games, such as role playing or alternate reality games.

As well as being about games and learning, this is a book about theory and research. By 'theory' I mean the abstract ways in which substantiated ideas and processes have been conceptualised and articulated; by 'research' I mean the evidence that has been generated through investigation into the field. While some scholars argue that theory is unhelpful because it is an overused and ill-defined term, uncritically lauded in itself, which propagates misrepresentations of reality (e.g. Thomas, 2007), for me, theory is about trying to better understand the complexities of the world, and the multiple perspectives that lie within it. It is not simply trying to explain or predict, but a tool with which to explore the different ways in which the world might be conceived. In this respect, theory is an abstraction of reality, or rather an abstraction of many different realities, but I do not see that, in itself, as problematic. The issue for me is about how we use theory, or what we believe it can do for us, not in the very idea of theory itself. Theory is a way of abstracting, of simplifying, of challenging, of offering differing perspectives, of representing in different terms and of providing a basis upon which to critically interrogate a phenomenon. Theory is not just a way of understanding 'what is', but a starting point for considering 'what might be' and 'what should be'.

Games and learning is a multidisciplinary field, bringing together disciplines as diverse as cultural studies, game design, computing, psychology, education and sociology. The multiple perspectives offered by these areas are one of the exciting aspects of the field, but also one of its challenges. Salen and Zimmerman (2004) call for the establishment of a critical discourse for game design, and highlight that a critical disciplinary vocabulary lets us "share ideas and knowledge, and in doing so, expands the borders of our emerging field" (p. 2). I believe that this is also true for games and learning, and it is the aim of this book to capture and begin to establish this critical vocabulary for the field of games and learning.

Book Structure

Games and Learning: Research and Theory is broken down into six parts; the book starts with an overview and introduction to the field. Second, there are parts for the four core themes, each focusing on one of four conceptions of games for learning: games as active learning environments; games as motivational tools; games as playgrounds; and games as educational techno-logies. Figure 1.1 below provides a graphical representation of these four conceptions of games and learning that provide the main structure for this book, and shows the ideas that are discussed in each part. Finally, the concluding part of the book examines the future for games and learning as a discipline.

This introductory part of the book aims to provide the reader with an outline of the field, an overview of the book as a whole and an examination of some of

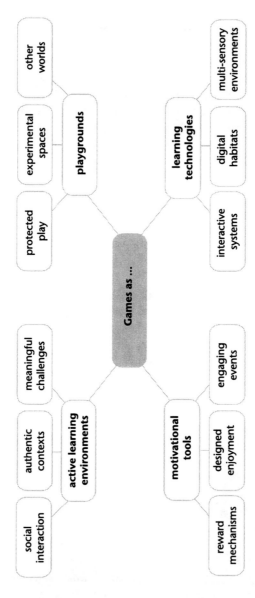

FIGURE 1.1 Perspectives on games and learning, and overview of the book structure

the key questions and evidence in relation to games and learning. It contains two chapters:

- *Chapter 1: Overview.* This introduces some of the key definitions and concepts, and the structure of the book.
- *Chapter 2: Evaluating digital games for learning* considers the rationales for games as tools for learning, and discusses the ways in which research is carried out in the field, the methods of evaluating the educational value of games, and the evidence base for games as effective learning tools.

The second part of the book, *Games as active learning environments*, highlights the first benefit of games for learning: the way that games can create constructivist learning environments in which players learn-by-doing from interaction with the game and the other players. In the context of learning, games are exciting because they are all about action and interaction, rather than passively watching or listening. Games require players to be more than spectators, and take part in the game in an active way. This part of the book explores the ways in which games embody paradigms of active learning and different theories of learning. In formal education, particularly at higher levels, teaching is still commonly didactic, based around a model of a knowledgeable teacher giving information to a classroom of students. Games simply do not work within this paradigm: they require discussion, practice, active problem-solving, learning through experience and reflection. Games support learning through gradual steps, guiding the player as he or she acquires greater competence; they provide appropriate, timely and meaningful feedback on the player's actions.

While these models of learning are certainly not unique to games, they are at the very heart of them. Games provide a way to bring active pedagogies into the classroom, and of course they are not simply used in formal educational settings. The active nature of games supports a variety of informal types of learning too. *Games as active learning environments* contains three chapters:

- *Chapter 3: Games as meaningful challenges* introduces different paradigms of learning and the idea of games as problem-solving environments. The chapter considers the different types of learning that can take place in game-based environments and the ways in which games provide intrinsic support structures to facilitate learning and seamlessly ease the transition from novice player to expert.
- *Chapter 4: Games as authentic contexts* discusses the value of games as authentic learning environments, supporting experiential learning and reflection, and providing context and purpose to the activities that take place within them.
- *Chapter 5: Games as social interactions* highlights the value of games as collaborative learning environments, and the potential of gaming communities to foster learning. It also looks at the role of competitive challenges in games,

considering aspects such as competing against oneself and the impact of competition in learning contexts.

The third part of the book, *Games as motivational tools*, looks at the ways in which games are structured and designed to enhance motivation to play the game as well as ongoing engagement, interest and immersion within it. As well as being motivational for many people, games have the power to engage and enthral long after any initial enthusiasm. Games have mechanisms that draw players in and keep them playing, and these mechanisms are discussed in the next three chapters:

- *Chapter 6: Games as engaging events* examines a range of theories and research associated with motivation and engagement and explores the different reasons why people play computer games as well as the relationship between games and learning.
- *Chapter 7: Games as designed enjoyment* considers aspects of game design such as the way in which goals, rules and game balance can be manipulated to create an experience that is motivational and enjoyable for different players with different preferences and perceptions.
- *Chapter 8: Games as reward mechanisms* focuses on the ways in which games engage players by rewarding them in different ways such as supporting the human urge to collect sets, or stimulating and satisfying curiosity. It also considers the role of formal assessment within a game-based context.

In Part IV, *Games as playgrounds*, I look at the playful aspects of the gaming experience that contribute to safe, enjoyable and fun learning. Play is one of the most important, yet most often overlooked, benefits of games for learning. Play provides safe, creative spaces for development and has long been accepted in the contexts of children and animals as being essential for learning. This section is also split into three chapters:

- *Chapter 9: Games as protected play* examines the roles of play and fun in game-playing and learning and their appropriateness in both contexts, considering the elements that make learning experiences fun.
- *Chapter 10: Games as experimental spaces* focuses on ideas of discovery learning, freedom, control and agency in games, considers how learning through exploration can encourage personal research and investigation and looks at the importance of creativity.
- *Chapter 11: Games as other worlds* considers the importance of games as spaces that are separate from the real world in which fantasy, storytelling and imagination can run wild. The ability to enter safe spaces of play and the benefits of play for learning are also discussed.

Part V, *Games as learning technologies*, focuses on digital play in particular, and the ways in which different gaming technologies can impact on the learning that takes place in games. There are three chapters in this part:

*   *Chapter 12: Games as interactive systems* explores the technological affordances of games for learning, looking particularly at the different ways in which digital interfaces can support or hinder learning, the use of simulation, feedback and interactivity. Issues of usability, accessibility and user experience design for learning are highlighted.
*   *Chapter 13: Games as digital habitats* explores the idea of games as cultural spaces, looking particularly at issues of identity and presence in virtual worlds, and the informal learning that takes place in shared digital spaces.
*   *Chapter 14: Games as multi-sensory experiences* considers the way in which digital games provide simultaneous visual, auditory and often kinaesthetic inputs and outputs, and the potential of these different sensory experiences for learning.

The book concludes with a chapter that aims to draw together the themes and ideas from across the previous 14 chapters, and highlight the future directions for the field of games and learning.

*   *Chapter 15: The future of games and learning* considers how games and learning can progress as a research discipline, and discusses the challenges for the future of the field, particularly in relation to issues of acceptance of the use of games in formal education, by learners, teachers and parents, drawing on the media discourses around games and violence, gender stereotyping and addiction, and discussing limitations to the use of games in practice.

In all, I hope that as well as providing a rounded overview of the field of games and learning, this book also makes a strong case for the relationship between games and learning, and serves to enthuse and convince readers that digital games are more than mere toys or amusements, but are a real tool to change the way that we practise, and think about, teaching and learning.

2

EVALUATING DIGITAL GAMES FOR LEARNING

At the heart of any discussion of games and learning is a single question: is there any evidence that digital games have an impact on learning, or on learners' motivations to learn? In this chapter, I will explore the evidence of the use of computer games, and games in general, to support and facilitate meaningful learning experiences. There are many examples of the use of games for learning in formal education, from the development of classification skills in early years (e.g. Sung, Chang, & Lee, 2008), to primary school geography (Tuzun et al., 2009), strategic and reasoning abilities (Bottino & Ott, 2006), arithmetic (Miller & Robertson, 2010) and learning vocabulary (Fisser, Voogt, & Bom, 2012). At secondary level there are examples from across the curriculum, including history (Huizenga, Admiraal, Akkerman, & ten Dam, 2009), science (Muehrer, Jenson, Friedberg, & Husain, 2012), language learning (Connolly, Stansfield, & Hainey, 2011), business (Lainema & Makkonen, 2003) and computer science (Papastergiou, 2009a). There are fewer examples from post-compulsory education, although some can be found, such as game-based induction in both further and higher education (Horne, 2013; Piatt, 2009) and examples of games used in university settings. There tends to be a bias towards games used in scientific and technical areas, such as food safety (Rooney & MacNamee, 2007), software engineering (Connolly, Stansfield, & Hainey, 2007) and mechanical engineering (Coller & Scott, 2009). In addition to these examples from formal education, there are examples in the research literature of the value of games to support learning in informal contexts, such as learning civic engagement (Ferguson & Garza, 2011), fire and street safety (Coles, Strickland, Padgett, & Bellmoff, 2007), diabetes education (Glasemann, Kanstrup, & Ryberg, 2010) and adult literacy (Kambouri, Thomas, & Mellar, 2006). However, while hundreds of case studies exist, it has been argued that the evidential underpinning of the field is based on an extrapolation from case studies rather than a unified theoretical basis (Klabbers, 2003). As a field there is still a lack of robust evidence regarding the value of games for learning and there is an identified need among policy makers for more robust empirical work to provide baseline evidence on how educational games can be used most effectively to teach (de Freitas, 2007); Van Eck (2007) argues that "we do not yet have the theoretical and research base we need to establish guidelines for practice" (p. 31).

Research into the effectiveness of digital games for learning is problematic for several reasons. First, digital games that are used in formal learning situations are typically small-scale game-based learning interventions, often used for a small number of hours only in total. This means that any effects that could be shown from the use of the game might be minimal and short-lasting since a small-scale learning intervention of any type is unlikely to have a significant impact on overall learning. Second, much of the research into games and learning is carried out by those with a vested interest in their success; often the teacher who created the game or researchers on a project. In this situation it is hard for total objectivity to be reached (although this point is true for many types of educational innovation, not just games and learning). Third, there is a general difficulty in measuring any type of learning in a meaningful way, particularly over time and in relation to transfer to other contexts, and game-based learning is no exception. In the next section, the difficulties involved in measuring learning will be discussed in more detail. Finally, there is the issue that much of the research in the field does not have a sound theoretical grounding. In their analysis of the games and learning literature based on learning theory orientation, Wu and colleagues (2012) suggest that the coverage of recent papers that consider learning theory is scant, and that the majority of studies on game-based learning were not based on theories of learning.

Measuring Learning

The most common way to measure student learning is through the development of measurable and observable performance indicators or learning outcomes, which are assessed in relation to a taxonomy of educational objectives (e.g. Bloom, 1956; Anderson & Krathwohl, 2001) to determine their level and scope. The degree to which a student can evidence these learning outcomes is then evaluated to indicate whether learning has taken place. In formal education this most often takes the form of an assessment such as an exam, essay, report or test at the end of a programme of study. However, in practice, meaningful assessment is not always possible in the case of game-based learning simply because the learning from the game forms a small part of a much larger overall set of learning objectives or because the learning from the game is not explicitly assessed as part of the formal course. If a computer game is only being used in one or two classes or as a small proportion of the course as a whole, then it may not have a large enough impact on the assessment to be evaluated in this way. There also needs to be some basis for comparison of assessment (e.g. the same class taught in a traditional way or the class in the previous year) and these data are not always readily available. In any research based on teaching two different groups using different methods, ethical issues arise in ensuring that each of the groups has a comparable experience. Particularly in the context of schools, teachers and researchers may not have access to assessment details beyond the top-level marks or grades (because they are often not the people who mark assessments) so available analyses are limited.

Another drawback of using formal assessment as the sole indicator of learning is that it does not take into account unintended learning (i.e. things that students learn that are not associated with the formal curriculum) from game-based learning that may be of interest to a researcher but may not be adequately represented in the assessment, such as problem-solving, teamwork or negotiation. Summative formal assessment, happening as it usually does as the immediate end of a course, may also not reflect the ability of a learner to appropriately apply the learning in real-life contexts or retain what he or she has learned over time. Problems can arise where learning practice has been mismatched to the assessment, leading to issues of assessment validity. For example, if a course is taught in an active way through the use of games or problem-based learning, a traditional assessment such as an exam may not be an appropriate way to capture what has been learned from the experience. Since teaching practice is often more flexible than assessment practice, this can lead to a mismatch of methods, where assessment scores are influenced by not only student performance, but also the suitability of the assessment instrument in that particular context.

In experimental design studies, where students are separated into groups that undergo different treatments and the differences in learning compared, the effectiveness of an educational game is usually measured using a test before the game (pre-test), followed by the game-play and other educational activities, followed by one (or more) equivalent test (post-test). The performance of students in the test condition (e.g. game-based learning) will be compared with that of others in a control group, which either has no intervention or a comparable intervention in a different mode (e.g. traditional teaching). Differences in the pre- and post-test scores for each group provide evidence as to whether the game has had a significant impact on learning in the test condition, or whether any variation could simply be due to chance.

Experimental research designs are common in studies on game-based learning; for example, Ebner and Holzinger (2006) tested theoretical knowledge in chemical engineering, Kambouri and colleagues (2006) evaluated basic literacy skills and Sung and colleagues (2008) examined children's understanding of taxonomic concepts. While this is the most common experimental model for evaluating skills and knowledge acquisition in game-based learning (Connolly, Boyle, MacArthur, Hainey, & Boyle, 2012), there are a number of potential problems with this approach. If the learning objectives are knowledge-based and involve the memorisation of facts then they may be easy to evaluate with a test, but it has been argued (Gee, 2003; Whitton, 2010a) that the real potential of games for learning is in their ability to help learners engage with the higher level learning outcomes, such as synthesis, creativity, teamwork, evaluation and critical thinking, that cannot easily be evaluated with a simple test. It may also be difficult, if not impossible, to persuade students to give up extra time for any additional testing and difficulties with getting students to cooperate with the pre-/post-test model because of the extra work required on their part are not uncommon. Squire (2005), for example, could not persuade the students in his sample group to complete a pre-test at all.

The timing of a post-test also has to be carefully designed to account for the retention of learning over time and application of learning in other contexts, and again it may be difficult to persuade the same students to take part after a period of time has passed, particularly when their participation will happen too late to influence the design of their own courses. There is also an issue of equivalence between pre- and post-tests and how researchers can ensure that they are of the same difficulty and assess exactly the same aspects of learning. Wouters, Spek, and Oostendorp (2011) offer structured assessment as an alternative to 'verbal' assessments such as knowledge tests. In structured assessment the way in which a learner's knowledge is organised is assessed, rather than the knowledge itself. They argue that, while verbal assessment provides a more nuanced picture regarding declarative and procedural knowledge, structural assessment provides an in-depth understanding of the learners' perceptions of the relative importance of knowledge, and thus allows the discovery of misconceptions.

Wideman, Owston, Brown, Kushniruk, Ho, and Pitts (2007) address the methodological limitations of experimental designs by proposing the unobtrusive recording of screen activity, with synchronised player audio recording, as an alternative way of evaluating the educational effectiveness of games. Another way of researching learning is by using student self-evaluation, both of the perceived increases in learning and of associated concepts, such as engagement, that are used to act as an indicator of learning. While the data gathered from self-evaluation of learning may not be robust – self-evaluation of this type is notoriously inaccurate (Falchikov & Boud, 1989; Mabe & West, 1982) – it does at least allow data gathering as to whether students think they have learned something from taking part in game-based learning. Alternative ways of evaluating learning with games include analysis of communication transcripts (e.g. to highlight evidence of learning behaviours) and other quantitative indicators, both external to the game, such as time spent playing and internal, such as points accrued, or levels reached. In addition, there are qualitative techniques, such as interviews, focus groups and observations, that can be used to gain a deeper understanding of the processes of learning that are taking place during a game. While there are a variety of possible methods, I believe that we can only gain robust evidence by using a mixed-methods approach, undertaking large-scale quantitative experimental research coupled with deep qualitative research to explore the nuances of the learning experiences. It is only by looking at the depth as well as the breadth of evidence that we will begin to develop a pragmatic and useful evidence base that gathers insights into the potential of games for learning and the factors and contexts that make it more effective as an educational paradigm.

Holistic and Diagnostic Evaluation

In addition to assessing learning that has taken place from an instance of game play, evaluation of factors that contribute to learning such as motivation and attitudes, and evaluation of other behaviours that indicate learning can provide greater insights into the effectiveness of games for learning, as well as diagnostic evaluation of a game environment before play to assess its suitability for learning. Connolly, Stansfield, and Hainey (2008) present a framework for the evaluation of game-based learning and propose that there are seven aspects that should be examined when determining the effectiveness of games and learning:

- *Learner performance.* Whether learning has taken place and there is an improvement in performance.
- *Motivation.* The levels of student motivation, interest and participation in the game.
- *Perceptions.* The views of the students towards areas such as the experience of time passing, the realism of the game, amount of complexity, support received and levels of perceived proficiency within the game.
- *Attitudes.* Feelings of the learners and teachers towards the subject itself and the use of games for learning within that subject.
- *Collaboration.* The regularity and effectiveness of working with others.
- *Preferences.* Inclinations of the learners and teachers towards, for example, different learning styles or modes of interaction.
- *Environment.* Factors associated with the game itself, such as the design of the environment, use of scaffolding, usability, levels of social presence and the way in which the game is deployed.

De Freitas and Oliver (2006) describe a four-dimensional framework for evaluating the holistic experience of games-based (and simulation-based) education. The four dimensions that they include in their analysis framework are shown in Figure 2.1 below.

In this model, the context considers the environment where learning takes place and how that affects learning, while the learner specification examines the characteristics of the learners, including their backgrounds and profiles. The pedagogic considerations reference the learning models and approaches used and the mode of representation is the way that the learning is presented in digital format, taking into account levels of interactivity, fidelity, immersion and realism.

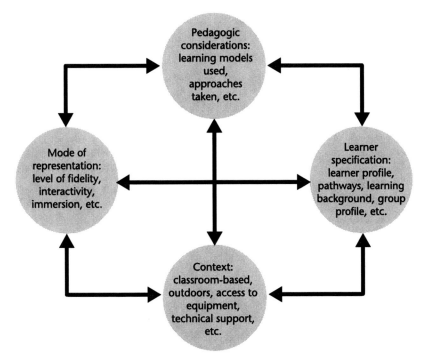

FIGURE 2.1 A framework for evaluating game- and simulation-based-education (de Freitas and Oliver, 2006)

Rice (2007) highlights the benefits of constructivist games, which he describes as those that support the development of higher-order thinking skills. He presents a rubric for evaluating games for their 'cognitive viability' (i.e. the likelihood of that game fostering higher-order thinking skills). In order for games to foster higher-order thinking skills, he says, it should be the case that:

- the user has to assume a role, forcing players to process information outside of their normal experiences;
- there is meaningful interaction with the environment and dialogue with non-player characters;
- the game has a complex storyline with characters that the players care about;
- there are complex puzzles that require effort to solve;
- the game uses three-dimensional graphics with multiple views;
- complex processes are simulated with variables that can be manipulated;
- interaction is allowed through the use of lifelike avatars;
- interactive virtual objects are available, for example objects that can be examined, manipulated and used;

- game knowledge is required beyond that which is prompted by the interface;
- gathering and synthesis of information is required;
- the real world is replicated, in terms of visuals, with recognisable real-life elements, or processes;
- non-player character interaction and dialogue is supported by artificial intelligence; and
- the game is replayable with varying results.

Two elements of this analysis are, I believe, contestable; first the requirement for three-dimensional views, and second the need for lifelike avatars. Rice (2007) asserts that three-dimensional graphics with multiple views increase cognitive viability because "complex three-dimensional VR affords users additional opportunities for cognitive processing" (p. 96). However, there is little evidence that this benefits learning, and it might in fact simply be a distraction or lead to cognitive overload, as discussed in Chapter 14. Kapp (2012) argues that three-dimensional environments create a sense of presence and embodiment that supports learning, which is an argument that carries more weight, but I would counter that the mode of the game (i.e. two-dimensional, first-person, third-person) is not a critical factor in determining whether that game might foster higher-order thinking skills. In respect to his argument for the need for lifelike avatars, Rice(2007) suggests that "[games with lifelike avatars] are typically the most advanced products on the marketplace, and consequently make the most use of cognitive strategies to enhance the gaming experience" (p. 96), which I feel is a fallacious argument for two reasons: first, not all advanced games use lifelike avatars; and second, it is impossible to infer anything about the quality of game design from the quality of game graphics.

In my own doctoral research (Whitton, 2007a), a review of literature and entertainment games suggested six areas of digital game design that could support learning. This model can also be used to provide a diagnostic evaluation tool for examining the potential effectiveness of a digital game for learning. These principles are:

1. Support for active learning – an environment is provided that encourages exploration, problem-solving and enquiry, with opportunities for collaboration, testing ideas and gaining feedback and practice and consolidation of skills.
2. Engenders engagement – the game presents: activities that have clear achievable goals throughout; a large world to explore and control, with a high level of interactivity with multiple ways to complete; an appropriate challenge that stimulates curiosity.
3. Appropriateness – the game fits with the curriculum and the method of assessment, matches the time available and is personally relevant and acceptable to the students.

4. Support for reflection – provides opportunities for reflection and debriefing on learning; supports meta-cognition of the learning process.
5. Provision of equitable experiences – the activity accounts for differing prior knowledge, allows for customisation and creates equal opportunities for participation.
6. Provision of ongoing support – provides orientation and overview activities, enables the learner to have quick initial success with the gradual introduction of complexity and the provision of hints and clues.

While there are many ways in which a game can be evaluated in relation to the overall learner experience, questions remain about whether or not the game has had an impact on learning, positive or negative. An overview of the research evidence that addresses this question is provided in the next section.

Evidence of the Effectiveness of Games For Learning

In recent years, there have been several meta-analyses attempting to draw together the evidence on the effectiveness of games for learning. Rather than presenting another extensive literature review here, I have conducted a search of previous meta-reviews in recent years, and then drawn together a total of the ten most prominent that have been published since 2005, which are summarised in Table 2.1 below.

In the section that follows, I have summarised and synthesised the key findings from the studies described here. This being a review of meta-reviews, I have naturally condensed a great deal of research into a few short paragraphs. For those interested in a more detailed analysis, I suggest reviewing the more recent papers described in Table 2.1. It is also worth noting that there is substantial duplication in the papers selected for each of these reviews, so where a point below is made by more than one author, it does not mean that there is an increased weight of evidence, but simply that they may have been drawing upon the same evidence base.

These reviews showed that a games-based approach to learning is being used across diverse curricular areas, most notably in health, business and social issues (Connolly et al., 2012) and in a variety of educational settings in pre-school, all stages of formal education, and workplace and informal learning, but studies with school-age children and college students dominate (Ke, 2009; Ng, Zeng, & Plass, 2009). The games used in research are typically simulations, puzzles, adventures, board games, action games, strategy games and business simulation games (Ke, 2009). The majority of the games are either educational games developed in-house for the study, or non-educational off-the-shelf games, and the majority are based on a personal computer (Ng et al., 2009). Most of the empirical studies focus on the effects of games on learning (Ke, 2009) and the majority these focus on knowledge acquisition or content understanding (Connolly et al., 2012).

TABLE 2.1 Reviews of the evidence of games for learning

Author/s	Scope of review	Articles examined
Connolly et al. (2012)	The potential positive impacts of gaming on users aged 14 years or above, especially with respect to learning, skill enhancement and engagement.	129
Girard et al. (2012)	A review of the results of experimental studies designed to examine the effectiveness of serious games (defined as video games intended to serve a useful purpose) on players' learning and engagement.	9
Huizenga et al. (2010)	A critical review of a decade of research into learning and motivational effects of digital game-based learning.	92
Hays (2005)	A review of the literature on instructional games with a focus on the empirical research on the instructional effectiveness of games.	105
Ke (2009)	Qualitative analysis and synthesis of research into computer-based instructional games.	89
Ng et al. (2009)	Descriptive overview of the different types of studies into the effectiveness of games for learning.	150
O'Neil et al. (2005)	Evaluation of learning outcomes in the context of the evidence presented in studies of the effectiveness of games for learning.	19
Papastergiou (2009b)	A critical review of the use of games for learning in health education and physical education.	34
Perrotta et al. (2013)	An examination of the impact and potential impact of game-based learning on learners' engagement and attainment.	31
Vogel et al. (2006)	A meta-analysis of studies examining cognitive gains or attitudinal change using comparative experimental design of traditional teaching against game-based learning.	32

A common theme was the lack of robust research, and flaws in methodology. There is a clear lack of empirical studies investigating the effectiveness of games in learning (Girard et al., 2012; O'Neil et al., 2005) and the current literature does not adequately evidence the presumed link between motivation, attitudes to learning and learning outcomes (Papastergiou, 2009b). Concerns about the research base include that the majority of game evaluation studies are: of short duration (Ng et al., 2009); typically less than two hours (Ke, 2009); the use of control groups is inconsistent, ranging from no intervention, to traditional teaching intervention, to alternative game-based intervention (Girard et al., 2012); the research literature is filled with ill-defined terms, and plagued with methodological flaws (Hays, 2005); and in several studies information is lacking, for example about how long interventions lasted and the sizes of effects (Huizenga, Admiraal, & ten Dam, 2010).

There is limited, and inconsistent, evidence of the value of educational games in formal settings. Research is inconclusive (Perrotta et al., 2013) although in one meta-analysis the finding was that "significantly higher cognitive gains were observed in subjects utilizing interactive simulations or games versus traditional teaching methods" (Vogel et al., 2006, p. 233). However, this positive finding is not replicated across the board in other analyses. There is some evidence that playing entertainment games in an informal context leads to improvements in attentional and visual perceptual skills (Connolly et al., 2012), that educational games may improve young people's knowledge, skills, attitudes and behaviours in relation to health and physical exercise, as well as potentially enhancing young people's physical fitness, motor skills and motivation for physical exercise (Papastergiou, 2009b), and that video games can impact positively on problem-solving skills, broader knowledge acquisition, motivation and engagement (Perrotta et al., 2013). Using games can also improve factual knowledge, but there is limited evidence that using games in education can improve students' cognitive skills (Huizenga et al., 2010). While research has shown that some games can provide effective learning for a variety of learners for several different tasks, it is impossible to draw general conclusions from this (Hays, 2005). There is no consistent effect of gender on learning from games (Ke, 2009) and gender does not seem to influence the effects of games on engagement, motivation and learning (Huizenga et al., 2010).

A more consistent finding in relation to learning design is that briefing and feedback are essential for learning (Hays, 2005) and instructional support features are a necessary part of educational computer games, as without such support within the game the learner will learn to play the game rather than learn domain-specific knowledge embedded in the game (Ke, 2009).

There is more evidence of the effectiveness of games in relation to engagement and motivation. Players seem to like the game-based approach to learning and find it motivating and enjoyable (Connolly et al., 2012) and research supports that game-based learning encourages engagement (Perrotta et al., 2013; Vogel et al., 2006). Using games in elementary and secondary education does engage students, as games can trigger enthusiasm, and supports students' on-task concentration (Huizenga et al., 2010), but relatively few studies explored changes in attitudes to learning as a possible outcome and their findings varied (Perrotta et al., 2013). There is no evidence to indicate that games are the preferred instructional method in all situations (Hays, 2005).

Overall, the evidence for the effectiveness of games is variable, due to the limitations of the research methods employed and variations in the contexts and types of game used, which make it difficult to draw general conclusions. Iacovides, Aczel, Scanlon, Taylor, and Woods (2011) suggest that the large variance in evidence for effectiveness could be due to a number of factors, including

> the environments within which games are played; differences in design between games designed for leisure and games designed for learning; difficulties inherent in tying game-play to required learning outcomes; aspects of choice, control, intention and mood of individual players; and the social dynamics associated with playing games.
>
> *(p. 10)*

It is important to note that the study of games and learning is not unique in this respect, and the difficulty of evaluating learning in a meaningful way coupled with the ethics and practicalities of any sizeable intervention mean that collecting evidence of effectiveness is problematic. For example, we do not have conclusive evidence that didactic teaching is the most effective way to learn (in fact, evidence to the contrary is mounting), yet its use is still widespread at all levels of education. What can be said, however, is that games certainly have the potential to have a positive impact on learning and engagement, but the use of a game does not ensure this as there are so many other factors that have to be taken into account. The most interesting research question for me is not *whether* games can be an effective way to learn, but how they can be made most effective, and cost-effective, and accepted; so that digital games have the opportunity to really make a difference to the practice of teaching and learning.

PART II

Games as Active Learning Environments

3

GAMES AS MEANINGFUL CHALLENGES

The use of games for learning is not new. Since the beginning of human existence, man has used forms of play to practise, test, experiment and learn new skills. Games are a long-accepted way in which children learn about the world in which they live and their places in it, how to interact with other people and ways of behaving appropriately. Educational games are not a new phenomenon, for example war games have long been used to teach strategy and assess military campaigns, and simulation games have been common in the corporate training world for years as a way of teaching management and business skills. There is a long history of academic research into traditional, non-digital games spanning at least the last 40 years; in comparison, the use of digital games for learning is a relatively new field.

Digital games for learning have been with us, in the mainstream, since the early 1980s, when computers became commonplace in homes and schools. Egenfeldt-Nielsen, Smith, and Tosca (2008) highlight three ways in which educational computer games are used in formal education: 'edutainment'; commercial entertainment games; and research-based educational video games. First, there is 'edutainment', described as games that are designed to teach basic skills such as spelling, memorisation or arithmetic, devised to look like mainstream video games. The model of edutainment is inherently problematic in the context of meaningful learning because edutainment games typically fail to create the same engaging game-play as commercial games and lack meaningful interactivity (Buckingham & Scanlon, 2003). Edutainment games are modelled on the learning principles of behaviourism, relying on extrinsic motivation with little integration between the game experience and the learning experience, often reliant on drill-and-practice learning and simple game play, and intended for use without a teacher present (Egenfeldt-Nielsen et al., 2008). Facer, Furlong, Furlong, and Sutherland (2003) describe the inherent problem of this model as being that

> in many of these educational software environments, learning is predominantly, and mistakenly, categorised primarily as the acquisition of facts and information. It is unsurprising, perhaps, that such a narrow definition of learning should require embellishment to render it more interesting.
>
> *(p. 208)*

Despite the flaws in this model of educational gaming, it is still prevalent today; possibly because these types of games are easy to design and build, and are less problematic to evaluate as learning outcomes are almost always of a type that can be easily tested, based on recall or simple application.

A second category of educational digital games in education is the use of commercial entertainment games in the classroom (also called commercial off-the-shelf or COTS games). There are some successful examples of their use (for example Squire and Barab's (2004) use of the historical strategy game *Civilisation*, Robertson and Howell's (2008) use of the role-playing game *Neverwinter Nights* and Miller and Robertson's (2010) use of brain-training console games) but opportunities to link entertainment games to formal curriculum content are limited. There may be some overlap between the goals of a game and the intended learning goals, but this is likely to be coincidental rather than by design, and the use of this type of game requires additional associated activities to help learners engage with the learning from the game in a meaningful, collaborative and reflective way. In practice, the use of commercial games in formal education is often limited to their use as a stimulus for discussion or as an incentive for learning, rather than integrated use of the game for deep learning. Commercial games may also be expensive to purchase, require powerful hardware and be difficult to integrate with institutional systems. While the motivational and playability aspects of this type of game are evidenced by their commercial successes, there is little evidence in most cases of their learning benefits, in the context of formal education, beyond that.

Third, there is the research-based educational game, a game typically designed as the product of a research project, which "often presents new approaches and has a strong documentation for learning outcomes" (Egenfeldt-Nielsen et al., 2008, p. 211). This category of game is the one that is the most interesting in the context of this book; games that provide active and meaningful collaborative experiences for learners, where learning from the game is closely aligned with intended learning outcomes to make an engaging and critical learning experience. It is these *constructivist* learning games that I make particular reference to throughout this book, particularly in this part on games as active learning environments, and later in the chapter I will discuss this in more detail.

This is not to say that deep and active learning does not take place in commercial games; however, there are few instances of this taking place effectively in formal education. To these three areas mentioned above, I could also add informal learning from games, learning through gaming communities, learning about the cultural impacts and implications of games and so on. The ways in which games can be used to enhance and facilitate learning, both within and outside of a formal classroom setting are almost endless. Gee (2003) argues that when people learn to play computer games they are actually learning a new literacy; understanding the multimodal symbols and representations of meaning embedded within the game itself, and the cultural practices that surround it. Bogost (2010) expands on this idea, arguing that video games provide "specific areas of experience" (p. 250) that enable development of 'procedural literacy', the ability to understand and critically interrogate the cultural and technological representations of real and imagined processes. Gee (2003) also problematises the deeply embedded idea that important knowledge is 'content' in the sense of "information rooted in, or, at least, related to, intellectual domains or academic disciplines like physics, history, art, or literature" (p. 21) and argues that any academic discipline is *not* primarily content (such as facts or principles) but is a dynamic set of social practices and discourses. Three conditions are involved in learning within this semiotic domain (an area with collectively constructed multimodal meanings and practices) in an active way: experiencing the world in new ways; becoming affiliated with the social group; and gaining resources to prepare for future learning and problem-solving. To learn in a critical way, learners must also, consciously or unconsciously, engage with the accepted and typical content and social practices within that domain and reflect upon them. Gee (2003) argues that digital games have the power to create active and critical learning in two ways because "[good games] are crafted in ways that encourage and facilitate active and critical learning and thinking . . . and [the people around the game] encourage reflective metatalk, thinking and actions in regard to the design of the game" (p. 46).

Games and Learning Paradigms

In this section I will explore the idea of games as learning environments from different paradigmatic angles, and consider the various theories and approaches that help us to understand the range of knowledge, skills, behaviours and attitudes that games can help us learn. The ways in which teaching and learning have been theorised have changed significantly over the last century. Behaviourism had long been the dominant school of thought, but cognitivism became popular in the late 1950s, and then grew to be the customary way of conceptualising learning. More recently the constructivist paradigm has become the prevailing way in which the theory of learning is described (Cooper, 1993). Behaviourists saw the mind as a black box that can be studied by observing behaviour, where knowledge can be transferred directly to a student by listening to an expert, and learning can be drilled and reinforced; in essence the mind was a vessel to be filled with knowledge. Cognitivist thinkers focused on the thought processes behind behaviours, and aimed to understand the ways in which the mind works, looking particularly at cognition, sensory systems, brain processes and memory. The constructivist perspective builds on some of the understanding of the workings of the mind developed through cognitivism but holds the view that, rather than there being a single truth that exists in the world, personal understandings of a phenomenon are constructed by individuals through experience, discussion and application.

Constructivism is not a single theory but a number of related theories and perspectives. Savery and Duffy (1995) summarise this highly complex collection of interwoven theoretical constructs. They state that there are three fundamental precepts:

1. *Situated cognition.* The idea that individuals' understandings are developed by interactions with their environments; they are formed by a combination of content, context, activity and goal and are individually constructed; they cannot be shared, but compatibility of understandings can be tested through discussion with others.
2. *Cognitive puzzlement.* Cognitive conflict – or puzzlement – is the stimulus for learning and determines the organisation and nature of what is learned; there is always a goal for learning something and this goal is a primary factor in determining what the learner attends to and what is constructed.
3. *Social collaboration.* Knowledge evolves through social negotiation and by testing the viability of individual understandings on others; the social environment is critical to the development of understanding, and other individuals are a primary mechanism for providing sources of alternative views to challenge thinking.

Games for learning are typically designed from either a dominant behaviourist or constructivist perspective. The early learning games developed from the 1980s onwards (often called 'edutainment', as described above) typically had two characteristics: first, they focused on low-level skills such as memorisation and recall; and second, they used the game characteristics as a reward for learning achievement. This model uses a behaviourist design, where the game provides extrinsic motivation for taking part. This model is often referred to as the 'chocolate-covered broccoli' approach to educational game design; the idea that you can make people engage with something they do not want to by adding motivating elements. Thirty years ago the idea of using any computer game – however repetitive and low-level – was exciting for most children simply because it was different and new. At that time behaviourist games still had novelty value over traditional learning methods, and may have increased motivation to engage because they were novel; the ubiquitous use of digital games means this simply is not the case nowadays.

Constructivist learning games are those that are richer and more sophisticated in content and purpose, and align educational goals directly with the goals of playing the game; the challenges and puzzles within the game provide an authentic learning environment in which players can undertake real-world tasks; the game and the 'content' are not separated but are integrated, and motivation is intrinsic rather than being external to the game. Wilson (1996) defines a constructivist learning environment as "a place where learners may work together and support each other as they use a variety of tools and information resources in their guided pursuit of learning goals and problem-solving activities" (p. 5). This definition can be applied to the vast majority of games that are developed for entertainment: at the heart of the game, players have a context in which they have to solve problems; they have a variety of tools and information at their disposal; and they work either collaboratively, or within gaming communities, to achieve these ends. Many digital games are single player and do not require collaboration to operate, but these also often have online community networks providing hints and tips to support the game. While there are some notable examples of constructivist games for learning in formal education (e.g. Akkerman, Admiraal, & Huizenga, 2009; Lainema & Makkonen, 2003) many educational games currently produced still rely on the behaviourist model of action and reward. Reasons for this could be the tested efficacy of the behaviourist approach, the fact that these games are relatively easy to design and create and the increased ability to evaluate games of this nature. As there is a long history of behaviourist learning games, tested design and development models exist, and as content is separate from the game framework, these models can be reused in different contexts, making them cost-effective. Behaviourist games, with their focus on recall, are also relatively easy to evaluate using a pre-test/post-test model, so their success can be easily measured; this is much more difficult for constructivist games that do not focus on skills that are easily testable or develop in short periods of time. There is evidence that behaviourist games are effective for what they are designed to do (i.e. support memorisation and recall) but learning facts is only the starting point of education: it is the application of knowledge and skills critically in different contexts, and developing an understanding of the processes underpinning learning that are key. There is nothing wrong with behaviourist games in themselves, and indeed they may be a valuable alternative to rote learning in the few instances where such an approach might be necessary. However, those areas in which this type of learning is actually required are few and far between, and they do not even scratch the surface of the potential of games to be active, experiential and collaborative problem-solving environments.

More recently, the educational paradigm of connectivism has highlighted the limitations of behaviourism, cognitivism and constructivism as they all assume that learning happens within individuals, and do not take account of learning that happens outside of people, for example learning that is stored and manipulated by technology, or learning that occurs within organisations. The theory of connectivism suggests that learning occurs through a process of connecting information and knowledge from a variety of diverse and conflicting information sources, including digital sources, and that nurturing and maintaining connections as well as the ability to see connections between fields, ideas and concepts is key to learning (Siemens, 2006). Connectivist courses involve the aggregation of information, re-mixing, repurposing, where learners share their insights with the community (Downes, 2011). This emerging paradigm can also be seen in the gaming communities that exist around games such as *Minecraft* and *World of Warcraft* to build, create and re-mix and share game artefacts and mythologies.

Learning Through Problem-solving

At the heart of every computer game, there is a challenge that revolves around problem-solving of one form or another. This could be working out how to complete a level in a platform game, discovering how to defeat the enemy in a shooting game, becoming powerful enough to defeat the level boss in a strategy game and so on. Although the types of problems encountered in digital games are many and various, as varied as the imaginations of the game designers, it is these problems that create the challenges that stimulate the desire in the player to play.

In education, the problem-based learning approach has clear parallels with the activities that take place in certain types of computer game, such as puzzle, role-play, strategy or adventure games. Problem-based learning (Boud & Feletti, 1998) is a teaching method that was originally motivated by the failures of traditional teaching methods in medicine, in particular failures of application where medical students were not able to apply what they had learned in the real world or adapt what they had learned to new situations, and involves small groups of students working together to tackle real-life, often cross-disciplinary problems. The teacher assumes the role of facilitator rather than the subject expert. Resources are made available to the students but information on how to tackle the problem itself is not provided, and work is carried out intensively on one problem at a time. This provides activity-based learning, with students taking more responsibility for their own learning, and learning in a real-world context. The Internet is also often central to facilitating problem-based learning as it allows students to research topics to a level and depth that is appropriate for them, and also means that there is a much reduced need for memorisation of content, but students need greater digital literacy skills in the application, evaluation and organisation of what they find online.

Researchers have highlighted that computer games have the facility to create real-life problem-solving experiences. Kiili (2005) argues that "games provide a meaningful framework for offering problems to students. In fact, a game itself is a big problem that is composed of smaller causally linked problems" (p. 17). In problem-based learning, learners are typically provided with triggers and assets, artefacts that highlight the problem or provide clues as to how solving the problem might be approached. Many types of games, but particularly adventure games, create environments in which problem-solving is the explicit aim and players have to engage with the story, characters and objects and situations presented in order to complete the game. Even when the context of a game is not directly relevant to a specific subject area, the transferable skills associated with problem-solving, such as lateral thinking, information gathering and analysis, and developing and testing solutions can be extremely valuable nonetheless. At the core of the problem-based learning approach is the idea that there is no single correct solution, getting students to explore alternatives and creative approaches (this is not always the case in games, particularly, for example, adventure games, that typically have a single set 'correct' path). At the heart of every game is a problem that needs to be solved. It is the challenge of the problem that drives the game forward, and motivates the player to complete the challenge of the game. The cyclical problem-based gaming model that Kiili (2007) presents highlights the importance of reflection on consequences as part of the problem-based learning cycle in games. Development of playing strategy leads to active experimentation, which has consequences in the game world; reflection on these consequences can either lead to further strategy development or directly to further experimentation.

A wide variety of problems exist that might typically be found in computer games. Table 3.1 below shows some of the most common types of problem, with a brief description and indication of the game genres in which each might most commonly be found.

The first problem type in this table, recall of knowledge, does not comprise 'problems' as such but requires the memorisation and recollection of facts, such as is common in quiz games; answers cannot be 'worked out' because players either know a fact or they do not (although sometimes correct answers can be deduced from the elimination of incorrect alternatives). A more sophisticated model of knowledge and recall problem-solving is the online treasure hunt, which does not assume that the player knows all the answers at the start of the challenges, but provides hints and clues to where the information can be found. As well as supporting the learning of facts, this also supports information literacy and evaluation skills.

Puzzles are problems for which there is typically only one solution (although this is not always the case for more complex puzzles) that can be solved by applying rules or systems to the problem. They are used in many types of computer game, for games that are puzzles in themselves (such as *Tetris* where players have to manipulate falling bricks into lines), games that use puzzles extrinsically to progress a storyline (such as the *Professor Layton* series for the Nintendo DS that reward players for solving puzzles) or those for which puzzles are intrinsic to the game play, such as the *Nancy Drew* series of adventure games, where puzzles are

TABLE 3.1 Types of problem that are employed in computer games

Problem type	Description	Game types
Knowledge	Recall of facts and information.	Quiz
Puzzle	Problem designed to test ingenuity in a specific domain, such as logic, verbal skills or spatial reasoning, usually with a single correct answer.	Puzzle, adventure, casual
Strategy	Problems that involve planning, decision-making, manoeuvres, developing tactics.	Strategy, god-games, shooters, action-adventure
Lateral thinking	Problems that involve inventive thinking to combine objects or ideas, and work out ways of achieving original solutions.	Adventure, role-play
Creative	Designing or making new objects that can be aesthetic or functional.	Alternative reality games, game-building
Physical	Problems that involve movement, rhythm, timing and other physical actions.	Fighting, sports, arcade, gesture-based
Social	Challenges that involve other people, such as team working, negotiation and group decision-making.	Online games, MMORPGs
Perseverance	Challenges that take time and energy but are not necessarily hard to do, such as clicking with the mouse.	Social network games

integrated into the adventure in the form of, for example, intricate locking mechanisms or codes that need to be solved.

There is a wide variety of types of puzzle used in digital games, including:

- Cryptic – using codes or ciphers, or conventions as in the case of cryptic crosswords.
- Lateral thinking – needing to be solved by thinking in an unconventional manner, or seeing things from a different perspective.
- Logic – the solver must use reasoning and deduction to work out the solution.
- Memory – such as repeating a pattern, or recognising objects that have been moved or removed.
- Musical – puzzles based on note forms, pitch or keys.
- Numeric – puzzles based around arithmetic or algebra, where the solver has to manipulate numbers in some way to arrive at a solution.
- Riddles – word puzzles that involve a pun or a play on words.

- Spatial – puzzles based around the movement or comparison of objects or moving around an environment, such as mazes.
- Tactile – using actual physical objects, such as puzzles that involve separating objects.
- Verbal – using language, letters or words as the basis for the puzzle, such as crosswords or anagrams.
- Visual – analysing pictures, such as spot-the-difference or finding a hidden object.

Of course, different puzzle types can be combined and there may also be puzzles that share elements of two or more puzzle types described here, such as Sudoku, which is both a numeric and logic problem. A good puzzle should be solvable, and amenable to checkpoints so that the solver knows that he or she is getting somewhere, appropriately difficult and tricky so that it uses some sort of misdirection, obfuscation or disguise, elegant and fit-for-purpose (Selinker & Snyder, 2013).

Strategy problems are those that require the player to plan a series of actions, review the effects of those actions and take a further series of actions based on the results. Strategy is required in a wide range of games including those that are seldom applied to education, such as first-person shooters, where players may have to work out how to clear an area, accessing appropriate equipment and health, while not losing so many life points that the character dies and the game ends. Problems of a strategic nature do not necessarily have only a single way of achieving the game goals but may have many alternative paths. This is also true for lateral thinking problems, which are like puzzles in some ways, in that there is a problem that needs to be solved using ingenuity, but there may be multiple solutions rather than a single one. Lateral thinking problems are common in adventure games, but also in role-playing and action-adventure, where the obvious course of action may not achieve the desired outcome.

Creative challenges are, I believe, one of the most powerful ways in which to stimulate and motivate learners. They differ from lateral thinking challenges in that their solutions need not have been previously considered by the game designer, but extend the game. They provide a meaningful and achievable challenge and also lead to all sorts of incidental learning, as students have to master new concepts and ways of thinking, software packages or transferable skills such as information literacy. Creative problems can involve activities including the development of artefacts, such as graphics, videos, songs, stories or animations, that become part of the narrative in games such as alternate reality games. This can involve using technology to make digital assets such as videos, graphics, animation or music, or can use offline technologies, for example writing a story or creating a physical object. As well as creative challenges within games, there can also be player-generated challenges that can involve activities extending, developing or modifying the game, creating artefacts around the game, such as character clothing or fan fiction, or game-creation itself (more about this in Chapter 10).

Physical challenges involve actually doing something with your body, such as 'twitch' and reaction time skills in computer games, as opposed to the primarily mental challenges of puzzles, knowledge and recall, and lateral thinking challenges. Modern computer game consoles, such as the Nintendo Wii, Sony PlayStation Move, or Microsoft Xbox Kinect offer great potential for movement-based challenges, but this is a little-studied area in terms of educational research. Social challenges are ones that involve working with, or against, other people. They can involve skills such as teamwork, negotiation, discussion and diplomacy. These types of challenge can help to build skills such as social literacy, interpersonal skills, communication skills and group interaction skills.

Games that utilise perseverance challenges are interesting because, in principle, they should not be engaging at all, and yet they are massively popular. It is a common form in social network games such as *Farmville* or *TinyZoo*, where play consists of simple actions, such as clicking or touching certain areas of the screen repeatedly (harvesting crops, or feeding animals) over extended periods of time. While, in theory, this does not sound like much fun, these games are designed to hook players by using techniques such as free play with low-cost enhancements known as 'micro-transactions' (typically game currency that gets things done more quickly), benefits for sharing or inviting friends, or rewards for coming back at regular intervals. The ethics of this type of game can be considered to be questionable (Rose, 2013) as, while they are typically advertised as 'free to play', they are designed to extract as much money as possible from the players.

Types of Learning in Digital Games

Games of different types can be used to learn a wide variety of knowledge and skills, from recall of facts, cognitive and physical skills, attitudes and behaviours. Table 3.2 below shows a variety of learning areas that different games incorporate, providing an indication of the types of skills and knowledge that could potentially be learned in seven of the most popular digital game genres.

This list is by no means intended to be exhaustive, but is simply to show that there is a vast array of different types of skills, knowledge, attitudes and behaviours that people can learn through playing games; even games that are designed primarily for entertainment, and those that at first glance may seem inappropriate for learning (such as shooter games). It is also worth noting that the vast majority of skills presented in this table are higher level than simple recall of facts, but involve synthesis, evaluation and critical thinking, which shows the potential range of skills that video games could be used to foster.

Games can support mentality change, emotional fulfilment, knowledge acquisition and reinforcement, thinking skills such as strategic thinking, interpersonal skills, spatial abilities and bodily coordination (Hong, Cheng, Hwang, Lee, &

TABLE 3.2 Overview of game genres and potential learning areas

Genre	Description	Potential learning areas
Adventure	A series of tasks or puzzles in which the player must interact with a virtual world and storyline, performing actions, talking to characters and manipulating objects in order to achieve the objectives of the game, often to solve some mystery or complete a quest.	Problem-solving, lateral thinking, creativity, empathy, critical thinking.
Platform	Moving a player character through a landscape (usually two-dimensional), jumping up and down between platforms, avoiding obstacles and enemies and picking up treasure, usually with some overall goal in mind and often in the context of a narrative.	Motor skills, problem-solving, spatial skills, planning, strategising.
Puzzle	Problem-solving, usually in a single domain such as verbal, logic, mathematics, visual or spatial.	Literacy, numeracy, logic, memory, application of skills, spelling, spatial awareness.
Quiz	Asking questions and providing feedback on correct answers; can also include various additions and gimmicks such as timers, methods of getting help and question selection.	Facts, recall.
Role playing	Taking on the role of a character in another (usually fantasy-based) world, the player can undertake a range of activities including solving quests, fighting, treasure hunting and interacting with other characters (either other players in the game world or non-player characters).	Decision-making, empathy, critical thinking, attitudes, understanding of complex systems, collaborative and social skills.
Shooter	Have the primary aim of using weapons (or sometimes spells and other special abilities) to defeat opponents, although the action is often embedded within a wider narrative context. They are generally played from a first person viewpoint and are played in real time.	Strategic thinking, working under pressure, timing, dexterity, planning, team working.
Strategy	Involve the player making strategic decisions within a scenario in order to meet the goal of the game, which is usually completing a level or solving a particular problem. They can involve, for example, movements of armies, progression of a group through various stages of development, management of resources or creation of environments to achieve specific purposes.	Time management, planning, strategising, hypothesis-testing, decision-making.

Chang, 2009). There is evidence that games can support the development of skills, knowledge and attitudes (Garris, Ahlers, & Driskell, 2002). Calvert (2005) argues, from the perspective of information processing theory, that video games have a range of cognitive effects, including:

- perception (initial intake of information) facilitated through rapid action, loud music, rapid pacing, and visual and audio effects;
- visual attention (highlighting important content) through, for example, auditory signals;
- representation and memory skills, such as the construction of schemas and mental maps, creation and articulation of strategies, and development of visual-spatial skills.

Kapp (2012) highlights the potential of computer games for stimulating episodic memory, where memories are stored in such a way that each is identified by a personal memory associated with a particular time and place. He argues that

immersive games have the visual and temporal-specific relations to provide a strong, rich association between what you are doing and your long term memory . . . in a well-designed and vivid game, episodic memory provides the learner with the ability [to] recall elements of the game, the game board or the game environment, and what was done to solve the problem.

(p. 68)

What is interesting to note here is that while Kapp starts the discussion talking about 3D immersive games, he subsequently broadens it out to include non-digital games; the real point here is that *any* game (or learning experience) that is emotionally engaging will be retained in memory longer (Medina, 2009). This also makes sense in relation to the neuroscience of learning, where there is evidence that emotionally arousing events tend to be better remembered than neutral events (Dolcos, LaBar, & Cabeza, 2004; LaBar & Cabeza, 2006). Games have the power to harness this emotion, through surprise, mystery, storytelling, excitement and in many other ways. They can be powerful tools for persuasion and attitude-changing, and can be used to present what Bogost (2010) refers to as 'procedural rhetoric' where players are exposed to arguments through interaction with the processes in the game.

Another way of looking at what can be learned from different types of computer game is the analysis undertaken by Kapp (2012), who has identified seven different types of 'learning domain' in which games can support learning. Table 3.3 provides a summary of the different domains described, with cognitive strategies used and examples of the types of game this could be employed in for learning (the examples are my own).

While Kapp's analysis does show that there are a range of skills that can be learned through gaming, it seems to overlook any of the higher level cognitive

TABLE 3.3 Learning domains and cognitive strategies employed in games (modified from Kapp, 2012)

Learning domain	Description	Cognitive strategies used	Example game
Declarative knowledge	Verbal or factual information.	Elaboration (linking new fact to previous knowledge), organising, association (linking a word or image to a definition), repetition, stories, sorting, matching.	Quiz games
Conceptual knowledge	Grouping of similar ideas, events or objects based on common sets of attributes.	Metaphor, examples and non-examples, classification, matching and sorting, immersion in the concept (first-hand experience).	Matching games
Rules-based knowledge	The relationships between concepts.	Examples, role play, experience consequences.	Simulations
Procedural knowledge	Step-by-step instructions.	Showing the big picture, explaining *how* and *why*, practice.	Repetition and practice games
Soft skills	Skills for dealing with social interactions.	Analogies, role playing.	Role play
Affective domain	Attitudes, interest, values, beliefs and emotions.	Encouraging participation, showing that success is possible, celebrity endorsement, immersion, providing success, encouragement from celebrity-type figures.	Role play
Psychomotor domain	Physical skills.	Observation, practice.	Haptic simulations

skills, such as analysis, evaluation, creativity, problem-solving and lateral thinking. I prefer the approach of a broader, but less detailed, range of the types of knowledge and skills that can be learned from games (Whitton, 2010a), with types of learning being categorised in six different areas: applying skills, such as undertaking a virtual chemistry experiment; developing strategies, for example working out the best way to defeat an enemy tribe; analysing information, like weighing up evidence to find a criminal; evaluating situations, for example determining how to escape from a locked room; changing attitudes, perhaps seeing the consequences of polluting a river; and creating knowledge by developing new games, modifications or levels.

However the skills, knowledge and attitudes that can be learned from digital games are classified, it is important to make the distinction between what is learned in a formal context, such as a school or university, and what is learned informally, simply by playing the game. When games are used in a formal educational context, whether they are designed explicitly for learning or not, they have intended learning outcomes (i.e. the teacher intends that the students will learn something specific that can be applied outside of the game) and can mediate this through appropriate briefing and debriefing activities. When games are used for leisure it is more difficult to control what is learned or see the relevance outside of the game world. In simple behaviourist games there is a much clearer link between game design and intended learning outcomes; the messy complexity of the entertainment or constructivist games makes this linkage much more difficult to ascertain or evaluate. Players learn *something* from playing all games; the question is whether that something is appropriate in formal educational settings or the development of broader life skills.

Supporting the Transition from Novice to Expert

Digital games contain many mechanisms and devices that support learning as the player moves from being a novice of the game to becoming adept and increasingly expert. Games are designed to support practice, as players move from level to level. They have a variety of inbuilt ways in which to support learning, such as the use of hints and tips, scaffolding, training levels and progress indications. They provide immediate and relevant feedback on progress to facilitate learning and movement through the game. By studying the mechanisms used in games, we can better understand how learning can be supported. Games, both behaviourist and constructivist, typically adopt a range of mechanics that support learning progress.

In describing the progression from novice to expert in games, Lewis-Evans (2010) draws on Rasmussen's (1983) framework of knowledge, rules and skills. This theory posits that all human behaviours are either knowledge-based, rule-based or skill-based, and that these are hierarchical in terms of cognitive effort: knowledge-based behaviours require the most effort and this is the level of reasoning, approaching new problems, and working things out, rule-based behaviours require less as they involve the application of previously learned rules, while skill-based behaviours are automatic and effortless. As players progress from novice to expert in games, they ideally move through these levels until flow can be achieved at the skill level. Dreyfus and Dreyfus (1986) suggest that there are five steps from novice to expert in terms of skill acquisition: (1) the novice, applying rules regardless of context; (2) the advanced beginner, using more sophisticated rules that appreciate the importance of the specific situation; (3) achieving a level of competence with the ability to prioritise, organise, plan and make informed decisions; (4) arriving at a level of proficiency using intuition based on past experience; before (5) finally becoming an expert where performance is fluid and unconscious. These levels also apply to game-players as they move from game "newbie" to master player, and games typically provide a variety of ways in which to facilitate this transition.

Kapp (2012) highlights four differences between novices and experts. First, he says that "experts represent problems at deep structural levels in terms of basic principles within a domain; novices represent problems in terms of surface or superficial characteristics" (p. 145). In essence, the expert has a more holistic view of the domain area; novices may focus on small (and possibly irrelevant) aspects. The second difference highlights the ways in which experts and novices approach problem-solving: experts approach problems with unknown solutions by using solutions already encountered in similar challenges; novices typically use a trial-and-error approach. Third, he suggests that because experts store knowledge in long-term, rather than short-term, memory that knowledge is more efficiently chunked and easier to access than for novices. Finally, novices are typically unaware of errors they make, and need to continually check solutions and assumptions, whereas experts have strong automatic self-monitoring skills.

In games, mistake-making is seen as an inevitable part of the gaming experience; it is by making mistakes and learning from them and trying again that players can make progress through the game. Instead of mistakes being seen as problematic, they are an integral part of game-play because they provide the opportunity for players to receive feedback, and change their game-play techniques or strategies. This is very different from the ways in which mistake-making is seen in education, where mistakes are commonly regarded as failure rather than as part of the learning process itself. Repetition and practice allow the brain to encode memories more efficiently and move them from short-term to long-term memory (Medina, 2009) so provision of an environment in which failure and practice are not only accepted, but part of the fun of play, is ideal for laying down long-term memories.

Digital games offer several structures that support meaningful practice, including progress indicators, reinforcement and adaptive play. Games usually have ways of indicating to players how they are performing, such as the use of scores and levels (either levels of content in the game, or levels of experience such as character levels in role-playing games). As players complete levels, as well as the motivational aspects (discussed in Chapter 6) they are provided with a framework in which to practise, consolidating learned skills as new ones are introduced.

As the game progresses, various means of guidance and context-relevant help systems are typical. Gee (2008) points out that

> there is a good deal of guidance in games: guidance from the game design itself, and from the NPCs [non-player characters] and the environment, from information given 'just in time' and 'on demand', from other players in

and out of the game, and from the resources of communities of practice built up around the game.

(p. 26)

Again, this guidance can be external to the game, such as hints or tips, or it can be part of the action of the game, such as advice from a character. Hirumi, Appelman, Rieber, and Van Eck, (2010) draw on Gagné's (1965) nine events of instruction to present a model of events of instruction in games.

1. *Gain attention*, for example through the use of motion, cut scenes, noise, music or speech.
2. *Inform of objective*, for example through the information on the back of the game box, documentation for the game, introductory movies, cut scenes, character speech or obstacles that make the aim apparent.
3. *Recall prior knowledge*, using for example environmental cues (puzzles that look like those used in tutorials), or familiar obstacles (where the search for solutions involves recalling solutions and events from earlier in the game).
4. *Present instruction*, using characters, the environment, objects, conversation; many games use situated learning and guided discovery strategies to embed learning in the context of the narrative.
5. *Provide guidance*, using for example cut scenes, non-player character or player character speech, hint books, cheats and walkthroughs, friends or partial solutions to puzzles. The actors and objects in the environment and the structure of the story also provide implicit guidance.
6. *Provide practice*, where players can refine skills and knowledge needed to advance, and mastery of challenges usually requires multiple attempts.
7. *Provide feedback*, again through mechanisms such as speech, sounds and motion; mastery of challenges followed by game advancement, cut scenes, new information, where every action has immediate feedback, even if that feedback is that nothing happens.
8. *Assess performance*, where advancement through the game *is* assessment; players learn skills in order to overcome challenges, each of which represents assessment of those skills.
9. *Enhance retention and transfer*, where things learned early in games are brought back in different, often more complex forms later and players know that what they learn in a game will be relevant in both the short and long term.

As can be seen from this analysis, games as learning environments intrinsically embody many of the events that support learners as they progress from a novice to an expert. I would question the final event; while this relates to retention and transfer within games, the real issue is whether skills learned in the game can be transferred to other contexts. This idea of games as authentic learning contexts and transfer of learning is discussed in more detail in the next chapter.

4

GAMES AS AUTHENTIC CONTEXTS

Games have the power to transport a player from the real world into the fictional context of the game world. This ability to create a realistic, often immersive context for play and learning is a key benefit of digital games. The framework of a role-playing or adventure game, for example, creates a setting in which challenges make sense and become meaningful within the context of the game. This constructs learning not as a set of abstract and unconnected tasks but as a meaningful and purposive series of activities leading to an end goal. If the goal of the game is aligned with the learning goals then this can result in a powerful learning experience.

In this chapter, I will explore theories that highlight the importance of the context of learning and the ways in which games provide a meaningful context and purpose for learning, even if learning is not the primary motivation for playing the game. First, I present and discuss a range of learning theories that are particularly relevant to games, including experiential learning, situated cognition and cognitive apprenticeship, epistemic games and pervasive learning. I have aimed to provide a broad theoretical overview of the importance of context for learning, as well as discussing the issues associated with the transfer of learning from one context to another, and highlighting ways in which digital games can create authentic and purposeful contexts for action.

Learning Through Situated Experience

The experiential learning cycle (Kolb, 1984) presents a model that emphasises the importance of active learning in a meaningful context, including planning, reflection and gaining theoretical understanding to underpin learning. According to this cycle, learning takes place as part of a sequence of steps where a learner starts by actively taking part in a learning activity that provides a concrete experience, which is followed by personal reflection on the experience. This reflection is then followed by the application of known theories to the experience, or the derivation of rules from it; and finally the learning is used to inform, modify action and experiment to create the next concrete experience.

Gee (2003) argues that computer games reflect the experiential learning cycle because players must examine the virtual environment of a game, reflect on the situation and form a hypothesis about what is happening, take action and then investigate the virtual world to see what effect their action had. For example, imagine you are playing an adventure game where you find a locked door (experience). Since the door will not open, you consider whether you need to access the door to progress or if there are alternatives (reflect). Next, in order to address the locked door problem, you think about doors you have encountered previously and perhaps check your inventory for any obvious door-opening objects such as keys; you then consider other ways of getting through doors in relation to what you already know about doors (theorise) and decide to try breaking the door down with a tree trunk (experiment), which produces a crack in the door but does not break it down. This feedback provides a clue to your next action because, while the door still refuses to open, it has shown that it can potentially be broken down, and the cycle begins again.

One of the benefits of digital games is the ability of a computer to provide the interaction and feedback that is crucial to the experiential learning cycle and to the whole process of learning. Computer games have the ability to facilitate many types of interaction from simple items that can be clicked and movement through a linear sequence to free exploration of highly complex interactive virtual worlds (see Chapter 12 for more detail about types of interactivity). However, while the experiential learning cycle may map onto learning within the game world itself, it does not necessarily provide students with scope for the meta-cognitive processes they require to enable transfer of learning from the context of the game into the real world.

This is why it is crucial that computer games for learning should be considered in relation to the other activities and reflection that surround them and not simply as stand-alone activities. The problem of transfer to learning from a game (or any educational context) into the real world is a perennial one. It is worth noting a key difference here between simulations and games. Simulations try to mirror the real world as closely as possible so that, in theory at least, transfer should be seamless, for instance from a high-fidelity flight simulator to an actual aircraft. Games, although they might be based on the real world, do not aim at the same level of realism, so transfer may become more problematic. In the case of games designed for entertainment, where real-life procedures may be truncated or altered to increase the game playability, there is still potential for using the game as a discussion point about how the game world differs from reality. Alexander and Brunyé (2005) suggest that the fidelity, the amount of presence experienced, levels of absorption in the activity and user acceptance are all factors that affect transfer of learning from a simulation game to the real world.

The issue of transferability can be addressed if the game is conceived as more than simply a stand-alone activity; associated debriefing activities can help to ensure that what is learned in the game can be meaningfully applied to the real world (Thiagarajan, 1993) and make the connection between the game and the curriculum, by developing skills such as reflection, observation, prediction or theory-building (Felicia, 2008). Garfield (2000) argues that every context for game playing is different, and that these interfaces between the game world and real life (what he calls 'metagames') need to be better understood. He highlights four types of metagame: what the player brings to the game, such as resources, preparation, reputation; what the player takes from the game, such as prizes, standing, access to future games; what happens between games, such as research and preparation; what happens during a game other than the game itself, such as fatigue or friendships and disputes outside of the game. While the game may try to provide a real-life experience, other external factors need to be considered to get the maximum learning benefit. Meta-cognitive strategies used during game-play that involve talking or observation, such as modelling or thinking aloud, were found to be more effective for enhancing learning and gaming achievements than those that use writing, such as note-taking (Kim, Park, & Baek, 2009).

Maharg (2004) argues that considering an authentic learning context, such as a game or simulation, to be a representation of reality in fact devalues both the role of education and complexity of reality. He suggests that educational processes such as reflection, variation, feedback and negotiated learning are more sophisticated than a simple mirroring of reality. In the fast-paced world of modern computer games, there is often little time to reflect or carry out other meta-cognitive processes during game play in game genres such as action-adventures or shooters, so it is crucial to build in reflection after or alongside play. Debriefing, post-game discussion and reflection are regarded by some as key aspects to ensuring that the learning is focused and appropriate (Kiili, 2007; Pannese, Ascolese, Prilla, & Morosini, 2013; Thiagarajan, 1993). It has been argued that one of the benefits of game-based learning is that learners are so engaged in the game that they learn almost without realising it (e.g. Prensky, 2007) – the idea of 'stealth learning'. However, this idea neglects the view that in order for learning (certainly at higher levels) to be retained and successfully applied to other contexts, critical reflection on the knowledge and skills learned and how they fit into the overall schema of knowledge and understanding is desirable. Therefore while stealth learning might take place, that learning may be very resistant to transfer to other contexts.

There is a variety of ways in which reflection can be built into the game-based learning process, both within the game and in the activities that surround it; a summary of different methods is shown in Table 4.1.

Experiential learning is not just about context, but also about the people who take part in the learning experience. Gee (2008) presents the situated learning

TABLE 4.1 Intrinsic and extrinsic game reflection mechanisms

	Reflection mechanism
Within game (intrinsic)	Required moments of pause/waiting
	Failure and replay
	Support resources (e.g. hints, helper)
	Character dialogue
During game (extrinsic)	Reflection moments, reviewing recent activity and failure points and looking at what was done from an outside perspective
	Cut scenes and recap
	Comments from others (virtual or in real time)
	Watching others play
After game (extrinsic)	Debriefing
	Reflective diaries
	Production of game artefacts (e.g. fan fiction, additional levels)
	Game critique
	Helping/mentoring others

matrix (see Figure 4.1) where "content is rooted in experiences a person is having as part and parcel of taking on a specific identity ... learning is situated in experience, but goal-driven, identity-focused experience" (p. 26). (Gee here uses the idea of 'content' in a broad sense, to refer to the whole range of skills and facts learned through playing a game, rather than having a specific focus on 'academic' content.)

In a game (the situated learning matrix), players assume an identity or 'way of being in the world', which is influenced by the goals of the character and the norms (or rules) by which that character operates. This can be a direct example such as playing a character in a role-playing game, or the more subtle form of taking on a character such as a property tycoon in *Monopoly* or 'a player of chess'. To achieve the goals of the character within the game, within the constraints of the character norms, the player has to gain knowledge and master skills required by the game (content), using the tools and technologies provided (objects that can be manipulated, characters that can be controlled, collaboration with non-player characters and other players). This means that learning always takes place within a specific, designed problem-space, which is one of

---

Identity ←→ Goals and norms (sometimes including ethical or moral values) ←→ Tools and technologies ←→ Context as problem-solving space that is one of a set of similar but varied problems ←→ Context

---

FIGURE 4.1 Gee's (2008) Situated Learning Matrix

many similar but varied problem-spaces, and as players experience more contexts within games they are increasingly able to generalise what they have learned from them.

Role playing, either in real life or in virtual environments, is a powerful way in which to give students direct experience of other contexts, situations, people and emotions. Based on an experiential learning model of virtual role play, Francis (2011) argues that learners develop an intuitive understanding of their places within the social context of the game, develop a holistic understanding of the social system through multiple modes of representation, learn about the game world as a by-product of achieving the personal game goals, and generate tentative hypotheses through iterative problem-solving. This ability to experience, investigate and interrogate both the 'physical' and 'social' worlds in games is one of their primary learning benefits.

Situated Cognition and Cognitive Apprenticeship

The theory of situated cognition (Brown, Collins & Duguid, 1989) supports the argument that learning needs to be placed in a meaningful context, making the case that knowledge cannot be something that stands apart from context, but that it is a product of the environment and culture in which it was created and applied. The theory of situated cognition suggests that learning, rather than being about the memorisation of facts, is about an enculturation into a domain, taking part in what Brown and colleagues (1989) term 'authentic' activities. These activities are described as the meaningful and purposeful "ordinary practices of the culture" (p. 34) and they make the argument that learning takes place through engagement in these activities. The related model of cognitive apprenticeship (Collins, Brown, & Newman, 1989) presents an approach in which formal learning takes place through gradual assimilation of the novice into the learning domain through a series of authentic activities. Cognitive apprenticeships use methods of learning that "try to enculturate students into authentic practices through activity and social interaction in a way similar to that evident – and evidently successful – in craft apprenticeship" (Brown et al., 1989, p. 37).

Games offer authentic activities, situated within meaningful contexts, with social interaction both within and alongside the game through collaborative gaming activities and the communities that surround them. Kapp (2012) gives a clear example of the process of cognitive apprenticeship in games:

> When you play the *Uncharted 3: Drake's Deception* game on the Playstation 3, you don't tell Nathan Drake what to shoot, you don't direct him where to go, and you don't give him commands to follow. No, you don't control Nathan Drake because you *are* Nathan Drake. By operating the character in the game, you learn the implicit rules of the world you inhabit. You rehearse the act of jumping from cliff to cliff until you master it. You practice

sneaking around undetected and use in-game money to unlock special actions. You are serving as an apprentice in the game environment.

(Kapp, 2012, pp. 69–70)

Collins (2006) presents a four-dimensional framework for designing the ideal learning environments to facilitate cognitive apprenticeship. The four dimensions are: content – the types of knowledge required for domain expertise (again, a broad definition of content that goes beyond memorisation of facts); methods for promoting the development of expertise within a domain; the ways in which learning activities are sequenced; and the social characteristics of the learning environment. Table 4.2 below provides an overview of the different aspects associated with each dimension of the framework.

TABLE 4.2 Aspects of the ideal learning environment to facilitate cognitive apprenticeship (adapted from Collins, 2006)

Dimension	Aspects
Content: Types of knowledge required for expertise	Domain knowledge (facts, concepts, procedures) Heuristic strategies (general techniques for accomplishing tasks) Control strategies (techniques for monitoring, diagnostics, remedial action) Learning strategies (knowledge and strategies for learning)
Method: Ways to promote the development of expertise	Modelling (performing a task that can be observed) Coaching (teacher observes and facilitates while student performs) Scaffolding (provides supports that are gradually removed) Articulation (verbalisation of knowledge and understanding) Reflection (replay and comparison of performance) Exploration (students problem-solve on their own)
Sequencing: Key to ordering learning activities	Increasing complexity (gradual increase in difficulty) Increasing diversity (presentation of a range of contexts in which to practise) Global to local skills (focus first on the overview then the specifics)
Sociology: Social characteristics of learning environments	Situated learning (learning in context from authentic tasks) Community of practice (sharing and support around the activity) Intrinsic motivation (learning is its own end) Cooperation (learners work together to achieve goals)

This framework can map onto the context of a digital game. A game typically will be about something; it will have a theme, a setting and a context, and a range of activities that can be carried out in the game world, however abstract or concrete. This is the 'domain knowledge' of the game, and involves applying problem-solving techniques (heuristic strategies) to achieve the game objects and meet the goals of the game. The control strategies are supported through devices in games such as progression indicators, points and feedback, while learning strategies can be developed through in-game help, watching other players or advice from in-game characters.

Games embody a variety of methods to promote the development of expertise. Modelling occurs throughout a wide range of digital games, where players can watch examples (for example in training levels) or other players (in multiplayer games), and are coached by other more experienced players, or within the game, for example through the use of a virtual guide. Provision of scaffolding is a key way in which games support learning; rather than having a manual or guidebook, modern computer games immerse the player in the game environment, but scaffold the immersion through gradual introduction to tools and activities within the game so that players gain more control and discover more about the game and what they can do in it. In some games this scaffolding happens only early on in introductory or training levels, while in others it can take place for the duration of the game, so that exploring and discovering the capabilities of the game interface becomes part of the game itself. Articulation, or verbalising, is not something that computer games typically support (although it is common in, for example, parlour games and some board games), but becomes apparent when a game is played with others, and strategies, techniques and ideas have to be articulated and discussed, for example during team play in massively multiplayer online role playing games. Computer games may also not naturally support reflection but it can be built in using techniques such as replay-and-review (in fighting games) and the provision of cryptic hints (in adventure games); it can take place away from the game as well through debriefing activities and discussion with others. Games can also be wonderful exploration and discovery-based environments, presenting rich and interactive virtual worlds in which players can move around, find new areas and objects, build and create things, and determine the full potential of the game activities.

Considering the sequencing dimensions of the Collins (2006) model, digital games match the characteristics by providing tasks that get gradually more difficult and more complex, in different and diverse contexts. The issue of sequencing from global to local is more problematic in games: on one hand, it could be argued that many games do this through training levels, which offer a microcosm of the entire game world and allow players a holistic view of activity; alternatively, many games focus on a small area initially and let the big picture emerge as the game develops, which adds to the mystery and suspense of the game.

In relation to the sociological aspects of the model, evidence was presented earlier in the chapter that games provide a forum for situated learning; their ability to foster communities of practice and cooperative learning is discussed in Chapter 5. Issues of intrinsic motivation are also discussed in more detail later in the book, specifically in Chapter 6.

Epistemic Games

The theory of epistemic games (Shaffer, 2005, 2006) links games, simulations and professional practices to provide a series of tools that support the design of games for learning. Shaffer (2005, p. 1) promotes the idea of learning contexts that are "thickly authentic" where "learners use real tools and methods to address issues they care about" that are "simultaneously aligned with the interests of the learners, the structure of a domain of knowledge, valued practices in the world, and the modes of assessment used". However, the creation of these rich and meaningful environments is difficult. In developing the theory of epistemic games, Shaffer draws on the ideas of epistemic frames (Shaffer, 2004a) and pedagogical praxis (Shaffer, 2004b). Epistemic frames are a way of understanding learning that takes place within the contexts of (professional or otherwise) communities of practice (Wenger, 1998, described in more detail in Chapter 5). Epistemic frames are described as

> a form of knowing *with* that comprise, for a particular community, knowing *where* to begin looking and asking questions, knowing *what* constitutes appropriate evidence to consider or information to assess, knowing *how* to go about gathering that evidence, and knowing *when* to draw a conclusion and/or move on to a different issue.
>
> *(Shaffer, 2004a, p. 476)*

The theory of pedagogical praxis assumes that, under the right conditions, technologies can make it easier for students to become actively and meaningfully involved in communities of practice, and that participation in professional communities allows students to learn from these experiences; technology 'builds a bridge' that allows students to participate in and experience the learning practices of professionals. An epistemic game, then, draws together the ideas of learning through meaningful technology-facilitated involvement in communities and the epistemic forms of knowing that occur in those communities, to create a "simulation that preserves the connections between knowing and doing central to the epistemic frame" (Shaffer, 2005).

The advantage of epistemic games is that they begin to address the issue of transfer of learning from the context of the game into other contexts (Shaffer, 2006). The problem with any form of learning is that it occurs in a context, and the more specific and closely aligned that context is to the knowledge or skills being learned, the more difficult it is for learners to see the relevance and apply what they have learned to other contexts. Shaffer (2012) highlights two dominant, yet conflicting, theoretical models of transfer:

1. *Learning as transfer of an individual,* where a solution to one problem is applied to an analogically similar problem, which is rare, difficult to achieve and limited.
2. *Learning as participation by individuals in communities,* where learners are mentored to do tasks within the context of the community, so skills do not transfer between settings.

However, he makes the argument that these two views need not be mutually exclusive and "we can understand learning – the transfer of experience from one context to another – as something that can be discussed, analysed, conceptualized and supported as both *transformation of an individual* and *participation in a practice*" (Shaffer, 2012, p. 405).

Brookes and Moseley (2012) build on Shaffer's work to make a compelling argument for what they call "pervasive learning activities" that attempt to bridge the "reality gap" between the learning experience and an authentic experience (see Figure 4.2 below).

They highlight that the gap is not just about the physical differences between the designed learning experience and the real world, but

> also includes anything that prevents the learner being able to engage with the intended reality – such as the learner's desires and expectations, their ideas of what is relevant to their subjects or contexts, their own perceptions of their learning potential from a particular type of activity, and a number of internal blocks that we all carry (which may include, for instance, a disdain for games as frivolous or pointless).
>
> *(Brookes & Moseley, 2012, p. 94)*

They suggest that pervasive learning activities require a suspension of disbelief and a blurring of the boundaries between learning activity and reality. The emerging field of pervasive games, alternate reality games in particular, can provide this intermediary context.

Standard lecture	Simulation Role-play Case study Computer-based simulation	Reality Gap	Authentic experience

Increasing degree of realism

FIGURE 4.2 The reality gap (adapted from Brookes & Moseley, 2012)

Pervasive Games for Establishing Context

Real-world games, pervasive games or mobile place-based gaming are all different terms that refer to games that use real-world locations as a backdrop to the fictional world of the game. Typically, technology is used as a mediator between the real world and the virtual world, using techniques such as augmented reality and GPS to add a game layer. Montola, Stenros, and Waern (2009) describe eight different types of pervasive game, from the established to the emerging; these are summarised in Table 4.3 below.

Pervasive games, particularly coupled with the increasing powers of mobile technologies, have massive potential for creating situated learning environments and meaningful contexts for learning. One type of game in particular, alternate reality games (ARGs), have been most commonly researched in learning contexts in recent years (e.g. Connolly et al., 2011; McGonigal, 2007; Moseley, 2012a). Alternate reality games provide an innovative learning context in which players can take part in a series of puzzles and challenges, on a collaborative and individual basis, both online and in the real world, as part of an overarching story that unfolds as the game progresses. This game format potentially provides engaging

TABLE 4.3 Pervasive game genres (summarised from Montola et al., 2009)

Established	Treasure hunts	Players find objects or locations within an unlimited game space (e.g. geocaching).
	Assassination games	Players have to locate other players and "assassinate" them.
	Pervasive LARPs	Utilising techniques from live-action role play, particularly physical acting and character-based make believe and pretend play.
	Alternate reality games	Collaborative games that merge the online and real worlds, and progress by puzzle-solving within a collaboratively constructed narrative.
Emerging	Smart street sports	Technology-enhanced, physical versions of children's games such as tag or pacman, played in urban spaces.
	Playful public performances	Similar in design to smart street sports, but with more emphasis on performance, playing and creating a spectacle.
	Urban adventure games	Combination of stories and puzzles in historical or cultural city spaces: hypertexts in physical space.
	Reality games	Conscious playing with concepts of real and reality, which encourages players to see reality in new and different ways.

collaborative learning spaces where students can work together to achieve desired learning outcomes that map onto the game challenges. ARGs differ from traditional digital games in that they blend real life and narrative into an 'alternate reality' using online artefacts such as web tools and social networking sites, as well as physical objects and places. ARGs have been described as "an obsession-inspiring genre that blends real-life treasure hunting, interactive storytelling, video games and online community" (Borland, 2005). The interplay between the real-world elements and fantasy narrative is a characteristic of the games, in that they

> take the substance of everyday life and weave it into narratives that layer additional meaning, depth, and interaction upon the real world. The contents of these narratives constantly intersect with actuality, but play fast and loose with fact, sometimes departing entirely from the actual or grossly warping it.
>
> *(Martin, Thompson, & Chatfield, 2006, p. 6)*

As well as the online environment, alternate reality games often use printed materials such as posters and business cards, or communication through means such as the telephone or conversations with real people; no medium is out of bounds and there is often no explicit distinction between the real world and the game world. For example, web sites within the game will be indistinguishable from genuine sites and similarly, an ARG will often not advertise itself as a 'game' and it is up to the players to distinguish between reality and fiction for themselves.

Brookes and Moseley (2012) highlight ten aspects of alternate reality games that they believe align them with pervasive learning activities (drawn from Brookes, 2009; McGonigal, 2003; McGonigal, 2011; Moseley, 2008; Whitton, 2007b):

1. The realistic, immersive and interactive nature of the game, which extends beyond narrative or simulation to blur the boundary between game and reality.
2. The 'doing' aspects of the game are identical to the real world, supporting authentic learning.
3. Players can influence outcomes as the game trajectory changes based on player actions and reactions.
4. Learning is organised and directed by the learner based on needs highlighted by the game, so that players have ownership of, and responsibility for, their own learning.
5. Progress, competition and rewards provide extrinsic incentives and motivation, which meets the needs of some players.
6. Pacing and regular delivery of new puzzles or storylines maintains engagement and interest.
7. Problems and puzzles at different levels of difficulty draw players in and provide an inclusive environment at all ability levels.
8. Active collaborative communities provide group learning and support environments.

9. The use of simple technologies and accessible media makes ARGs accessible to educators and learners alike.
10. The novelty of the approach may be surprising and fun, motivating some learners.

In theory, alternate reality games should provide an engaging context for collaborative problem-solving and learning within a community of practice, and there are some examples of perceived motivational and learning benefits (Connolly et al., 2011). However, in practice their use in educational settings has highlighted many challenges such as low take-up, lack of understanding of the nature of the game world, limited value for learning and lack of motivation for students to take part, and the tension between the niche nature of ARGs and accessible and inclusive educational curricula (Piatt, 2009; Whitton, Jones, Wilson, & Whitton, 2012). In spite of the discord between ARGs as games and as formal learning activities, I still believe that these problems are not insurmountable; there is lots of potential in the genre to create meaningful learning activities that provide an authentic context, in a way that is accessible for both teachers and learners.

Recent developments in mobile devices have also opened up a new world of possibilities for mobile gaming using technologies such as smartphones, handheld computers, PDAs, cameras, portable media players and tablets, situating the gaming world in the real world. These devices are usually location-aware, in that they use GPS to accurately pinpoint the position of a player in space, they present a range of built-in communication devices, from the basic functions of telephone, text and email to internet video telephony and social networks. These devices are light-weight and can access the Internet from anywhere, and so information is available exactly when needed, and they typically have the capabilities to allow the user to view and capture data in a range of multimedia forms, including video, photographs and audio. These capabilities offer a wide range of possibilities for mobile educational games. For example, Facer and colleagues (2004) describe the use of a mobile game in which children learned about animal behaviour using their mobile devices to map out and interact with a virtual savannah, while Huizenga and colleagues (2009) discuss the effectiveness of a mobile game set in Amsterdam used to teach medieval history to secondary school students, and Holden and Sykes (2011) explore the potential of using an augmented reality mobile game for language learning by enabling students to interact with a historical neighbourhood and solve a fictional mystery overlaid onto the real world.

Alternate reality games, mobile games and other pervasive games provide a model for creating context in education, but they are not the only options. The majority of games are designed in such a way that the creation of a context for play is integral to the activities of the game, and it is this context that helps the learners to become involved and immersed in authentic activities and problems, in theory at least, increasing learning and the ability to use the skills and knowledge learned in real-world situations.

5

GAMES AS SOCIAL INTERACTIONS

Game playing is, with a few exceptions, inherently social. Before the advent of computer games, most games were played with other people, either competitively or collaboratively. Games provide a reason to be with other people and a context for activity, as well as acting as a social facilitator, for example at family gatherings or social events where people do not know each other well, making social interaction easier by giving it a focus. While there are some examples of pre-digital games that are solo activities (solo card games such as Patience being a notable example), the advent of computer games initially made gaming a more solitary practice, as the growth in un-networked home computers in the 1980s spawned a range of genres for 'play-alone' games, such as adventure or platform games. Even though these games were designed to be played by one person, they were still often used in social situations with players working collaboratively to solve problems, or taking turns to play while watching others.

The growth in networked computers has led to a massive increase in the numbers of networked games and the ways in which games support collaborative activities. Some genres, such as online role-playing games and first person shooters, have a long history of multiplayer collaborative design, while other genres, such as casual games, are relatively recent additions. As well as fostering collaboration with others online, games can also be played competitively, while still creating a feeling of community and fun that is as important as, if not more so than, the competition element. Playing games with other people, whether collaborating with or competing against them, provides the important social interaction that games foster so well. Koster (2005) provides a useful overview of this distinction in what he calls the 'human activity matrix'. This matrix can be used in the context of any human activity, but the example in relation to gaming is particularly insightful here. The matrix shows three approaches to an activity: collaborative,

TABLE 5.1 Gaming in the human activity matrix (from Koster, 2005)

User goal	Approach		
	Collaborative	Competitive	Solo
Constructive	Team game design	Commercial game development	Modding and skinning
Experiential	Cooperative player-vs.-environment gaming	Player-vs.-player gaming	Single-player games
Deconstructive	Strategy guide writing	Hacking and cheats	Writing a book about gaming
	Many participants		One participant

competitive and solo, and three ways in which users might engage in activities: constructive (building or creation), experiential (taking part in the activity), and deconstructive (taking apart and analysing the experience). The example of Gaming in the human activity matrix is shown in Table 5.1 above, which shows example activities for each quadrant.

This grid shows the different approaches to playing and working with other people in the context of game creation, playing, analysis and discussion. This is a particularly useful model as it shows that the potential of games for learning and playing together is not just about 'playing games' (the experiential user goal) but about creating games, and understanding the processes that surround them (more about this in Chapter 11). In this chapter three areas relevant to games and learning with others are discussed: first, a selection of theories that highlight the importance of collaborative learning are presented; second, the ways in which learning from others can be incorporated into games, as happens informally in gaming communities, are considered; and finally I explore the role of competition in games and learning.

There are many learning theories that assert that more can be learned by working with others, and learning from them, than can be learned alone. Social learning theory argues that people learn from one another through observation, instruction and modelling (Bandura, 1977). Kapp (2012) highlights the relevance of this theory for game-based learning because of the potential for the use of avatars to model behaviour, which allows learning to happen at any time in a variety of contexts in a way that can be replayed, saying that "[a video game can] simultaneously expose the player to modelling, rehearsal, and reinforcement of the social behaviour that is involved in the games's theme" (p. 71). While social learning theory offers a basic understanding of some of the more straightforward ways in which games can support learning through virtual 'social' interaction, it misses the far greater potential for actual interaction. One of the important advantages in the growth and ubiquity of personal networked devices is the potential to develop virtual communities of learners. Collaborative online learning communities involve the "bringing together of students via personal computers linked to the Internet, with a focus on them working as a 'learning community', sharing resources, knowledge, experience and responsibility through reciprocal collaborative learning" (McConnell, 2006, p. 11). Emerging collaborative game forms, such as alternate reality games (see Chapter 4 for more detail) can help to harness 'collective intelligence', the idea that the ability of the internet to support a rapid, open and global exchange of ideas can generate new and unexpected ways of generating, sharing and curating collective knowledge, wisdom, skills and experience (McGonigal, 2007).

Social Constructivism and the Zone of Proximal Development

Social constructivism focuses on the importance of constructing shared meanings and understandings with other people; highlighting that knowledge evolves through social negotiation and through the evolution of the viability of individual understandings, that the social environment is critical to the development of understandings, and other people are a primary mechanism for testing those understandings and providing sources of alternative views to challenge thinking. Central to the ideas of social constructivist learning is the idea of students working together, sharing and clarifying ideas and opinions, developing communication skills and learning from one another (Jonassen, Davidson, Campbell, & Bannan Haag, 1995). Working collaboratively enables students to work to their strengths, develop critical thinking skills and creativity, validate their ideas and appreciate a range of individual learning styles, skills, preferences and perspectives. Social constructivism highlights the importance of context and culture in forming meaning; it views learning as not simply an internal process, or a passive shaping of behaviours, but as a social construct that is mediated by language via discourse (McMahon, 1997).

Vygotsky (1978) is a particularly influential social constructivist, and his work is concerned with the collaborative aspects of learning, theorising that learning takes place at a social level first and then at an individual level. His theory of zones of proximal development contends that the zone of proximal development is the difference between what a student can learn working alone, and what he or she can achieve when being supported and guided by a teacher or some other expert. The zone of proximal development is described as "the difference between the actual development level as determined by independent problem solving and the level of potential development as determined through problem solv-ing under adult guidance or in collaboration with more capable peers" (Vygotsky, 1978, p. 86). This highlights that students can learn more under the mentorship or guidance of others with more advanced understandings or knowledge, and the fact that learners can only progress within a certain range with support from others. This also supports the notion of scaffolding, the idea that learners can progress faster with guidance that is gradually removed as they make the transition from novice to expert; this is discussed in more detail in Chapter 3. The theory of connectivism, which was also introduced in Chapter 3, also supports the notion of learning with other people. It posits the idea that learning takes place through gathering and organising information, re-mixing and re-purposing and sharing that information as part of a community (Downes, 2011). Knowledge is not something that is 'owned' by an individual, but something that exists in the collective consciousness of a community.

Communities of Practice

A community of practice (Wenger, 1998) comprises a group of people who share a craft, profession or common interest. Participating in these communities provides a legitimate and on-going way of learning from others as part of a group through apprenticeship and education in the context of the group norms, processes and identity. Wenger (2000) describes these communities of practice as "the basic building blocks of a social learning system" and states that "participating in these 'communities of practice' is essential to our learning. It is at the very core of what makes us human beings capable of meaningful knowing" (p. 229). He describes three modes of belonging to a community:

1. Engagement – doing things with other people, talking together and discussion, creating things collaboratively.
2. Imagination – constructing a (real) image of yourself and your place within the community, and the place of the community within the world. This allows members of the community to orientate themselves, reflecting on the community and explore future possibilities.
3. Alignment – the coordination of individual and local activities within the overall processes, codes and identities of the group.

As well as the action that takes place directly before, during and after game play, there is a great deal that can be learned through engagement with the communities that support the game, and the ways in which engagement in the community supports the development of identity. Belonging to communities, through doing things with others, and feeling a sense of group identity and purpose and undertaking activities within a common overall ethos and goal, is key to learning, and this is one of the critical arguments behind the use of computer games for learning. However, Gee and Hayes (2012) argue that the idea of communities of practice has been so overused that it has become essentially meaningless, and that the concept does not bear much relation to "the geographically distributed, technologically mediated, and fluidly populated social groupings" (p. 132) that are common in online communities such as gaming fan communities.

Squire (2011) makes the point that the "educational potential of video games is not just about the *software*, but also about the participatory communities that games often inspire" (p. 61). He argues for the importance of "participatory media spaces" outside of formal education, that "provide opportunities to forge new identities, follow one's passions, develop unique expertise, make social connections, and ultimately participate in real practices" (p. 61). Erickson (1997) suggests that communities need: membership (and therefore exclusion); relationships between and among members; commitment to the community and helping others simply because of their membership; shared values, practices, goals, procedures, histories, artefacts and places; creation, control and distribution of collective goods; and assumptions about the longevity of the community. Hand and Moore (2006) highlight a key criticism of the idea of 'virtual communities': that the ethical dimension has been removed, that the fact that "they are formed through bonds of transient mutual interest rather than mutual obligation or proximity, makes them something other than communities" (p. 173). Perhaps this is somewhat of a semantic argument: groups of people gather around games, share ideas and learn together, whether or not we call them communities.

Affinity Spaces

Learners need opportunities to build on and take part in their own group and learning communities, and key to this is the ideas of affinity groups (Gee, 2003) and affinity spaces (Gee & Hayes, 2012). An affinity group is composed of the people associated with a particular semiotic domain (defined as an area in which people share common values and ways of thinking about the area of interest, see Chapter 3 for more detail) such as chemists, geographers or video game players. They share a passion for the domain and shared ways of thinking, behaving, believing and being within that domain. Gee (2003) describes affinity groups as groups in which: members bond first through a 'common endeavour' and second through affective ties; the common endeavour is organised around a whole process rather than discrete or separate tasks; group members have 'extensive' and 'intensive' knowledge (i.e. knowledge of many or all stages of the endeavour as well as deep and specialist knowledge of one or more areas); much of the knowledge of the group is tacit (embodied and unwritten), distributed (spread among members) and dispersed (spread among different sites and institutions); and group leaders are not 'bosses' as such, but have the role of designing and resourcing the group, while helping members turn their tacit knowledge into explicit knowledge that can be shared outside the group. These affinity groups manifest in all areas of life, where people have a shared passion and wish to voluntarily communicate and share knowledge and practices, and can be physical or virtual. Squire (2011) argues that not all affinity groups are communities as the latter typically have a longer history, more established culture, stronger social ties and group commitments, and mechanisms for becoming familiar with the culture of the community.

In his more recent work, Gee (Gee & Hayes, 2012) states a preference for the term 'affinity spaces' over 'affinity groups' stating that

> often in the modern world a group is defined by a space in which people associate rather than by some readily identifiable criterion such as registering with a political party or completing professional training. On a fan site devoted, say, to *Age of Mythology*, who 'belongs' and who does not? What does *belonging* really mean?
>
> *(p. 132)*

The organisation of the space (including web spaces and real-world spaces) is as critical as the organisation of the people. Squire (2011) suggests that online affinity spaces provide a model for education; they are open to anyone, although they do police behaviour both formally and through member action and activities, and provide a mixture of 'official' (editorially approved) and 'user-generated' content. Learning to interact as part of such a group and evaluate group contributions and assess their validity, credibility and value is a key digital literacy skill. Egenfeldt-Nielsen and colleagues (2008) distinguish between the player cultures that develop in gaming communities within the game, which facilitate in-game relations (such as strategies) but can extend beyond the game (for example through the use of additional voice tools in multi-user gaming), and meta-cultures that exist around and beyond the game such as fan sites, online discussions, and game magazines. Gee and Hayes (2012) also highlight the importance of the social practices that take place within and around games, and describe 'nurturing affinity spaces', arguing that "human learning becomes deep, and often life-changing, when it is connected to a nurturing affinity space" (p. 134). They describe 15 features of affinity spaces in general, and discuss how these manifest in nurturing affinity spaces (they stress that these features are not 'absolute' or 'ideal'). These features are summarised in Table 5.2 below.

It can be seen from this table that affinity spaces are not unique to those who are passionate about computer games, and they need not be wholly online (although in practice a great many are, and characteristics such as age, race or sex become less visible). Operating in collaboration and in communities, and in affinity spaces is a key way in which to learn. In the section that follows, the different ways in which digital games can facilitate and enhance learning through collaboration and communities are discussed.

Models of Collaboration

In this chapter so far, I have presented and discussed theories of collaborative learning, and started to discuss their relevance to game playing. In this section, I will move on to explore some of the theories that are specifically associated with learning through collaborative computer game playing. While collaborative

TABLE 5.2 Features of affinity groups and nurturing affinity groups (from Gee & Hayes, 2012)

	Feature	Implementation in nurturing affinity spaces
1	A primary common endeavour based around a shared passion.	Encouraging and supporting new members.
2	Not segregated or judged by age; people are judged by their passion, desire to learn and skills.	Older members set a standard of appropriate, respectful behaviour and younger members readily follow.
3	Novices are not segregated from experts. Not everyone must be fully committed to the passion, but all are respectful of it.	Easy entry for newcomers.
4	Anyone can create and design, as well as consume.	Support high standards of production through respectful and encouraging mentoring.
5	Content is dynamic and transformed by social interaction.	Sensitivity of content producers to the views and values of other members of the space.
6	Both specialist and general knowledge development are encouraged.	Specialist knowledge is recognised as only partial and the need for supplementation with the knowledge of others appreciated.
7	Both individual and distributed knowledge are encouraged.	Expertise viewed as residing in the space or community and not in individuals' heads.
8	Use of dispersed knowledge (knowledge that can be found outside of the space) facilitated.	Links to other spaces, with greater inclusivity of link choice.
9	Tacit knowledge is honoured, explicit knowledge encouraged.	Tolerant of a wide range of abilities in articulating knowledge.
10	Many different forms and routes to participation.	The variation in forms of participation is wider.
11	Many different routes to status.	More variation in routes and acceptance of those who do not desire status.
12	Leadership and membership is fluid and leaders act as resources.	Removal of hierarchies and view of leadership as teaching.
13	Roles are reciprocal, any person can be: learner/teacher; mentor/mentee; leader/follower, etc.	Highest experts view themselves as always having something to learn from the community.
14	Learning is viewed as individually proactive, but does not exclude help.	View requests for help as a way of extending the knowledge base of the space. Tolerance for newcomers with redundant questions.
15	Encouragement and feedback from an audience of peers.	Support and encouragement is the norm.

gaming is often viewed as people playing in real time in the same virtual space, there are many ways in which collaboration and learning can happen before, during, around and after game play; there follows a list of some of the more prevalent models:

- *Synchronous distributed.* Online games that allow collaboration to take place in real time as the game progresses with two to many people simultaneously active in the game space (for example *World of Warcraft*). Interaction can take place through the use of in-game chat or voice communication, or by using additional software such as multi-party audio or video conferencing.
- *Asynchronous distributed.* Games that are spaced over time by turn-taking, with one person making a move and then waiting for the next person (or group) to make theirs (for example, email chess or social media quizzes). Games of this type can be slow, however, and involve one person waiting for the next person to make a move, which forces time inter-dependency between players.
- *Synchronous co-located.* Two or more players using the game at the same time while present in the same physical space (for example, exploring the same game world with separate handheld consoles, or playing a console driving game with two sets of controllers).
- *Asynchronous co-located.* These involve turn-taking in the same physical space, for example console games where each player takes a turn and then watches as the other players take their turns. These games can be designed for multi-player (i.e. they keep separate scores and records and compare profiles) or single-player, where players simply take it in turns to play the same game.
- *Single-player.* The use of a game designed for one player by one or more players, either in the same physical space (for example, players sitting together with one computer to solve the puzzles in an adventure game) or in distributed spaces (for example, players in some online adventure games can communicate through a real-time chat channel to offer hints and tips to one another).
- *Team.* Games where groups of people work together (either online or offline) to achieve the goals of the game and compete against other teams (for example, the management game *Marketplace* where teams of businesses have to make periodic company decisions to compete with other teams).
- *Community-supported.* Games that are either played with others or individually that have associated online communities, web sites and asynchronous messaging offering hints, help and support.
- *Reflection-supported.* Games that are either played with others or individually that are supported by break-out activities and discussion with others.
- *Collective.* Games that require the inputs of large numbers of players, typically asynchronously, in order to solve the challenges of the game, for example in alternate reality games where a large amount of diverse knowledge or processing power is required.

Note that while some of the models describe situations where players are competing during game play, this is still a collaborative enterprise as the players agree to collaborate in 'playing the game' as well as in taking part in any or all of the activities that surround it (for this reason all games that are experienced by more than one person can be considered to be collaborative to some degree).

There are examples from the research literature of different ways in which to implement collaboration using games, from the use of a single-screen with multiple input devices with learners co-located (Infante et al., 2010) or two players working together on a single game (van der Meij, Albers, Leemkuil, & Meij, 2011) to the use of *World of Warcraft* in formal undergraduate teaching (Dickey, 2011) and McGonigal's (2003) description of 'extreme networks' that harness the power of the collective intelligence of massive disparate groups of people in order to solve real-world problems. Collaborative play also does not assume multiplayer gaming. It is very common for single-player games to be used in collaborative contexts, despite the initial intentions of the game designer. In their analysis of the activities and interactions that take place during face-to-face play, Schott and Kambouri (2006) found that single-player games were able to incorporate cooperation with others playing in groups, and that this approach was seen as quite natural and consistent as the players progressed through the game.

There is also some empirical evidence of the processes of collaboration in educational games. For example, Hämäläinen and colleagues (2006) found that students playing a multiplayer educational game could easily collaborate on practical problems, but that higher levels of collaboration were more difficult to achieve, something they attribute to the design of the game problems as being "relatively simplistic and unthreatening problems that could be addressed through risk-free trial-and-error procedures" (p. 58). They suggest that more sophisticated collaboration could be promoted through the integration of time pressures, greater risks and the need for more creative behaviours. Later research using the same game (Bluemink, Hämäläinen, Manninen, & Järvelä, 2010) found more evidence of 'true and constructive' collaborative activity, and highlighted the impact of previous experience and existing social ties on collaboration in the game. Dickey (2011) found evidence of peer mentoring within a game, but this was not transferred to the classroom; in contrast, the collegiality fostered in the game was transferred to the classroom setting, so that in a sense "the classroom became an extension of the playspace as they blended game and non-game spaces" (p. 207).

In a long-term study of 100 gamers in an educational MMORPG designed to teach English language skills to Chinese primary school children, Hou (2012) found that although the game was equipped with situated learning scenarios and problem-solving quests, 'battles' were the behaviours that were found to most frequently trigger learning (battles in this context are not violent). This could be related to the more instant gratification and rewards from the battles rather than the more in-depth engagement needed for the scenarios or quests, or perhaps that they do not require the learners to engage in a narrative, which is not motivational for everyone.

The role of the teacher in collaborative game play is important, and there is evidence that teacher facilitation can lead to greater effort to share information on the part of the game players, as well as a greater focus on the game task, with less off-task discussion (Hämäläinen & Oksanen, 2012).

Competing with Others

Competition is a fundamental part of many games; even in games where there are no other players (such as the card game Solitaire or single-player video games), there is still the element of either competing against yourself on a previous occasion, or competing to beat the game system, that is, to 'win' the game. It is possible to argue that this type of solo play is not strictly competitive because it does not involve other people, but is focusing on the challenge of the game. What then about the case of the artificial opponent in computer games, so that the player is competing against the game system that takes the form of another person? The distinction is blurred. Salen and Zimmerman (2004) argue that all games are competitive because "all games involve a conflict, whether that conflict occurs directly between players or whether players work together against the challenging activity presented by the game system" (p. 255). In contrast, they also argue that all games are cooperative, because players voluntarily cooperate by entering the 'magic circle' together, upholding the rules of the game and creating the game experience (including an individual colluding with the game system to play a game in the first place). It holds, therefore, that cooperation and competition cannot be mutually exclusive because they both exist in all games.

Competition is perhaps one of the more controversial aspects of game-based learning. It can add rationale and tension to game play, but it can also demotivate those who prefer non-competitive activities, and distract from learning. Competition occurs when one person is working against one or more others in a situation where only one person can win, and therefore the others lose. There are negative aspects of competition such as the fact that in group contexts, learners typically give attention to the moment rather than the longer term, and focus on winning above all else; it gives rise to a lack of trust and sharing, and creates a hostile environment where people think only of their own interests (Johnson & Johnson, 2003). Competition can also be a distraction, with some players focusing on winning to the detriment of learning (Harviainen, Lainema, & Saarinen, 2012). While it might be logical, therefore, that competition in education would have a negative impact, it is, however, implicit in any formal education system that awards marks (or grades) that relate to achievement and can be compared with others in the class. Assessment is in itself a competitive system, made more so in circumstances where the grade of one student affects those of others (such as when grades are normally distributed, or 'graded on a curve') or when there is an additional prize (such as a class medal or internship to the top student). Johnson and Johnson (1999) argue that cooperation is preferable to competition, or the efforts of one person alone in many learning and work situations, but they also highlight situations in which competition supports learning, such as when it is between groups rather than individuals. Van Eck (2002) showed a link between the relative effectiveness of video advice provided in the game and whether the game was played competitively or not, suggesting that use of competition might have unintended effects on other aspects of the learning process. While competition is, for many, a key aspect of game play, it is one that needs to be applied with caution in an educational environment.

In some learning situations, however, direct competition can provide the motivation and specific goals to enhance learning, for example using a tournament format (Squire, 2011). Squire (2011) argues that is it not competition per se that is harmful to learning, but the fact that it is high-stakes, separates winners and losers and provides only one chance to win (such as normally distributed tests, class rankings and competition for places on courses), and unsurprisingly this leads to drop-out and disincentives. He uses the competition that is inherent in sports as an analogy to show that competition can be motivating and increase learning; however, this merely shows that competition in sports is (highly) motivational for some people, but equally alienating for others, who may drop out even earlier. The key point is that "the trick is to create good competition that is engaging, fair and equitable. In that spirit, we need to not only critique competition in games, but also critique competition in schools just as carefully" (Squire, 2011, p. 175).

The question, then, is how appropriate are different degrees of competition; how explicit and overt can competition become and still be appropriate in games for learning? Moseley (2012b) argues that competition in formal education in inevitable, suggesting that

> we are all constantly involved in small personal competitions of both a positive or negative nature. For one child, in school, their personal competition might be to get through the day without receiving a warning; or to perform better in a team sport and score a goal; or to be the first to the front of the dinner queue. All these competitive actions are taking place all the time, regardless of whether competition is designed in or not.
>
> *(p. 59)*

He argues that because competition is inevitable, we should look to harness the positive aspects of competition in education through clever design and cooperative elements. Matthew and Sayers (1997), on the other hand, describe how competition in their group activities led to a 'must win' rather than a 'must learn' attitude, and that by shifting the focus from competition to collaboration they were able to see an increase in enthusiasm and energy. Zaphiris, Ang, & Law (2007) found lower learning gains when an educational game was played competitively than when it

TABLE 5.3 Models of competition in games

Model of competition	Examples
Single player vs. single player	Chess, singles tennis
Pair vs. pair	Doubles tennis
Team vs. team	Football
Single player vs. many	Tag
Every man for himself	*Monopoly*, running a race
Single player vs. game system	Adventure games, Solitaire
Individual players side by side	Casino blackjack
Group vs. game system	*World of Warcraft, Forbidden Island*

was played in an individual context, and Ke and Grabowski (2007) found that cooperative (as opposed to competitive) game-playing was most effective for fostering a positive attitude to mathematics.

Salen and Zimmerman (2004) identify seven different forms of competition (in its widest sense) that can be present in a game structure. These are shown in Table 5.3 above; I have added some additional examples. I have also added an extra model, 'pair vs. pair', because there is a different dynamic in pairs compared with small groups, particularly in the context of education.

Salen and Zimmerman (2004) argue that, as well as competition, games offer enjoyment from other sources, such as the joy of play, as well as the competitive struggle and outcomes of winning and losing. Competition can threaten to undermine the playfulness of the gaming situation, if the focus is put too much on winning and not enough on fun. Huizinga (1955) makes this point nicely, saying that "a passion to win sometimes threatens to obliterate the levity proper to a game" (p. 47). Different people will have different motivations for winning; winning leads to respect, esteem and honour, which readily passes from the individual to the group. The competitive instinct is not a desire for power or a will to dominate, but a desire to excel others and be honoured for that (Huizinga, 1955).

There is a variety of different ways in which competition can be built into games (and learning) to create more or less intense competition between players, and these are techniques also often used in the context of gamification. Some of the most common techniques are discussed in the list below.

- *Points and leaderboards* – allow players to put a numerical value on their achievements and compare that value with those of other players. Leaderboards can simply show the top ten players (which is not terribly motivating for the player at position 100), a zoomed-in section of the total leaderboard relative to the player (i.e. if you are at position 100 you might see positions 95 to 105, which gives a more realistic attainment goal by showing you competitors of approximately your own level), or a leaderboard that shows your position relative only to other players who you have tagged as 'friends' rather than the whole playing community.

- *Direct conflict* – in some game genres such as fighting, shooters and multiplayer role-playing games players can go head-to-head into battle so that there is one loser and one winner.
- *Competing for resources* – there are limited resources (such as money, food, other goods) in the game and players have to compete for them. While gaining these resources will not ensure success, it will certainly aid it.

It has been argued that motivation by competition has a gender bias, that men and boys are much more likely to be motivated by competition than are women and girls. Squire (2011) found this not to be the case and gives anecdotal evidence that girls were just as competitive as boys, but had more limited access to games consoles at home because they were often kept by their brothers; he concludes that "attitudes towards gaming are influenced by many variables, including cultural notions of womanhood" (p. 172).

In this chapter, I have examined the role that other people play in games, as collaborators, competitors or simply others sharing the game space. There is a variety of different ways in which these social aspects can support learning, in face-to-face or distance contexts, and with the growth in online games in shared spaces, these aspects are of increasing importance in the context of digital games and learning. These spaces are, however, relatively new and in years to come I would expect a growth in research in these areas as well as an increased sophistication in the ways in which we understand the impact of this type of social interaction on learning.

PART III

Games as Motivational Tools

6
GAMES AS ENGAGING EVENTS

There is something about games that excites and enthuses people, that pulls them in and keeps them playing, that motivates them to play again. Of course, I am not referring to all games and all people, but there is *something* in games that is compelling and fascinating, and in this chapter I am going to look at what this might be and how the engagement inherent in games for many people might be theorised. In the second part of this book, I looked at the ways in which games can facilitate active learning by providing experiential problem-solving environments. In this third part I will move on to consider the theories and research that are related to the use of digital games for motivation and engagement. While computer games are certainly not motivational for all people, particularly adults, they do provide structures that draw players into the game and keep them playing. This provides additional support for the benefits of digital games for learning (beyond the argument that they are effective learning environments in their own right) as there is some evidence of a link between intrinsic motivation in games and learning (Cordova & Lepper, 1996), although there is also a danger that high engagement with a game – particularly emotional engagement – may become a distraction, and that high engagement with a game does not necessarily mean the intended learning is taking place unless the intended learning outcomes are closely aligned with the gaming outcomes.

Games are intrinsically motivating for many players; people will take part voluntarily for no other reason than to play the game. Of course, this is problematic in formal educational games where the primary motivation is to learn rather than to be entertained. This highlights a paradox of formal educational gaming: one of the benefits often cited for using games to learn in formal contexts is that they are intrinsically motivating (although this is a gross over-generalisation) and players take part voluntarily in game play. Leaving aside the fact that many people do not find games motivating, and certainly are not motivated by all types of games, there is still the issue of the voluntary nature of gaming in educational settings. By making a game a compulsory part of a formal educational curriculum, extrinsic motivation is automatically imposed and the freedom of choice removed. While for some players this might be a necessary driving force to ensure participation in the game, for others the external motivation may negatively impact upon the genuine intrinsic motivation. Using a game in a compulsory setting is, in effect, undermining the game itself and making it, by definition, cease to be a game.

Creating an appropriate level of challenge is the key to creating a motivational environment. In the literature on games and learning, the notion of 'motivation' is typically used in two related, but distinct, ways. There is the initial motivation to engage in game playing and to play a particular game, what Salen and Zimmerman (2004) refer to as the 'seduction' into the magic circle that must necessarily occur before a player is willing to take part in the gaming activity at all. Second, there is the sustained motivation to continue to participate in the gaming experience as it takes place, which is commonly termed 'engagement'. Appropriate challenge will influence both types of motivation; the motivation to play a game on subsequent occasions, and the motivation to continue playing at a deep level. In this chapter, I will first examine the motivations that players might have to play games, before looking in more detail at engagement, its definition, the relationship between engagement and learning, and the factors that make games engaging.

Motivations for Playing Computer Games

In order to understand the different ways in which games can motivate and engage learners, it is useful to consider why people play games, and computer games, in the first place. Ferrara (2012) describes a number of common motivations for playing digital games, including immersion (flow), a feeling of autonomy and control, a feeling of competence, catharsis and an outlet for our aggressive impulses, accomplishment at no personal risk, social image and reputation within the game community, social interaction and as an outlet for creativity. Malone (1980) produced some of the original and most influential work on computer games and motivation: he investigated the elements that make computer games motivating, and initially highlighted three aspects of games that positively influence motivation: challenge, fantasy and curiosity. In his later work, a fourth aspect, control, was added to this list (Malone & Lepper, 1987). These factors are summarised in Table 6.1 below.

Each of the elements in this motivational model is discussed in more detail elsewhere in this book: challenge in Chapter 7; curiosity in Chapter 8; control in Chapter 10; and fantasy in Chapter 11. This research was carried out over 30 years ago, when computer gaming was in its infancy and the novelty of games had a bigger role to play in motivation, so it is obviously dated. It also focuses specifically on the motivations of children so may be of limited value in the context of other

TABLE 6.1 Taxonomy of individual intrinsic motivations for learning from games (from Malone & Lepper, 1987)

Motivation	Elements impacting on motivation
Challenge	Goals
	Uncertain outcomes
	Performance feedback
	Self-esteem
Curiosity	Sensory curiosity
	Cognitive curiosity
Control	Contingency
	Choice
	Power
Fantasy	Exogenous versus endogenous
	Emotional aspects
	Cognitive aspects

learners. However, Malone's work is still regularly cited in academic books and papers and I believe that it still provides a useful starting framework for exploring game elements and motivation. There are other limitations such as a lack of focus on the social dynamics surrounding games or alternative user interfaces. Iacovides and colleagues (2011) argue that while the work of Malone and Lepper is hugely influential, "there is a need to update our ideas in order to really understand why people play different games and what they get out of the experience" (p. 10).

In a small-scale phenomenographic study with gamers and non-gamers, I identified three primary and two secondary motivations for game playing (Whitton, 2007a). All of the interviewees who considered themselves to be game players exhibited one (or more) of the primary motivations for game playing: mental stimulation, social interaction and physical challenge. The participants who did not consider themselves to be game players still played games under certain circumstances: killing time and social facilitation. In the case of these two motivations, the game was seen as a means to achieving another end (i.e. passing time or making a social occasion easier) rather than being motivational in itself. Hence the game players were intrinsically motivated to play, while non-gamers required extrinsic motivation.

Also highlighted in the study was a range of other factors that affected motivation for different individuals. There emerged two factors that seemed to be motivating for all those who mentioned them, four that were universally de-motivational, and a further 15 factors that were either motivational or de-motivational depending on the individual. The two motivating factors were: 1) continual improvement, being able to see swift and steady advances; and 2) perceived proficiency, a feeling of being skilled and adept. The four factors that were considered by all to be demotivating were: 1) difficulty starting, problems beginning to play, understanding the concept or mastering the rules; 2) getting stuck, reaching a dead end and being unable to make progress; 3) unfairness, a lack of trust in the game, where it is seen as being inequitable or unjust; and 4) boredom, intrinsic lack of interest in the subject matter or game itself.

In addition, 15 elements emerged, each of which was seen by some respondents as being positively motivational and by others as negatively so. The 15 additional elements were:

1. *cerebral activity* – the extent to which the game is seen to be intellectually challenging;
2. *chance* – the degree of random input into the game;
3. *collaboration* – whether the activity is undertaken collaboratively or individually;
4. *competition* – the importance of playing against others and winning;
5. *complexity* – the degree to which the rules are hard or easy to master;
6. *difficulty* – whether the game is easy or hard to play;
7. *involvement* – the degree of active participation required;
8. *length* – whether the game is quick or time-consuming;
9. *open-endedness* – whether the game has a fixed end or could continue indefinitely;
10. *playfulness* – whether the game is serious or light-hearted;
11. *physical activity* – the extent to which the game requires physical exertion;
12. *realism* – whether the game is realistic or fantastic;
13. *sociability* – whether the game is played alone or with others;
14. *speed-dependence* – the degree to which speed of action is important; and
15. *stimulation* – whether the game is relaxing or stimulating.

Each individual who mentioned an element found it to be either motivating or demotivating to different degrees. Some preferences seemed to be relatively static for an individual, while others were more fluid depending on the particular circumstances and context of the game playing (e.g. mood, purpose, other players). An individual's preferences determine whether he or she is generally more likely to play games (as opposed to other leisure activities) as well as influencing the types of games played. These motivational preferences also contribute to the explanation of whether, and when, a person stops playing a game.

In a study looking at reasons for playing video games, Hoffman and Nadelson (2010) found that the three primary reasons that emerged were: escapism and fun; social connectivity; and the achievement of task-related goals. Their research suggests that players take part in computer gaming to fulfil recreational, social and esteem needs and that levels of motivation are influenced by the perceived ability to control the game and the perception that there are few consequences of failure. Calleja (2010) argues that games present an opportunity for escapism because they allow immersion in other worlds, and because they present a playful juxtaposition to the seriousness of work. In a three-year longitudinal study looking at the differences in motivation between players of single-player and multiplayer games, and online and offline players, Hainey, Connolly, Stansfield, and Boyle (2011) found that challenge was the top motivation and fantasy and recognition the lowest overall, and that multiplayer game players were more motivated by competition, cooperation, recognition, fantasy and control than were players of single-person games. In a survey on children's motivations for playing games, Kutner and Olson (2008) found four categories of motivation: excitement and fun; sociability and playing with others; a way to deal with emotions, such as getting out anger or feeling less lonely; and as a way of overcoming boredom. Bostan (2009) analysed player motivations in relation to psychological needs, highlighting the importance of materialistic needs such as building things, gaining and retaining possessions, power needs including aggression and dominance, affiliation needs including nurturing, achievement and recognition needs, information needs and sensual needs. Kallio, Mäyrä, and Kaipainen (2010) argue that there are (at least) nine different ways in which players approach gaming, based on three main mentalities: social (playing with kids, playing with friends and playing for company), casual (killing time, filling gaps and relaxing) and committed (having fun, entertainment and immersion). As well as positive motivations for game playing, there are negative ones, including a desire to release aggression (Ferrara, 2012), habit and lack of behaviour regulation (Lee & Larose, 2007), causing grief to other players (Schell, 2008) and motivations to disrupt game play through activities such as cheating, trifling, sabotage and spoil-sporting (Remmele & Whitton, 2014).

Myers (2010) describes the role of 'bad play', of which he says there are two generic types: "play that is threatening, risky, or otherwise harmful to the self or others; and play that is against the rules" (p. 16). He argues that forms of 'bad play' in computer games are "a necessary and unavoidable consequence of the peculiar and related representational forms of simulations, games, and play" (p. 28) because the exploration, manipulation and transformation of the game rules is, in itself, an integral part of play. Where these rules are sufficiently incomplete this process can go on indefinitely, but if the rules become fixed then players must either conform to the rules or abandon the game rules entirely. Harviainen and colleagues (2012) argue that when educational games are framed competitively, dishonest play becomes acceptable because players adopt game logic rather than real-world logic, which is particularly detrimental when game objectives and learning objectives are not closely aligned, and highlights the need for reflection on the gaming process.

There are many reasons why people play games with other people, including the opportunities for competition, the possibility of collaboration, provision of a focus for meeting up with other people, a way of exploring the 'real selves' of our friends and as a way of exploring ourselves and the ways we interact with others (Schell, 2008). Bartle (1996) provides a framework for understanding the different 'player types' that engage in multiplayer games, focusing on the motivation of each type for undertaking play. While the original framework was

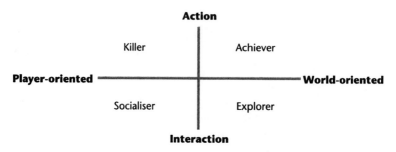

FIGURE 6.1 Typography of MUD player types on two dimensions (Bartle, 1996)

developed in the context of the early Multi-User Dungeons (MUDs), and was not developed scientifically (it is offered as a framework for enhancing game design), it still offers insights into the ways in which different players might approach the multiplayer gaming experience (although it does not tell us anything of the motivations of those people who choose not to engage in this type of game at all for leisure). The framework is based around two axes: action vs. interaction and player-oriented vs. world-oriented (see Figure 6.1).

The four player types are described as:

1. *Achievers* – people who want to succeed within the game context by accomplishing the game goals.
2. *Explorers* – people who want to explore and discover as much of the virtual environment as possible.
3. *Socialisers* – people who use the game as a means for social interaction and role-playing.
4. *Killers* – people who use the game to cause distress to other players (or, less commonly, with the sole purpose of helping others).

Bartle (1996) suggests that while players will drift between different player types, depending on mood or playing style, they will tend to have a dominant style; he argues that a good game will accommodate all playing styles and that balance is about keeping the proportions of each player in the game steady. Understanding that different motivations for taking part in multiplayer games exist also helps us to understand the learning that happens within them. More recently, Yee (2007) presented a model of motivations for play in online games, which has three factors made up of ten subcomponents.

- **Achievement**
  o Advancement: progress, power, accumulation, status
  o Mechanics: numbers, optimisation, templating, analysis
  o Competition: challenging others, provocation, domination

- **Social**
  - o Socialising: casual, helping others, making friends
  - o Relationship: personal, self-disclosure, find and give support
  - o Teamwork: collaboration, groups, group achievements
- **Immersion**
  - o Discovery: exploration, lore, finding hidden things
  - o Role-playing: story line, character history, roles, fantasy
  - o Customisation: appearances, accessories, style, colour schemes
  - o Escapism: relax, escape from real life, avoid real-life problems

The achievement, social and immersion aspects of Yee's model map closely to the achievers, socialisers and explorers in Bartle's framework, but the negative motivations associated with killers are not included in this framework as a key factor (although some may be present in the subcomponent of competition). Also in relation to online role-playing games, Burn and Carr (2006) suggest that three principal motivations are: playing with representations of the self (this is touched on through role-playing and customisation in the previous model but also has more to do with performance and exploration of identity); ludic motivations related to achieving the objectives of the game (like achievement in the previous model); and communal motivations (similar to social above). They highlight that these motivations are not separate from one another but are 'entangled' and combine during play.

Crawford (1984) differentiates between a motivation to play games in general, and motivations to play a specific game. He argues that people play games for fantasy fulfilment, to overcome the social restrictions of real life, to demonstrate competence or prowess, for social lubrication, mental or physical exercise or to satisfy a need for acknowledgement. When selecting a specific game, he suggests that there are two factors at play: the game play itself, and the sensory gratification inherent in the game.

While it is interesting to consider the various motivations for playing games for entertainment, there is no guarantee that someone who is motivated to play games in their leisure time will be motivated to play them for learning, or that the types of games played by choice for fun will be those more appropriate for learning in an academic context. For example, in a survey of computing students, I found in my doctoral research that by far the most popular type of game for playing in leisure time for the group of undergraduate computing students in my sample was first person shooters, whereas the game genres most appropriate for academic learning are typically adventure, role-playing and strategy games (Whitton, 2007a).

Continuing my interest in games and motivation, in a later research study I investigated the motivations of players of an alternate reality game, and found indications of six different motivations (Whitton, 2009). The six motivational elements described by alternate reality game players are described below (note that these elements are not mutually exclusive but that there tended to be one primary and one or more secondary motivations for each player). While this motivational model emerged from a study of alternate reality games, I am presenting it here because I believe that it is much more widely relevant to a range of different types of computer games, and even to non-digital games.

- *Completion.* Some players will simply want to complete the game and achieve all the tasks or challenges, similar to wanting to complete a jigsaw to see the full picture. This can be facilitated using techniques like making all the tasks apparent up front and allowing them to be checked off, or linking subtasks to some overall reward such as completing a picture.
- *Competition.* An element of competition can motivate some people, although it may turn off others, so it has to be applied carefully and should not be too overt, or linked to the overall rewards of completing the game. Adding a leader board or high scores list will enable players to see how they are performing in relation to others.
- *Narrative.* A compelling ongoing story with an element of mystery can help to stimulate curiosity and keep students engaged, as well as embedding activities within a purposeful context. Fantasy narrative may be less appropriate in this context but it will really depend upon the particular student group.
- *Puzzle-solving.* Ongoing puzzles, riddles and problems that need to be solved also serve to stimulate curiosity and heighten engagement. These should start relatively easy so that players are drawn into the game and receive early gratification from playing, but can then get gradually more difficult as students become more experienced.
- *Community.* Supporting play outside the game and encouraging players to talk to one another and work collaboratively will be motivational for some players. Ways of facilitating this include the provision of forums or other online community space, and tasks that require collaboration (either explicitly or because they are too difficult for one person to achieve alone).
- *Creativity.* The opportunity for players to be creative, either through lateral thinking and creative problem-solving or through the creation of their own artefacts within the game (e.g. creating posters, video or stories) allows people to become more immersed in the game and shape its direction.

There is a wide variety of reasons why people play computer games in the first place, but in the next section I am going to examine why they continue to play and stay engaged in the game.

Defining Engagement

The idea of ongoing 'engagement' is a complex one with the notion of 'engagement' being constructed in many different ways, for example the idea of 'learner

TABLE 6.2 Types of student engagement (from Appleton et al., 2006)

Type	Indicators
Academic	Time on task, credits earned towards graduation, homework completion.
Behavioural	Attendance, suspensions, voluntary classroom participation, extra-curricular participation.
Cognitive	Self-regulation, relevance of schoolwork to future endeavours, value of learning, personal goals and autonomy.
Psychological	Feelings of identification or belonging, relationships with teachers and peers.

engagement' is common in the context of UK Higher Education, and generally refers to the amount and type of student participation in activities over the course of academic study (e.g. Trowler, 2010). The idea of games and engagement is constructed differently, with engagement being the subjective experience during play, encompassing ideas of enjoyment, immersion, flow and presence (e.g. Boyle, Connolly, Hainey, & Boyle, 2012). This leads to a problematic conception of engagement when the ideas of 'engagement with learning' and 'engagement with games' are put together to examine gaming engagement and its relation to learning. Appleton, Christenson, Kim, & Reschly (2006) describe four different types of student engagement, with associated indicators, shown in Table 6.2 above.

While this model applies to all engagement with all types of learning, it does not highlight the use of engagement as 'absorption' or 'flow' as it is commonly used in the context of games. I am particularly interested in the ways in which engagement is theorised in the field of game design, and the insights these might provide into learning engagement. I used a game-based construction of engagement that focuses on the elements of the subjective experience that influence learning to create a five-factor model of learning engagement with games (Whitton, 2010b), which is shown here:

- *Challenge.* The motivation to undertake the activity, clarity as to what it involves, and a perception that the task is achievable.
- *Control.* The fairness of the activity, the level of choice over types of action available in the environment, and the speed and transparency of feedback.
- *Immersion.* The extent to which the individual is absorbed in the activity.
- *Interest.* The intrinsic interest of the individual in the activity or its subject matter.
- *Purpose.* The perceived value of the activity for learning, whether it is seen as being worthwhile in the context of study.

The five-factor model of learning engagement described here supposes that each of these factors contributes to an overall sense of engagement with an activity and that the greater the extent to which each factor is present, the greater the engagement; it does not attempt to assign an order of importance to these factors. This model has some commonality with the motivation theories of Pink (2009) from the business perspective, which suggest that the three key motivational aspects are: autonomy over task, time, technique and team; mastery, a long-term movement towards expertise in a task; and purpose, that a task is seen as useful and meaningful. These three elements map neatly onto control (autonomy), challenge (mastery) and purpose in the previous model.

Calleja (2007; 2011) presents a conceptual model for 'digital game involvement' called the 'digital game experience model', with a variety of experiential dimensions corresponding to six broad categories of game features on two levels of involvement: macro and micro. Macro involvement relates to factors that shape the players' thoughts, plans, feelings and expectations of the game before and after play. Micro involvement refers to the moment-by-moment engagement of game-play as it happens. The categories in the model are:

- *Tactical involvement* – engagement with the decision-making within the game, including interaction with the rules, the environment and the other players.
- *Performative involvement* – engagement with modes of avatar or game-piece control.
- *Affective involvement* – engagement with the cognitive, emotional and kinaesthetic feedback loop that is formed between the game process and the player to influence the player's moods and emotions.
- *Shared involvement* – engagement with other players, sentient objects or characters within the game world.
- *Narrative involvement* – engagement with the 'designed narrative' of the characters, plot, backstory and so on, and the 'personal narrative' that is each player's interpretation of his or her individual journey through the game.
- *Spatial involvement* – engagement with the player's location in the wider game world rather than just seen on the screen through tools such as maps and directions.

Poels, de Kort, and IJsselsteijn (2007) present what they call a comprehensive categorisation of the digital game experience, consisting of nine dimensions: enjoyment (pleasure, fun, relaxation); flow (concentration, absorption); imaginative immersions (character identification, absorption in a story); sensory immersion (presence); suspense (tension, thrill); competence (pride, accomplishment); negative affect (frustration, anger); control (autonomy, power, freedom); and social presence (empathy, cooperation). Immersion is another term that is used in many different ways in the literature, for example it has been deconstructed into three separate levels: engagement, engrossment and total immersion (Brown & Cairns, 2004), while Calleja (2011) highlights the difference between 'immersion as absorption', where to be immersed in a game is to be thoroughly engrossed in it without any sense of spatiality or actually 'being there', and 'immersion as trans-portation' is the sense of being transported to another reality. Immersion in the first sense is strongly related to a sense of engagement and flow, in the second sense to presence (see Chapter 13).

Another theory commonly used to explain the way in which players engage with games is flow theory (Csíkszentmihályi, 1992). Being in the state of flow is described as being in a state of optimal experience: "the state in which people are so involved in an activity that nothing else seems to matter; the experience itself is so enjoyable that people will do it even at great cost, for the sheer sake of doing it" (p. 4). Clearly, this is very relevant to the experiences that people have when playing computer games. Flow theory posits eight elements that create this 'optimal experience'; the more of these elements that are present, the more enjoyable, engaging and immersive an activity. (For clarity, I have grouped the original eight elements into those that are associated with the activity itself, and those that are embedded in the participants' subjective experiences of the activity.)

A flow activity has:

* a challenge that requires skills with an attainable goal and known rules;
* clear goals;
* immediate feedback;

during which participants experience:

* complete absorption in the activity;
* a sense of control, lacking the sense of worry about losing control;
* concentration on the task in hand;
* loss of self-consciousness;
* transformation of time.

Csíkszentmihályi (1992) presents a graphical model of the flow state, which shows challenge level mapped against skill level (Figure 6.2 below). When skill level and challenge are balanced (not too hard, not too easy) then a state of flow can be achieved, but when the skill level is greater than the challenge level the task is too easy and the participant becomes bored; by increasing the level of challenge the flow state can be maintained. When the challenge level is far greater than the skill level then the task is too difficult and anxiety ensues; in this instance flow can be achieved by increasing skills. As a person becomes more competent at an activity, it is only by increasing levels of challenge over time that the flow state can be maintained.

In a later work, Csíkszentmihályi (1997) presents a more complex version of the flow model (see Figure 6.3), which shows different emotional outcomes at different combinations of skill and challenge level. At low levels of challenge, players move through apathy, to boredom and finally relaxation as skills increase;

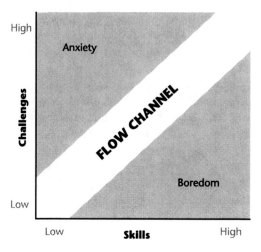

FIGURE 6.2 Flow channel (from Csíkszentmihályi, 2002)

at higher levels of challenge players move from anxiety, to arousal and finally into flow, when both challenge and skills are high. This posits that a combination of above-average skills and above-average challenge is required to achieve flow, which is somewhat at odds with the earlier model.

Although flow theory is a useful starting point for considering the nature of engagement, a problem arises in using it for measurement because, while some of the indicators it uses can be objectively analysed (e.g. the existence of goals and rules), others are based on the subjective perception of the player (e.g. loss of

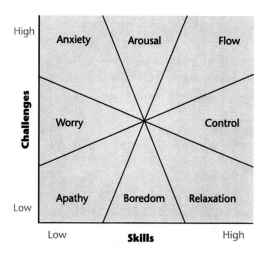

FIGURE 6.3 Quality of experience as a function of the relationship between challenges and skills (from Csíkszentmihályi, 1997)

self-consciousness). In his analysis of flow theory, Draper (1999) adds that engagement only occurs where a connection exists between the activity and the player's core values and beliefs, while Salen and Zimmerman (2004) argue that flow is not intrinsic to a game, but is dependent on the state of mind of the players as they play the game. In the context of the research presented here, engagement is considered to be a subjective state observable only to the individual taking part in the activity, so that it is not the activity in itself that is engaging but rather an individual's interaction with the activity at a specific time.

Engagement and Learning

Engagement is often used in research on games and learning as a proxy for learning. In theory it is easier to measure the subjective experience than the actual learning. If the learner was engaged, it follows that he or she would have learned more. Unfortunately the evidence for this is scant. Jacques, Preece, and Carey (1995) argue that designing interactions to be engaging can encourage and facilitate learning, and Lepper and Malone (1987) provide some evidence that there is a link between intrinsic motivation to learn, engagement and instructional effectiveness. It is important to note that there is a distinction between player engagement with a game and engagement with the intended learning from the game. Ideally, the game outcomes should be aligned with the learning outcomes so that engagement in the game supports learning, but even with the cleverest design there is no guarantee that this is the case. Koster (2005) argues that it is the learning inherent in games themselves that makes them engaging: "fun from games arises out of mastery. It arises out of comprehension. It is the act of solving puzzles that makes games fun. In other words, learning is the drug" (p. 40), stating that games become boring when they fail to provide new information to integrate into existing understandings and that creating an engaging game is about getting the balance right between providing the right amount of information to stimulate curiosity while not producing sensory overload.

The most common methods employed in the literature to measure engagement in educational settings are the use of questionnaires and learner surveys. There are a number of different questionnaires that have been used in research to measure engagement and related concepts, and some of these are summarised in Table 6.3 below in order to give a flavour of the variety of ways in which engagement, and related constructs, have been theorised and measured.

While questionnaires are a common way of evaluating engagement with games, they are not unproblematic because games are typically large exploratory environments that require many hours of game-play to become fully engaged, yet laboratory tests of engagement typically happen after far shorter periods (Chen, Kolko, Cuddihy, & Medina, 2011). Other techniques for measuring engagement include analysis of facial expressions and body language (Hughey, 2002), measurement of physiological factors such as heart rate and brain activity

TABLE 6.3 Questionnaires in the literature pertaining to engagement and related constructs

Authors	Scale	Construct	Sub-scales
Appleton et al. (2006)	Student Engagement Instrument	Cognitive and psychological engagement	Control and relevance of school work, future aspiration and goals, extrinsic motivation (cognitive); teacher–student relationships, peer support for learning, family support for learning (psychological)
Brockmyer et al. (2009)	Game Engagement Questionnaire	Engagement with video games	Absorption, flow, presence, immersion
Engeser and Rheinberg (2008)	Flow Short Scale	Experience of flow	Flow
Fu et al. (2009)	EGame Scale	Enjoyment of e-learning games	Immersion, social interaction, challenge, goal clarity, feedback, concentration, control, and knowledge improvement
Jennett et al. (2008)	Immersion Questionnaire	Immersion	Cognitive absorption, flow, presence
Kiili and Lainema (2008)	GameFlow	Flow in games	Flow antecedents, indicators of flow state, flow consequences
Lafrenière et al. (2012)	Gaming Motivation Scale	Gaming motivation	Intrinsic motivation, integrated regulation, identified regulation, introjected regulation, external motivation and amotivation
Whitton (2010b)	Game Engagement Questionnaire	Engagement with learning games	Challenge, control, immersion, interest, purpose

(Nacke & Lindley, 2008), eye movements (Jennett et al., 2008), frameworks for evaluation (Sweetser & Wyeth, 2005), interviews and video analysis (Chen & Johnson, 2004; Davies, 2002), observations (Read, MacFarlane, & Casey, 2002), attendance rates (Chapman, 2003) and voluntary time on task (Virvou, Katsionis, & Manos, 2004). What is clear is that there is a great deal of research taking place that looks at how to conceptualise and measure engagement, and there is evidence that engagement in the sense of 'time on task' and 'participation' has a positive influence on learning (Kuh, Kinzie, Schuh, & Whitt, 2010), but that there is a lack of real evidence that engagement, in the sense of being part of an engaging experience as it is commonly used in the context of games, relates to learning in any direct or indirect sense. There is a need for further work in the field to investigate this connection.

In this chapter I have aimed to examine the reasons why games are motivational, and to consider the different ways in which engagement and related concepts have been theorised and measured. There is a great deal of variation in the terminologies and constructions used in the different discourses around engagement, from the perspectives of game design and student learning in particular. I think that a greater recognition of these two parallel conceptions would greatly increase the potential of more deeply understanding the types of engagement that happen in games and their value for learning.

7

GAMES AS DESIGNED ENJOYMENT

In the previous chapter I examined theories of motivation and engagement. In this chapter I will move on to look specifically at the ways in which game structures create a designed experience that supports and enhances enjoyment and engagement. One of the main difficulties with game design is ensuring that the levels of challenge are appropriate for players so that the game is fun to play. A game that is too easy or where the player does not have any control, such as games of chance like *Snakes and Ladders*, are boring to older players who will soon lose interest; games that are too hard or complex or where players keep 'getting stuck' quickly become frustrating because the level of challenge is greater than the ability of the player. Taking into account that different players have different skill levels, persistence and preferences, and that challenges become easier as skill levels increase, getting the right level of challenge for different players at different times is a difficult balancing act.

The right challenge is at the heart of the design of computer games that people want to play, and want to keep on playing. Challenge creates a motivation for taking part, and enables players to set goals and see improvements in their performance as they progress through the game. Getting the type and level of challenge right is key to creating a playable game, whether this is a game for pure entertainment or a game for learning. A challenge is an activity that is difficult to do and requires thought and effort, and therefore provides a feeling of satisfaction when a goal is achieved. Different types of challenge will appeal to different people: some will prefer physical to mental challenges; others will prefer to measure themselves against their own previous performances, while others will prefer to compete with others. Whatever the type of challenge, what is crucial in terms of engagement is getting it at the right level for the player, so that it is not so easy as to be boring, not so hard as to be unachievable.

In recent years, the idea of 'gamification' has become one of the most hyped concepts in game-based learning. It is defined as "the use of game elements and game-design techniques in non-game contexts" (Werbach & Hunter, 2012, p. 26) or, more specifically, "using game-based mechanics, aesthetics, and game thinking to engage people, motivate action, promote learning and solve problems" (Kapp, 2012, p. 10). So gamification is wider than using game techniques for learning in a formal context, but can encompass it; it is not about using entire games, but about using the techniques from games that can promote learning and engagement, and applying them to different contexts. Werbach and Hunter (2012) describe what they see as the three core elements of gamification: points, badges and leaderboards (PBL). They admit that "PBLs are so common within gamification that they are often described as though they are gamification. They are not, but they are a good place to start" (p. 71). Gamification has the advantage of being relatively cheap and easy to apply (compared with, for example, development of a high-end video game) but, because the elements used in gamification (commonly points, badges and leaderboards) promote extrinsic motivation with the activity, they can be viewed as simply adding a further layer of motivation to a task rather than fundamentally re-thinking the task itself. As gamification is growing in popularity, not just in terms of education but also in areas such as social media and marketing, there will be a danger that use of the approach will simply be seen as jumping on the latest bandwagon. Recent research shows that students who completed a gamified class had higher initial motivation and got better scores in practical assignments but performed poorly on written assignments and participated less in class activities (Domínguez et al., 2013). While the use of the term 'gamification' is relatively new, similar ideas have been expressed in the literature for several years, such as the concept of 'game-informed learning', which suggests that educational processes should be informed by the experience of game-play (Begg, Dewhurst, & Macleod, 2004).

This chapter will first explore the core structural elements that form the backbone of what it is to be a game: challenges, rules, progression and outcomes, and ends by looking at the issue of game balance and exploring the ways in which games can be designed to make them appealing and enjoyable to a wide audience.

Game Structures

Games contain structural elements that support engagement and motivation, and in this section I will consider the elements of a game that come together to create an appropriate challenge for the player, one that is not too hard, not too easy. Schell (2008) describes four basic elements that come together to make games: mechanics – the procedures and rules of the game; story – the sequence of events that unfold during the game; aesthetics – the look and feel of the game; and technology – the medium and artefacts through which the game operates (this does not have to be digital technology). The mechanics of the game, which hold the game together and make it fun and engaging, are at the very core of the game design. Schell (2008) defines six main categories of mechanics, from the perspective of the game designer.

1. *Space.* An abstract construct of the places that exist in the game and how they relate to one another. Game spaces can be discrete (such as the spaces on a chess board) or continuous (such as the playing area of a pool table), one-dimensional (*Monopoly*), two-dimensional (chess) or three-dimensional (football) and may be bounded or nested within other spaces. Schell argues that it is useful to think of games that are not played in physical space (such as *Twenty Questions*) as happening in zero-dimensional game spaces because information on the state of the game has to exist somewhere, even if it is only in the minds of the players.
2. *Objects, attributes and states.* Objects are the things that can be manipulated in the game space (e.g. characters, tokens, swords), which have attributes (categories of information about the object such as 'colour' or 'cost') that can be static or dynamic. States are the values of attributes at a given time, so for example a ball might have the state of 'blue' for the 'colour' attribute.
3. *Actions.* This is what the players can do with the objects within the game space. Schell distinguishes between operative actions (the base actions that a player can take, such as 'move a chess piece forward') and resultant actions (the overarching strategies of play, such as 'sacrifice a piece to make a gain'). He argues that 'emergent game-play' is what makes a good game, and that this is the consequence of meaningful resultant actions.
4. *Rules,* which are "the most fundamental mechanic. They define the space, the objects, the actions, the consequences of the actions, the constraints of the actions, and the goals" (p. 144). A more detailed discussion of rules follows in a later section.
5. *Skill.* Focuses on what the player needs to do in order to achieve at the game; these skills can be physical – such as strength, dexterity or coordination; mental – such as memory, observation or puzzle solving; or social – such as 'reading' the intentions of an opponent or collaborating with others.
6. *Chance.* The uncertainly generated by random elements in the game.

The way in which the term 'game mechanics' is used differs depending on the context and the author. For example, from a game design perspective, Thompson, Berbank-Green, and Cusworth (2007) use mechanics and rules synonymously and talk about the use of luck, strategy, diplomacy, resource management or territory control; while Brathwaite and Schreiber (2009) also use mechanics as rules, and define dynamics as "the pattern of play that comes from the mechanics once they're set in motion by players" (p. 30), such as gaining territory or winning a race. The mechanics-dynamics-aesthetics (MDA) framework provides a formal game design model that differentiates between the mechanics, which implement the rules of the game, the dynamics that make up the game system as the game is being played and the aesthetics, which are the emotional responses to the game elicited by the player (Hunicke, LeBlanc, & Zubek, 2004).

Werbach and Hunter (2012) suggest a three-level game element hierarchy (see Figure 7.1 below) with: five dynamics, the top level abstract elements; ten mechanics, the basic processes that drive forward action and generate engagement; and 15 components, ways in which dynamics or mechanics are implemented.

Whatever taxonomy or classification system is used, the important thing to take away is that games have certain structural elements, and it is these structural elements that influence how the players interact and, ultimately, how enjoyable the game-playing experience is for the players. There is a variety of structural elements in games that support and enhance engagement and motivation to play. These can be analysed as ways in which to understand how and why games draw people in and keep them playing, allowing these elements to be identified and applied to other contexts (gamification). Four of the most important structural elements of games are:

1. *Challenges and goals* – the explicit aims and objectives of the game.
2. *Rules* – the constraints that are set within the game, including the goal of the game and the limitations on being able to achieve that goal.
3. *Progression* – a visible indication that the player is moving towards achievement of the game goals.
4. *Outcomes* – the results of the game (or level); whether the goal has been achieved or not.

In the four sections that follow, I examine each of these areas in more detail.

Challenges and Goals

Malone (1980) says that "in order for a computer game to be challenging it must provide a goal whose attainment is uncertain" (p. 162); this is achieved through goals with uncertain outcomes. Games, by their very nature, present players with goals that must be achieved in order to win or to complete the game. The challenges that games present are one of the features that draw people in and keep them playing, but also a key reason why they are such effective tools for learning. Here, I examine the ways in which games can support problem-solving through active experience, reflection and presentation of challenges. The constructivist viewpoint discussed in Chapter 3 also puts forward the idea that people learn better by undertaking an active role in the learning process, by exploring and experiencing the authentic contexts for themselves and discovering their own meanings from the experience.

Goals are the aims of the game, the tasks that need to be completed in order to progress or win. They can be critical to the completion of the game, or optional,

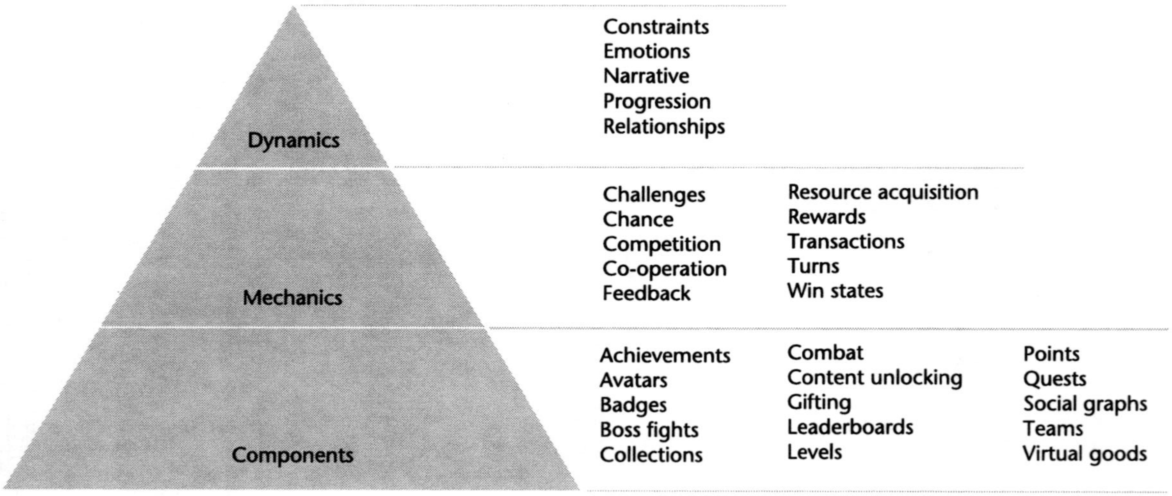

Dynamics

Constraints
Emotions
Narrative
Progression
Relationships

Mechanics

Challenges
Chance
Competition
Co-operation
Feedback

Resource acquisition
Rewards
Transactions
Turns
Win states

Components

Achievements
Avatars
Badges
Boss fights
Collections

Combat
Content unlocking
Gifting
Leaderboards
Levels

Points
Quests
Social graphs
Teams
Virtual goods

FIGURE 7.1 Game element hierarchy (from Werbach & Hunter, 2012)

such as side-quests in a role-playing game; they can be immediate or long term; they can be simple, or complex and multi-faceted. Effective game goals are obvious and compelling, so that players know what they need to do and are motivated to do it, but also practical and intrinsic to the game (Malone, 1980). Game goals are more meaningful if they are logically consistent with the narrative and action of the game, so that the player has a meaningful motivation, which is consistent with the role adopted within the game world. For example, a problem in an adventure game might involve finding a way to open a door, but the challenge is much more powerful if there is a reason for the player to open the door (beyond simple exploration) that is in line with the overarching narrative (such as another character being trapped inside). Games typically also include mechanisms that tell players when they are getting closer to a goal, such as a progress bar or a score; and in environments where no explicit goals exist (such as simulations or virtual worlds) games are commonly designed so that users can easily generate their own goals of appropriate difficulty. Goals can also be absolute (such as completing the quest or finishing the level) or relative (such as being top of the leaderboard or achieving a personal best).

Having uncertain outcomes means that a player does not know at the start of a game whether he or she is going to win or lose, or manage to achieve the goal. If achieving the goal is certain, the game will be boring; if it cannot be achieved, the game will be pointless. Uncertainty in gaming can also increase levels of motivation (Howard-Jones & Demetriou, 2008) and there is some evidence that it can also increase levels of learning (Ozcelik, Cagiltay, & Ozcelik, 2013). Malone (1980) suggests four ways to ensure that the outcome of a game is uncertain for players over a wide range of abilities:

1. *Variable difficulty levels*, which can either be determined by the game, by the user or by a (virtual or real-life) opponent's skill. Levels can also be progressive, supporting players through a chain of events or levels, or adjust dynamically to a player's current skill.
2. *Multiple-level goals*, such as short-term and longer-term goals (which can be in conflict), and meta-goals where the object is not simply to achieve something but to achieve it faster or more efficiently. These meta-goals provide a relative element to an absolute goal, and scoring and timed responses are two ways of facilitating this within the game.
3. *Hidden information*, such as making certain information only available at certain points within the game (e.g. talking to the mage reveals the location of the map). Additional information revealed later in the game has to be consistent, however, or else the game may be perceived as unfair by the players and this can be de-motivational. This hidden information can provoke curiosity as well as creating uncertain challenge.
4. *Randomness*, so that there is an element of chance to the outcome of the game. There is a fine balance between adding an element of uncertainty, and

making players feel like they have no control over the game. For example in *Snakes and Ladders*, a game that is entirely driven by chance, the outcome is uncertain because it depends upon the random throw of a die, but the players have no control over whether they win or lose.

Malone (1980) also highlights the relevance of self-esteem as an important aspect of challenge, and suggests that therefore feedback in game play should be designed to promote perceptions of personal competence and effort while players strive to meet the challenges that the game sets. This also highlights the importance of gradually increasing difficulty levels so that players of all abilities can perceive themselves as achieving, and increase their self-esteem levels. In relation to this, goals need to be personally meaningful to the learner, such as being perceived as a useful goal to achieve, being set in a motivating context for the particular learner (e.g. a fantasy context for a fan of that genre) or having socially relevant goals, such as gaining recognition among peers (Malone & Lepper, 1987).

Rules

Rules are fundamental to every game, without rules a game cannot exist, instead we are looking at a form of free play. As Egenfeldt-Nielsen and colleagues (2008, p. 99) put it: "Rules, arguably, are the most defining characteristics of games; they are the element shared by everything we usually understand as a game, and are the element that sets games apart from linear media such as novels or movies".

Salen and Zimmerman (2004) argue that games are systems, and rules provide the formal structure of the game. They define six characteristics of rules:

1. Rules limit player action to specific sets of instructions.
2. Rules are explicit, complete and unambiguous.
3. Rules are shared by all players.
4. Rules are fixed, and do not change during game play (even in games in which changing the rules is part of the game play, the ways in which rules can be changed are strictly governed by rules).
5. Rules are binding and contain their own authority.
6. Rules are repeatable and portable from game to game.

They highlight the difference between personal motivations (character) or global motivations (world) – when these are brought together they are described as a 'die-hard' motivation. Parlett (2005) provides a detailed discussion of the different types of game rules that exist, which are summarised with examples in Table 7.1 below. The final rule type was added by Schell (2008) in his discussion of the original list.

Myers (2010) highlights the motivations for computer game players to play outside of the rules, but still engage within the game, so that their play is in conflict

TABLE 7.1 Different types of rules (adapted from Parlett, 2005 and Schell, 2008)

Rule type	Description	Example
Operational rules	The explicit rules that describe the set of procedures for playing a game.	Noughts and crosses is played on a 3 × 3 grid where players alternately take turns to add a 0 or an × to one of the squares and the aim of the game is to make a line of three in any direction.
Foundational rules	The formal logical and mathematical structures underpinning the game.	The underlying mathematical logic in noughts and crosses.
Behavioural rules	Unwritten rules that are the normal or accepted way of playing the game.	There is a reasonable time limit between making moves in noughts and crosses.
Written rules	Rules that have been formulated in writing.	The rule sheet that is provided with a boxed game, such as *Monopoly*.
Official rules	Rules that have the status of authority, both prescriptive and proscriptive.	The book of official *Scrabble* words.
Laws	Explicit rules of behaviour, proprieties, sanctions, corrections.	A person caught cheating will be excluded from the game.
Advisory rules	Rules of strategy, tips to help players play better.	Strategy guides for video games.
House rules	Localised versions of the operational rules that are adapted to make the game more fun.	Modifying *Monopoly* so that no one can buy a second set of houses until everyone has at least one set, to make it fairer for young children.

with both the game rules and the spirit of the game, commonly called 'exploits', suggesting that "despite the programmed and tangible nature of rules embedded in game code, computer game players seem to play as often in disregard of these rules as they do in accordance with them" (p. 18). However, he also notes that given this tendency for players to "explore, manipulate and transform game rules to their advantage" (p. 19), many games employ special rules that are, in essence, simply there to be broken and become an integral part of the game play.

Of particular relevance to educational games is the idea of a rule enforcer: who is responsible for ensuring that players keep to the rules, but what are the sanctions if players ignore them? For digital games, the rules are to some extent embedded within the game structure itself, and it may be impossible to cheat the game code, although help forums, hacks and walkthroughs mean that cheating is still possible. Different levels of cheating within and around the game may be acceptable to different degrees by the player community and it is important in a game-based learning situation that the rules (or 'laws' in the model above) are made explicit. There are also the implicit rules of a particular game genre to take into account: for example, if a player is familiar with a certain genre, say adventure games, he or she will know that a locked door will require a key, a fire a bucket of water (or some play or in-joke on these ideas) because they are common starter puzzles; however, someone new to the genre may not have the necessary background knowledge or experience to know how to approach a puzzle, or 'get-the-joke'. It is this idea of 'gaming literacy' or implicit knowledge of the rules of a genre (which does not just apply to computer games, but to sports too, for example) that presents a barrier to entry and needs to be considered when using games in formal educational settings. Zagal (2010) argues that understanding games goes beyond playing them but involves the interpretation of games as cultural artefacts, in the context of other games, in the context of their technological platform and "by deconstructing them and understanding their components, how they interact, and how they facilitate certain experiences in players" (p. 24).

Progression

The concept of progression is the idea that players can see themselves gaining skills and making advances in the game. In order to measure progress, a very common method is to use points. Points provide a universal currency that allows players to determine how near completion of the game they are, and to measure achievement against other players, and against previous occasions when they have played the game. Points are a measure of the performance of the player, the proficiency and level of skill attained and how far the player has progressed through the game (Ferrara, 2012).

Points can be used in six ways in gamified systems (Werbach & Hunter, 2012):

1. To keep score and let the player know how well he or she is doing, and determine progress relative to previous occasions and other players.
2. To determine when someone has achieved the goals of the game (i.e. won the game).
3. To create a connection between the game system and real-world extrinsic rewards (e.g. collect 100 points to win a toaster).
4. To provide explicit and frequent feedback.
5. To provide an external display of progress in multi-user environments.
6. To provide data for the game designer.

Points can be simple or complex; they can, at their most basic, be a straightforward indication of how much of a game is completed, or be based upon a single variable, for example how many aliens have been shot. It is more common for points to be kept on multiple variables (e.g. health, time, aliens shot) that are combined into an overall score. These multiple scores may take place in the background and may not be visible to the player. What game actions increase the scores (and whether the player realises that this is the case) will impact on the way that the player plays the game. Players (like learners) are often strategic – if they realise that they will not get a score for an action then they are less likely to do it. Points can also be used as a form of implicit assessment, where there is a direct link between points scored in the game and real-world educational assessment (Moseley, 2012c); a more detailed discussion of assessment in games is provided in the following chapter.

As well as simply showing points to the player, scores can be used to indicate progress in a variety of different ways such as through progress bars, visual representations (e.g. number of lives left) or use of auditory feedback (such as music increasing in volume or tempo as the score increases). Of course, not all game genres use (explicit) scores, for example they are uncommon in adventure games (although early text adventures often provided a score as an indication of progress, but all it showed was how many actions had been achieved towards the overall goal) but genres like role-playing games make heavy use of scores and provide all manner of character data for the player to view and evaluate. The use of scoring (and the underlying mechanisms of objects and attributes) allows for greater replayability of a game. Without a score the result of a game is simply a binary outcome (achieved/not achieved); with a score there is always the impetus to complete the game faster or in a different way to achieve a better score.

Outcomes

As well as being able to see a score, that score has to translate into something meaningful; a score on its own is irrelevant without something to compare it to. Any score will translate to an outcome, meaning that the player has won or lost, completed a level, achieved better than last time or better than another player. Outcomes are the results of game activity, and rewards (discussed in Chapter 8) are what is gained as a result of those outcomes. Badges of achievement are one way in which outcomes are made visible to the players themselves as well as to others (usually called 'badges' in the context of gamified systems and 'achievements' in the context of games). They provide a visible representation that the player has reached some skill level or ability, or has successfully completed a task or challenge. Badges can be used to represent a certain level of points, or to signify that some other activity has been carried out, and one of their chief benefits is their flexibility: different badges can be awarded for different things at different levels (Werbach & Hunter, 2012).

Antin and Churchill (2011) suggest that there are five primary functions of badges, from a social psychology perspective:

1. *Goal setting* – setting of a challenge for the player to achieve.
2. *Instruction* – they provide information about the types of activity that can be undertaken in the game.

3. *Reputation* – a visible encapsulation of a player's expertise, interests and interactions, which determines trustworthiness and reliability to other players.
4. *Status and personal affirmation* – symbols of achievements, accomplishment and status to others and as a personal reminder.
5. *Group identification* – to be recognised as part of a group undertaking a shared experience.

As well as in the context of badges in gamification, the same idea is applied as an 'overlay' to many games nowadays, so that in addition to the core game, there may be different achievements for playing for a certain length of time, unlocking certain areas of a game or achieving tasks in efficient or unusual ways. This additional level of game play enhances the replay value of games, as players, on completing the game, can then look for different ways in which to attain all of the achievements. To the list above, I would add three additional motivational benefits of using badges or achievements.

6. *Set-building.* They cater for the human desire to create collections and sets, so there is the motivation to continue collecting the complete set of badges or achievements.
7. *Playfulness.* As the badges or achievements are typically a non-compulsory additional layer to the main game, there is scope for playfulness and fun and perhaps more silly achievements (for example, in the game *Scribblenauts* players have to solve puzzles by creating and using objects; there are achievements for transforming a creature into a toad and destroying the world).
8. *The unexpected.* As well as providing instruction, some achievements are cryptic, so that players know that they can do something but are just not sure what or how, leading to additional exploration of the game to work out how to achieve the badge; conversely badges can be gained 'by accident' leading to surprise (for example, in *Plants vs. Zombies* there is an achievement called 'Peking Express' that you gain by scrolling all the way through the achievements list (which is shown as a hole in the ground) until you get to China).

There is a growing interest in the use of badges as a way of recognising and authenticating educational achievement too. Mozilla's OpenBadges framework (see http://openbadges.org) provides a combination of free software with open standards, which allows people to create and give badges for anything that they want, that users can then display on their own web spaces.

Drawing on games and motivation theory and research, as well as my own experience, there follows a set of eight principles of badge design for learning that I have developed in the course of my work.

1. *Simplicity.* Badges need to be clear without too much information encapsulated within a single badge. A two-by-two (for example, type and level) matrix is

sufficiently complex, and each badge can then have a clear, uncluttered visual identity.

2. *Variety.* One of the key benefits of badges is their flexibility (Werbach & Hunter, 2012). This means it is possible to provide a large number of badge types so that different learners on the same course can develop completely different badge sets but can still identify as part of a group. This also allows for exploration and identification of possibilities.

3. *Exponential progression* As learners move through levels, badges should become increasingly difficult to achieve as skills increase, in order to keep the learner in a state of flow (Csíkszentmihályi, 1992). Early badges should be gained quickly to give learners a feeling of mastery; later ones can take longer and be more complex.

4. *Fairness and clarity.* It is crucial for the integrity of the learning system that badges are perceived to be fair to gain and are a meaningful representation of accreditation, so that the criteria for achieving one are clear and transparent (not necessarily before it is achieved, however).

5. *Surprise.* The unexpected can be a massive motivator, and it is possible to create badges that are not known in advance (but are still fair, with the reason for their awarding clear in retrospect) or that are cryptic with learners having to work out how to achieve them (as long as these are optional since they will not appeal to all learners).

6. *Achievability.* Each subsequent badge should build on previous ones to be seen as achievable, yet still challenging. If a badge is seen as being too hard then it will not be a motivating challenge (Malone, 1980).

7. *Collections.* Humans like to arrange things into sets and complete collections, so grouping badge sets into collections can add another motivational layer (but with associated complexity).

8. *Humour.* Not all badges have to be serious and, depending on context and appropriateness, adding a layer of fun and silliness can be engaging and motivational as well as removing some of the pressure of the system.

A second way of showing outcomes is through the use of levels, which may be linked to badges ('I have achieved a Mage Level 4 badge') or can be intrinsic to the game design itself. Many genres of game (for example platform games and strategy games) consist of a series of levels rather than a single narrative from start to finish. Each level is harder than the previous one, adding new elements and additional complexity. As players complete levels they can see how far they have progressed in the game as well as having a definite level of achievement. Levels are, in a way, microcosms of the whole game and need to be balanced in the same way. Badges and levels provide two ways for players or learners to show what they have achieved. In the next section, we will look at the variety of different types of rewards that can be given in games, and the implications of different types of reward for learning and motivation.

Game Balance

One of the hardest aspects of game design is ensuring that the game starts off as enjoyable, is just challenging enough to keep the player engaged but not so easy that it is boring, and that it continues to be interesting and keeps the player immersed, forever striving to meet the next goal or achieve the next task. This is the idea of balancing a game, and going back to flow theory (Csíkszentmihályi, 1992), as described in Chapter 6, it is the balance between boredom and frustration as the player's skills increase throughout the lifecycle of a game.

From a game design perspective, Schell (2008) suggests that

> keeping someone in the flow channel is a delicate balance, for a player's skill level seldom stays in one place. As their skill increases, you must present them with commensurate challenges. For traditional games, this primarily comes from seeking out more challenging opponents. In videogames, there is often a sequence of levels that get gradually more challenging.
>
> *(p. 120)*

Schell (2008) suggests a model for ongoing challenge within the flow zone with a repeating cycle of increasing challenge and reward, often of more power, which makes things easier for a time, followed by a further increase in challenge and so on (see Figure 7.2). He suggests that this fluctuation of challenge and success is one of the core ways in which to balance a game so that a player is neither bored nor frustrated. Methods for ensuring this balance include: increasing difficulty with each success, enabling skilled players to get through easy parts fast; creating layers of challenge so that different players can play to different levels, for example by having bronze, silver and gold levels of success (this is similar to Malone's

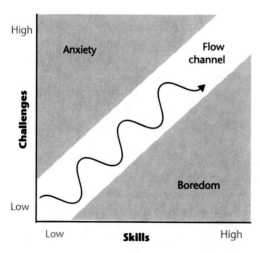

FIGURE 7.2 Cyclical progression through the flow zone (Schell, 2004)

(1980) idea of meta-goals); letting players choose the difficulty level; and play testing with a mixture of skilled and novice players to ensure that a game has an appropriate level of challenge for all levels of player.

So levels of challenge need to be mapped to appropriate skill levels over time in order to keep the interest of the player and ensure that the game continues to be engaging for a variety of players for its duration. Thompson and colleagues (2007) echo this idea of an undulating progression through the flow zone, and suggest adding 'dips in the difficulty curve' to "give the player some time to relax and prepare for the next rise" (p. 66). They highlight a range of different ways of setting pace, such as through the game story, adjusting difficulty or focusing on the learning curve or the development of character skills.

Schell (2008) describes three components of player interest. First, there is inherent interest. Some things are simply more interesting than others because they have novelty, appeal to our base and higher instincts and create dramatic situations. Second, there is the poetry of presentation, the aesthetics and inherent beauty of the entertainment experience. Finally, there is the interest of projection, the extent to which individuals use empathy and imagination to see themselves as central to the experience, by creating characters that players can relate to and people and places that capture the imagination. Salen and Zimmerman (2004) highlight the importance of emergence in relation to game balance; the idea that fixed rules can lead to an infinite variety of outcomes, and that it is the variety, novelty and surprise of the outcomes that make a game engaging: "The infinite possibility that arises out of an emergent system is a key design strategy to encourage repeat play" (p. 165). Schell (2008) also states that goals that can be achieved in more than one way support players looking for interesting strategies and interactions with objects, and help to develop emergence in play. He suggests that there are 12 common types of game balance:

1. *Fairness.* All players feel that they have a reasonable chance of winning and that it is within their own control.
2. *Challenge vs. success.* Creating the right balance between the level of challenge and skills required to be successful, so that the game is neither too easy nor too difficult.
3. *Meaningful choices.* Giving the player choices that have an impact on what happens next, where no choice is obviously preferable.
4. *Skill vs. chance.* The balance between which elements of the game are within the control of the player and which are random.
5. *Head vs. hands.* The balance between mental and physical activities and challenges in the game.
6. *Competition vs. cooperation.* Whether players play together towards a common goal or whether they play against one another.
7. *Short vs. long.* Ensuring that the game is long enough for the player to get into it but not so long that he or she becomes bored.

8. *Rewards.* What the player receives for achievements in the game.
9. *Punishment.* What happens to players if they fail to achieve.
10. *Freedom vs. controlled experience.* Creating a balance between the amount of freedom the player has to move around and interact with objects.
11. *Simple vs. complex.* The degree to which the game is simple or complex.
12. *Detail vs. imagination.* Which details should be provided and which should be left to the imaginations of the players.

Game design is not just about what is in a game; what is left out is often just as important. Fullerton, Swain, and Hoffman (2008) describe five features of games, which they describe as 'fun killers'. These are: 1) micromanagement of overly complex game variables, essentially giving the player too much control over too much detail; 2) stagnation, where nothing seems to happen for a long time and decisions stay at the same level of importance and impact; 3) insurmountable obstacles, or ones that seem that way to a large percentage of players because they lack the experience or intuition to approach the problem; 4) arbitrary events, which happen without warning or a logical reason, particularly if they have negative consequences; and 5) predictable paths through the game, so that the outcomes become obvious, anticipated and boring.

The use of chance in games delays or prevents the solvability of the game, and makes it competitive for all players so that anyone has the possibility of winning, regardless of skill level. It increases variety and unpredictability in game play, creates dramatic moments where, for example, everything rests on the roll of a die and makes decision-making more interesting because players have to weigh up the risks and benefits of events with known and unknown probabilities (Brathwaite & Schreiber, 2009). Juul (2013) includes chance in what he calls 'three paths to fairness' in game design, i.e. three ways in which players can progress and be rewarded in modern computer games. These are skill, chance and labour. The third is a relatively new aspect and is common in casual social network games, such as *Farmville*, where players take part for very short times, often as small as a couple of minutes, and gradually accumulate goods or achievements by doing something trivial and repetitive, such as clicking the mouse on certain areas. These types of game have been criticised because they reward very low-level activity and are designed in such a way as to keep the players 'hooked' on returning regularly to the game.

The aim of this chapter has been to examine the core structural elements of digital games and examine how they can be used to create games that engage players and keep them engaged. The elements of challenge and goals, points, progression and outcomes provide the core mechanics for many games and are fundamental building blocks for game design. They also help us to understand what it is about games that makes them compelling, and how they can be balanced in order to enhance the gaming and learning experiences of players. These ideas are at the heart of what makes the difference between a good, engaging, playable game and a poor one.

8

GAMES AS REWARD MECHANISMS

In this chapter, I will look at another motivational element of games, the rewards that players get for winning, or simply for taking part. There is a wide variety of different types of rewards, some that support extrinsic motivation, such a prizes or esteem, while others, like the simple pleasure of completing a difficult puzzle, are more deeply associated with the intrinsic motivation within the game. In this chapter I will start by discussing reward systems in games, looking at the types of rewards that exist and evidence of their impacts on learning. In the second half of the chapter I will look at the most common extrinsic reward used in education – formal assessment – and the ways in which game-based assessment can be implemented.

The reward is what the player receives for successfully completing the game (or a stage within it) or winning over other players. Rewards can be intangible, such as the kudos of winning or the satisfaction of having solved a difficult puzzle, or tangible, such as a prize or trophy; in addition to the esteem of winning, every game has a stake, which can be of material or symbolic value. "The stake can be a gold cup or a jewel or a king's daughter or a shilling; the life of a player or the welfare of a whole tribe" (Huizinga, 1955, p. 50).

Types of Reward

There are many different ways in which theorists have classified rewards in games. Hallford and Hallford (2001) describe four distinct categories of reward (their analysis is undertaken in relation to the design of role-playing games but Salen and Zimmerman (2004) suggest that their use is applicable to other digital game types too):

1. *Rewards of glory* – rewards that are associated with prestige and self-affirmation, but make no difference to the game play, for example finishing a level or beating a particularly tricky opponent.
2. *Rewards of sustenance* – in-game items that enhance or prolong the game, such as medicine packs that restore health, mana potions that increase spell ability or bags that enable the player to carry more objects.
3. *Rewards of access* – the ability to access new areas within the game.
4. *Rewards of facility* – the ability to do things that the player could not do before. This can be intra-game, such as learning a new spell, or extra-game, such as unlocking a new mini-game.

Schell (2008) suggests nine common types of reward, shown in Table 8.1 below, mapped against the categories described above. These are specifically focused on rewards that are provided within the game.

TABLE 8.1 Types of reward (from Schell, 2008, mapped against Hallford & Hallford's, 2001, categories of reward)

Type of reward	Description	Category
Praise	The game telling you that you have done well, through words, sounds or an in-game character talking.	Rewards of glory
Points	Either as a measurement of success, or as a pathway to other rewards.	Rewards of glory/ sustenance/access/ facility
Prolonged play	The ability to play longer by providing increased play time, extra health or an extra life.	Rewards of sustenance
A gateway	Entry to new parts of the game that can be explored.	Rewards of access
Spectacle	Beautiful or interesting music, animation or sight.	Rewards of glory/ access
Expression	The ability for the player to make a mark on the world, through access to special clothes or items.	Rewards of glory
Powers	New or improved skills or abilities that allow the player to achieve things in new and better ways.	Rewards of facility
Resources	Virtual resources that can be used in the game, or virtual money that can be spent.	Rewards of sustenance/facility
Completion	The feeling of closure gained from completing the game.	Rewards of glory

A different classification of rewards is provided by Oxland (2004), who suggests that there are four types of reward: game-play rewards that are given to a player for progress in the game (which could be a range of types according to the previous classification, praise, points, power or resources, for example); hidden rewards and secrets that surprise the player because they are unexpected (again, they could be almost any of the above with the exception of completion); impetus rewards that pull the player towards a particular goal, such as solving a puzzle or reaching an object that is currently unobtainable, so that achieving the goal is its own reward (this could apply to gateway, powers or resources); and visual rewards such as big explosions, special effects and things that the player has never seen in the game before (this is similar to spectacle).

The use of punishments can be thought of as 'rewards in reverse'; a game might punish players to show that game resources are scarce and valuable, to increase risk and excitement and to increase meaningful challenge if there is a risk of punishment. Common types of punishment in games include shaming, loss of points, shortened or terminated play, setbacks, removal of powers or resource depletion (Schell, 2008). Use of punishments need to be considered carefully because they can be demotivating (particularly in the context of educational gaming) and a reward is almost always a better choice, but light punishments can have the motivational effects mentioned previously.

As well as the rewards associated with abilities or powers within the game, there are also tangible rewards such as prizes or trophies. While these are uncommon in the realm of digital games, excepting the big-budget fighting championships that happen in the Far East, they are common in the realm of sports, and small physical rewards such as badges are common in mixed-reality and pervasive games. These are extrinsic rewards, rewards outside of the game structure, while intrinsic rewards are those that have meaning within the game (e.g. access to another level, increased powers). Another type of reward is the social or competitive reward, such as the use of badges to signify competence and recognition within a community, or leaderboards to show how a player is performing compared with other players (or how well the player performed compared with his or her last game or over time). Leaderboards in educational gaming may be problematic; while they can be motivational for some players, they can also demotivate those who are less competitive or less comfortable with openness regarding performance.

McGonigal (2011) suggests that in life, intrinsic rewards fall into four major categories: satisfying work; the experience (or hope) or being successful; social connections; and meaning – the chance to be something larger than ourselves. She argues that good games can help us achieve these rewards:

> Games, after all, are the quintessential autotelic activity. We only ever play because we want to. Games don't fuel our appetite for extrinsic reward: they don't pay us, they don't advance our careers, and they don't help us accumulate luxury goods. Instead, games enrich us with intrinsic rewards.

> They actively engage us in satisfying work that we have a chance to be
> successful at. They give us a highly structured way to spend time and build
> bonds with people we like. And if we play a game long enough, with a
> big enough network of players, we feel a part of something bigger than
> ourselves – part of an epic story, an important project, or a global community.
>
> *(McGonigal, 2011, pp. 50–51)*

Games also provide emotional rewards to the players, such as the satisfaction of
curiosity by solving mysteries and uncovering secrets; using hidden or secret
information that is revealed at key points in the game to reward the player and
enhance interest. Salen and Zimmerman (2004) describe four different ways of
using digital games to reveal hidden information:

1. *The fog of war* – strategically showing map areas as the game progresses.
2. *Secret locations and hidden moves* – known in advance or surprises.
3. *Item economies* – the ability to purchase new objects as the game progresses.
4. *Rules as information* – trial and error to discover the rules of the system and
   point of the game.

Ferrara (2012) describes 'meta-rewards' that exist outside of the game but are
about the experience of playing the game, including 'Easter eggs' and cheats.
Easter eggs are secrets hidden within the game interface itself, such as the famous
flight simulator that was hidden within early versions of Microsoft Excel if users
performed a certain set of actions in the spreadsheet. Since Easter eggs are not
a logical part of a game they can only be stumbled on by chance (or found on
Easter egg web sites) so cannot be used to directly motivate players. Cheats are
codes deliberately built in by designers, usually for testing purposes, that use
unlikely key combinations to, for example, unlock areas, restore health or provide
unlimited lives. These cheats provide an alternative experience for players who
may prefer the easier experience to the one intended by the game designer, and
in the case of single-player games the word 'cheat' may be misleading for it is
simply the system that is being cheated in order for the player to create a more
enjoyable and engaging experience. Also, bugs or glitches in the game can become
meta rewards in themselves, for example players can find unintended odd effects
or shortcuts in the game such as passing through an apparently solid corner into
a secret area, caused by a programming error or a testing shortcut left in by
developers. These are often shared on fan forums and sought out by other players.

Motivational Effects of Rewards

Werbach and Hunter (2012) suggest that extrinsic rewards have to be used with
caution because they can 'crowd out fun' and be profoundly demotivating: "for
tasks that are interesting, intrinsic motivation dissipates when extrinsic rewards

are tangible, expected, and contingent" (p. 60). That the expectation of an extrinsic reward decreases motivation has also been shown in research studies (Lepper & Greene, 1972). Werbach and Hunter (2012) argue that extrinsic motivation has a negative effect when a user is already intrinsically motivated, but has benefits when the user is amotivated, and the task is boring, tedious and repetitive. In the context of pure entertainment games, it would be logical to suppose that this type of task does not exist because there is no reason to motivate players to carry out a boring, tedious or repetitive task for pleasure. However, there is evidence to the contrary: for example, the 'grind' in massively multiplayer online role-playing games, where players have to repetitively kill monsters or other such tasks for long periods until they have achieved a new level, or the massive popularity of *Farmville*, in which players have to do little more than repetitively click at regular intervals in order to gain levels.

The type and regularity of a reward can also influence its motivational effect. Players get inured to regular and consistent rewards, so rewards that are variable and gradually increase in size are more motivational than regular and predictable (Oxland, 2004; Schell, 2008); uncertain rewards are more motivating (Howard-Jones & Demetriou, 2008; Schell, 2008) and there is evidence that motivation is at its greatest when the outcome is most uncertain (Atkinson, 1957). Salen & Zimmerman (2004) differentiate between macro-level uncertainty (winning or losing) that happens in all games, and micro-level uncertainty (relating to specific chance occurrences within the game) that does not occur in all games, highlighting that "the feeling of randomness is more important than the randomness itself" (p. 176). From a behaviourist perspective, different reward schedules (i.e. changing the frequency and timing of rewards) can create different patterns of behaviour. So, for example, continuous reinforcement, where each correct action triggers a reward, allows new behaviours to be picked up quickly but can lead to negative results if it is suddenly inconsistent. Fixed-ratio schedules occur where a reward is given after a fixed number of tries, and leads to an increase in pace. Variable-ratio schedules occur when a reward is given after a number of tries, but this number changes over time, and this results in a fast response rate with little pause after the reward, for example in the case of slot machines, which work on a variable-ratio reward schedule. Fixed-interval schedules provide rewards after set amounts of time, and in this case players quickly get a feel for the timings and step up their efforts at the appropriate times, taking it more easy at others. Variable-interval schedules provide rewards based on time intervals, but these change so they are indistinguishable from randomisation and have the lowest impact on behaviour as there is no apparent link between behaviour and reward (Ferrara, 2012).

In this section I have considered the motivational effects of rewards on game players. In relation to formal learning, where assessment takes place, the manner and methods of assessment used, the ways in which it is implemented and how it interacts with the game elements will have implications for motivation. In the sections that follow, I consider the implications of games and assessment.

Games and Assessment

Assessment in the context of game-based learning is an ambiguous term that can actually mean several different things. Table 8.2 below shows the important distinction between a) the assessment of game-based learning activities and b) using games as an assessment tool in themselves. Note that while the term 'assessment' is often used interchangeably in the game-based learning literature with 'evaluation', assessment in this context refers to the formal assignments that need to be successfully completed in order to pass accredited courses.

So, as can be seen from this model, assessment of game-based learning can refer to three specific situations: the use of games for learning, but with traditional assessment (e.g. Whitton & Hynes, 2006); traditional teaching (used here to refer to teaching without games) with game-based assessment (e.g. Charlier & Clarebout, 2009; McAlpine, van der Zanden, & Harris, 2011) or a combination of both game-based teaching and assessment (e.g. Brookes & Moseley, 2012; Sheldon, 2011). The use of a pure game-based teaching model is perhaps the most common because of the small scale of most game-based learning implementations, in non-formal contexts, and the political and acceptability aspects of game-based assessment. However, while the use of games for formal assessment is less common, their benefits in relation to formative and informal assessment are well known. External assessment is more time consuming and labour intensive than in-game assessment, but also more flexible and creative. There is a variety of different ways of assessing game-based learning using external methods. For example:

- Reports on actions taken and decisions made, with critical analysis of the consequences of decisions, or on future planning based on the endpoint of the game.
- Presentations on aspects of a game using roles from within the game (e.g. in a business game this could involve making a group presentation to the board of directors explaining the rationale for decisions taken).
- Creation of artefacts based on and extending the action in the game (e.g. posters, digital video, audio, graphics).
- Discussion posts can be assessed for their contribution, critical engagement with and reflection on the game.

TABLE 8.2 Types of assessment with games

		Teaching method	
		Game-based	Traditional
Assessment method	External	Game-based teaching	Traditional learning and assessment
	In-game	Game-based teaching and assessment	Game-based assessment

- Collaborative web sites, using tools such as blogs or wikis can be used to encourage students to work together to create an ongoing log of actions taken and learning from the game.
- Narratives associated with the action in the game (e.g. characterisations, back stories, future scenarios).
- Personal reflective accounts of the actions taken in the game and the learning acquired from it.
- Portfolios detailing the use of the game, decisions made, artefacts created, consequences and learning.

In-game assessment is a far less well researched area than game-based learning. While games offer a host of pedagogic advantages mentioned throughout the earlier chapters of this book, they are typically poor at fostering reflection or meta-cognition about the learning process; and this is one way in which well-designed assessment can play a role. In-game assessment has the advantage of being automated, repeatable (and therefore theoretically equitable) and can be undertaken without breaking the flow of the game – players can be assessed with-out even realising it (this does, however, have ethical implications). Moseley (2012c) makes a distinction between stealth assessment, where the learner is unaware that he or she is being assessed, and implicit assessment, where there is a link between some element of the game score and the formal assessment marks but students are made fully aware of this. External assessment of game-based teaching offers more creativity and teacher control, but is more time intensive. Linking lower level learning outcomes (such as recall and comprehension) to game scoring and progression mechanisms is relatively straightforward, but this becomes trickier at higher cognitive levels (for example analysis and critical thinking) because the game is essentially using a quantitative method to assess a qualitative aspect; it is only the product that is being assessed, not the process.

There are a number of issues with in-game assessment, which makes it important to consider whether the benefits really outweigh the pitfalls. The first problem is related to the purpose of assessment, which many researchers and academics think should not simply be to test, but should be an integral part of the learning process. With their focus on action, many games do not offer space for reflection, or for the player to consolidate what has been learned or consider how to apply the learning to other contexts or situations. This can be remedied though additional out-of-game activities such as discussions, structured reflective activities, debriefing activities or assessment. Assessment can provide this space for reflection, meta-cognition and evaluation of progress in relation to feedback but in-game assessment does not facilitate this if it is covert. Linked to this is the fact that in-game assessment does not provide any evidence of the transferability of learning to other contexts; there is no evidence that just because someone can achieve something in the game context, he or she will be able to apply that learning to the real world (pervasive games being a notable exception).

Another issue with in-games assessment is that of validity: whether the game-based assessment is measuring what it is intended to measure. When using a game for formal learning it is difficult to ensure that the intended learning outcomes are aligned with the gaming outcomes, and this is compounded in the case of assessment; it is difficult to separate measurement of learning from measurement of skills in the game (which are seldom completely equivalent). For example, skills such as timing, mouse control or hand–eye coordination may impact on game performance but have little to do with the intended learning from the game. Assessing game performance directly is also problematic because poor game performance does not mean that a student is not learning from the game; one of the key benefits of games is the ability and space to make mistakes, reflect and learn from them (more about this in Chapter 11). Game-based assessment that uses a single 'snapshot' of performance may be problematic, whereas allowing multiple attempts within the game until an outcome has been achieved would make the most of the ability of digital games to support repeated practice, assisted by the well-developed forms of feedback provided in games. Poor game performance could also be due to factors such as low gaming literacy (where the player is not familiar with the implicit norms and conventions of the game type), navigation problems (such as movement in a three-dimensional environment using keyboard and mouse) or usability issues (including the transparency of the interface and clarity of functionality), so assessment of game performance directly may have equity issues that need to be considered.

There is also the wider point that it is difficult to fully automate any meaningful assessment, not just in respect of game-based assessment. The role and judgement of a teacher is important to ensure that assessment is appropriate and fair. While the use of the data that are collected in the background of digital games designed for entertainment might provide some evidence of learning, its use in formal contexts (particularly schools) is problematic because game performance does not provide evidence of relevance to the real world, and the knowledge and skills acquired playing entertainment games are unlikely to map onto any formal curriculum. Even in recognition and recall games, when the facts of the game are relevant to a specified curriculum, the game itself may detract from learning them (Dumbleton & Kirriemuir, 2006).

Shute and Ventura (2013) highlight that traditional classroom assessments are detached events, separate from learning, that they rarely influence learning and have issues with validity. They offer what they term 'stealth assessment' as an alternative. Stealth assessments are "woven directly and invisibly into the fabric of the gaming environment ... evidence needed to assess the skills is thus provided by the players' interactions with the game itself (i.e., the processes of play)" (p. 42) so that they are valid, reliable and unobtrusive. However, the importance of transparency of the outputs of assessment and the ability for players/learners to gauge their performance at any time are also highlighted. Shute and Ventura (2013) developed a game, *Newton's Playground*, that embedded assessment for conceptual physics, as well as transferable skills (conscientiousness and creativity) by linking evidence of a skill to performance in the game. For example, persistence (a component of conscientiousness) was indicated by time spent on problems within the game, and understanding of certain laws of physics was indicated by completion of certain tasks within the game. While this model clearly shows how assessment can be linked to game activities in such a way that levels of learning can be indicated, it does not get over the overarching issue that if a person knows that an activity is assessed (be it a game or traditional assessment) then levels of anxiety will increase. In this case the tight coupling of game activities to game content may have led to a reliable and valid assessment, but this may not always be possible in other domains. The key issue is whether assessment is competency-based and allows for repetition and practice so that learners can have multiple tries (i.e. they achieve the assessment when they have completed the game to a sufficient level), or whether the game is used as a one-off assessment activity.

Zapata-Rivera and Bauer (2012) argue that there are some components of games that can enhance assessment, but highlight issues that need to be taken into account (they mainly discuss formative assessment, but say also that these issues apply to summative). These include:

- requirement of skills and knowledge to play the game that are not relevant to the construct being assessed;
- behaviours such as trying to 'game the system' or repeatedly exploring interactive effects such as sound or visuals that can skew the results of assessment;
- increased cognitive load because of attention being given to irrelevant game factors and interaction;
- accessibility issues with rich, immersive graphical environments;
- tutorials and time required for familiarisation to interact with a novel graphical environment.

Assessment systems also need to consider: the type and amount of feedback provided to students; the potential for replay and the number of attempts that need to be taken into account when making assessment evaluations; and that dependencies among actions and events can be hard to model and interpret. Zapata-Rivera and Bauer (2012) make an assumption that game-based assessment necessarily has to be immersive and with a high level of graphical fidelity. They argue that learners will expect this type of graphical quality for the game to be accepted, but this assumes that learners compare game-based assessment with playing entertainment games, whereas I would contend that learners compare game-based assessment with traditional assessment so, from a motivational perspective, any game is better than none.

As well as considering game-based assessment that is embedded in the game itself, it can also be about using ideas from games to improve assessment, for example making it less stressful or more engaging. Moseley (2012c) points out that there are ways in which game elements can be directly mapped onto formal educational assessment systems, stating that there is little difference between scoring points based on actions in a game and rating student performance based on actions in an assessment, and that there is a parallel between increasing difficulty in games and increasing difficulty in assessments over time. He argues that "there is no reason why we can't utilize some of the contextual and open aspects of game scoring and feedback, and mould them to fit an educational context" (p. 132) and suggests four principles from games that could be applied to educational assessment:

1. *Contextual assessment* – the subject of the assessment matches the skills that the students are learning.
2. *Open assessment* – marking students on particular activities as they do them and on separate scales, thus providing immediate and explicit feedback.
3. *Negative feedback* (as in the creation of a negative feedback loop rather than damaging or harmful feedback) – giving students harder or easier assessments based on their previous performance.
4. *Positive feedback* (as in the creation of a positive feedback loop) – such as giving assessment bonuses for four high scores.

Sheldon (2011) took the idea of embedding gaming principles in assessment one stage further to develop an entire module of study based around the metaphor of a massively multiplayer online role-playing game, with students working for experience points rather than for grades. In this case, the class was for game design students, who might be assumed to be more favourably disposed to the use of this type of metaphor than students from other disciplines. However, this still presents a very interesting model for structuring assessment in innovative and engaging ways.

In this chapter, I have explored the different ways in which games can reward their players and the effects of these different strategies on game play and learning. The issue of game-based assessment is a thorny one, particularly in relation to the appropriateness and acceptability of games where the assessment is meaningful in an academic context. Of particular interest to me is the way in which assessment could be re-conceptualised, based on the ways in which game failure is seen as a learning process, which is not the case in terms of assessment failure. If formal assessments could be seen as developing indicators of cumulative experience rather than single-shot profiles then, I believe, they would be a much more effective way of motivating students as well as providing meaningful levels of performance.

PART IV

Games as Playgrounds

9

GAMES AS PROTECTED PLAY

In this part of the book, I will move on to look at theories and research in the area of game-based learning that is perhaps most neglected in the literature, that of games for play. In the 'serious' context of learning, the frivolous, playful aspects of games are often passed over because they are seen as being inappropriate or not acceptable, particularly in the context of adult formal education. However, it is the very playful, or ludic, quality of games that gives them so much power for learning; the fact that they offer an 'other' world in which mistake-making is taken for granted, and taking on other characters or ways of being is integral to the activity. In this chapter I will first provide an overview of play and learning, before discussing the related concept of fun and considering the relevance of fun to learning.

Play and Learning

Play is a powerful influence on learning that is fundamental to the development of both adults and children (Rieber, 1996), promoting creativity (Howard-Jones, Taylor, & Sutton, 2002), engagement and mastery of developmental tasks (Colarusso, 1993). It is a fundamental part of the evolving human experience and the way in which we learn, providing the opportunity to practise and explore in a safe environment, teaching skills like aiming, timing, hunting, strategy and manipulation of power (Koster, 2005).

> The very existence of play continually confirms the supra-logical nature of the human situation. Animals play, so they must be more than merely mechanical things. We play and know that we play, so we must be more than merely rational beings, for play is irrational.
>
> *(Huizinga, 1955, p. 4)*

However, play is difficult to define, although everyone can recognise it, and it is culturally and politically constrained. Play can also not be defined, as commonly happens, as the opposite of work because "work becomes play when one's job is so satisfying and rewarding that getting paid to do it is of secondary importance" (Rieber, 1996, p. 44); although, conversely, Yee (2006) argues that games can become like work when players spend such large amounts of time making progress in the game that it feels like obligation. He suggests that "the central irony of MMORPGs is that they are advertised as worlds to escape to after coming home from work, but they too make us work and burn us out" (p. 70).

Huizinga (1955) describes play as a voluntary activity, encapsulating freedom, which is separate from 'real life': "a temporary sphere of activity with a disposition all of its own" (p. 8), and 'not serious' with no material interest, but with its own limitations and boundaries, and rules about what is appropriate in the play-world. Play promotes the creation of social groups that separate themselves from the 'common world' with their own rites and secrets. Caillois (2001) notes that this description is flawed on two points, first that the secretive nature of the play-world actually reduces mystery because it is the role of play to expose and highlight those secrets, and second that Huizinga's definition does not account for gambling or other games of chance in which money is exchanged. He argues that play has to be defined as "an occasion of pure waste: waste of time, ingenuity, skill, and often of money" (p. 6) so gambling, as it does not produce anything, is included in the definition, but professional sportsplayers, he says, do not play, but work. A second distinction Caillois (2001) makes is that "play has to be defined as a free and voluntary activity, a source of joy and amusement. A game which one would be forced to play would at once cease being play" (p. 6). Brown and Vaughan (2010) present a definition of play that is based on properties, some of which can be objectively observed about the activity and others that are subjective to the participant. They say that play:

- Has apparent purposelessness – it is done for its own sake and does not have any extrinsic value.
- Is voluntary – it is not obligatory or required by duty.
- Has inherent attraction – it is fun, provides relief from boredom and makes people feel good.
- Provides freedom from time – it makes players lose the sense of the passage of time.
- Creates a diminished consciousness of self – so that players stop worrying about how they look.
- Has improvisational potential – there is not a fixed way of doing things.
- Provides a continuation desire – so that the player wants to keep playing.

Brown and Vaughan (2010) themselves note the similarity of the play experience to the characteristics of flow (Csíkszentmihályi, 1992, see Chapter 6 for more detail), particularly in relation to freedom from time and the lessened sense of self. Again, the notion that play is a voluntary activity is present. This presents an interesting consideration for the field of games and learning: for if a game is used in a formal context, where the learner has no freedom of choice over whether to take part, does that mean that it can no longer be considered play? I agree with the first point, that play has to involve freedom, joyfulness and fun, but disagree that this is contingent on the voluntary nature of the activity. In educational settings, a game may not be voluntary (in that the players have no option to opt out) but it can still be something entered into in a spirit of play; given the external goal of learning (which may, or may not, be voluntary). The activity may not be voluntary, but may still be preferable to an alternative activity, and is undertaken as part of the overall engagement in education. Of course, there may be individuals who refuse to 'play' a game (as there may be in any educational activity) who will have a different type of learning experience. Caillois (2001) also considers play to be an activity that is voluntary, and one that is separate from the real world, uncertain, unproductive and governed by convention and make-believe. He presents four categories of play: agon (competitive play); alea (games of chance); mimicry (role-play and children's games) and ilinx (play through physical sensation, such as fairground rides).

Brown and Vaughan (2010) also describe a framework created by play historian Scott Eberle, which shows a six-stage process that he says people go through as they play. The stages are as follows:

1. *Anticipation.* Waiting with expectation, curiosity, perhaps a little anxiety.
2. *Surprise.* Discovery of the unexpected, a new sensation, idea or shifting perspective.
3. *Pleasure.* A good feeling.
4. *Understanding.* The acquisition of new knowledge or a synthesis of existing knowledge.
5. *Strength.* The mastery that comes from experience and understanding, and the empowerment of coming through an experience unscathed.
6. *Poise.* Contentment, composure and a sense of balance in life.

Salen and Zimmerman (2004) identify three forms of play: game play; ludic activities (all the non-game behaviours considered to be playing – a kitten batting a ball, children playing house); and being playful (the spirit of play). They argue that "play is a free movement within a more rigid structure" (p. 304) and that it is this rigid structure that means play can exist in opposition to the structure. They describe the idea of transformative play, which "occurs when the free movement of play alters the more rigid structure in which it takes shape. The play doesn't just occupy and oppose the interstices of the system, but actually transforms the space as a whole" (p. 305). This makes sense in relation to the model described by Brown and Vaughan (2010) above, where the play experience also takes on the role of transformative experience, leading ultimately to learning and a greater understanding of the world.

Salen and Zimmerman (2004) argue that "the goal of successful game design is meaningful play" (p. 33), where the essence of creating great game experiences is to create games that have meaning and are meaningful. They point out that this can take an infinite variety of forms and that "meaningful play emerges from the interaction between the players and the system of the game, as well as from the context in which the game is played" (p. 33). Meaningful play is defined in two separate ways: the first, which they term *descriptive*, is the way in which game actions and decisions result in outcomes giving meaning to the actions (intrinsic to the way in which all games operate); the second, termed *evaluative*, looks at the degree to which the outcomes of actions are 'discernible and integrated' into the wider game (emotional and psychological) experience. These definitions are integrated in the sense that decisions have immediate significance but also affect the experience at a later point in the game.

Games, Play and Fun

At the heart of understanding play is the notion of fun. Huizinga (1955) describes fun as the 'essence of play', but argues that fun "resists all analysis, all logical interpretation ... it cannot be reduced to any other mental category" (p. 3). Sutton-Smith (2001) agrees that fun is fundamental to play, repeating the claim that it is the essence of play. He presents seven 'rhetorics' of play, which include: play as development, such as the games of children; play as fate through games of chance; play as power, such as sports; play as confirmation of identity through traditional celebrations; play through creativity and innovation; play as relaxation or escape; and play as frivolous activity. Each of these rhetorics can provide a context for developing a sense of fun, although there is also a serious side to many of them (for example, the solemnity and ritual of celebrations or the rivalry of sports players) so that play can clearly exist without fun; the two concepts are not interchangeable. Fun is a crucial concept in the entertainment games industry; in a survey of 63 game developers, educators and researchers, Michael and Chen (2006) found that 21 respondents (33%) felt that fun was very important, and an additional 30 (49%) felt it was important. While there is an obvious relationship between fun and games designed for enjoyment, in relation to education and learning, the role of fun is much less clear.

Koster (2005) suggests the root of the word fun is either 'fonne' ('fool' in Middle English) or 'fonn' (pleasure in Gaelic). He defines fun simply as 'a source of enjoyment' and emphasises the importance of the chemistry of fun, arguing that "fun is all about our brains feeling good – the release of endorphins into our system" (p. 40). The most important source of fun is when our bodies reward us chemically with that "moment of triumph when we learn something or master a task" (p. 40). He argues that the idea of fun necessarily links with learning and says that "fun, as I define it, is the feedback that the brain gives us when we are absorbing patterns for learning purposes" (p. 96). From a neurological perspective, Schmidhuber (2010) presents a formal model and definition of fun, also highlighting the link between learning and fun in his definition. He defines fun as the internal joy for the discovery or creation of novel patterns, where a pattern is interesting or surprising if "the observer initially did not know the pattern but is able to learn it" (p. 230). Since fun and learning have such a close link, it is interesting that the term 'serious games' has been widely adopted to refer to games used for purposes other than entertainment, such as learning. Klabbers (2006) argues that the term does not make sense because it excludes play, saying "players can be both playful and serious, while playing. Therefore, the play concept is much broader and of higher order than is seriousness. Seriousness seeks to exclude play, whereas play can very well include seriousness" (p. 5).

Draper (1999) argues from a psychological angle that a key characteristic of fun is intrinsic motivation, where it is not done as a means to an end; that fun is play for pleasure, one type of enjoyment. He suggests that "fun is not in fact a property of an activity, but a relationship between that activity and the individual's goals at that moment" (p. 118). Carroll and Thomas (1988) distinguish fun from ideas of ease, or ease of use, by describing fun in terms of its complexity. They suggest that jokes that are too obvious or games that are not challenging enough are not fun; whereas those that we expect to be "of moderate complexity (interesting and tractable) and then in fact find them to be so" (p. 21) lead to a sense of fun.

Other concepts commonly used (particularly in games design research) in association with, or as synonyms for, fun, are 'enjoyment', 'amusement', 'pleasure' and 'fulfilment'. Gajadhar, de Kort, and IJsselsteijn (2008) suggest that fun is part of enjoyment, which is described as comprising four elements in total: positive affect (fun); competence (feelings of strength and skill); challenge (stimulation, effort); and (lack of) frustration (tension, irritability). Prensky (2007) argues that academics use both 'amusement' and 'enjoyment' to define fun, but that these are not the same. While "amusement may be frivolous, enjoyment and pleasure are certainly not" (p. 108). Csíkszentmihályi (1992) distinguishes between pleasure and enjoyment, saying that pleasure is "a feeling of contentment that one achieves whenever information in consciousness says that expectations set by biological programs or by social conditioning have been met" (p. 45), while enjoyment occurs when "a person has not only met some prior expectation or satisfied a need or a desire but also gone beyond what he or she has been programmed to do and achieved something unexpected, perhaps something even unimagined before" (p. 46). Salen and Zimmerman (2004) also discuss the nature of pleasure, saying,

> when we speak of pleasure in games, we are referring to the fundamental feelings derived from the intense concentration of a game of Memory, the

exhilaration of winning a touchdown, the charged socio-sexual manoeuvres of Twister, the hypnotically satisfying patterns of Tetris. Pleasure can include any physical, emotional, psychological or ideological sensation.

(p. 330)

Oxland (2004) adds the notion of fulfilment, described as "the feeling you get when you have just solved a puzzle, beaten a big behemoth or completed a difficult section of the game" (p. 90). Koster (2005) defines 'delight' as when we "recognise patterns but are surprised by them" (p. 94) such as the moment when reading a mystery novel that everything falls into place.

The notion of fun and associated concepts is difficult to pin down as researchers and academics from different disciplines use the language in different ways; Figure 9.1 below attempts to synthesise the concepts and theoretic models described above, to separate two distinct aspects of fun, those that are fundamental, immediate and sensual, and those that build up over time, engage the mind and provide a sense of satisfaction. In relation to learning, both aspects of fun may play a part, but it is likely to be the longer term and more cerebral aspects that have a greater impact upon learning.

Hunicke and colleagues (2004) argue that terms such as 'fun' and 'game-play' are a too limited vocabulary for discussing the aesthetics of games. They present an eight-factor taxonomy, shown in Table 9.1 below, with my own examples.

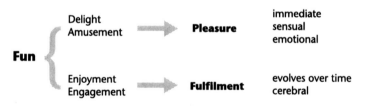

FIGURE 9.1 A synthesis and summary of aspects of fun

TABLE 9.1 Types of fun (Hunicke et al., 2004)

Type	Description	Example game genres
Sensation	Game as sense-pleasure	Physical games, sports
Fantasy	Game as make-believe	Role play
Narrative	Game as drama	Adventure, role-playing games
Challenge	Game as obstacle course	Shooters, platform games
Fellowship	Game as social framework	Social network games, board games
Discovery	Game as uncharted territory	Adventure, simulation
Expression	Game as self-discovery	Game building, sandbox games
Submission	Game as pastime	Casual games

Schell (2008) adds additional factors, which he calls pleasures, to the original eight listed above, although he acknowledges that even now this is not a complete list. These additional pleasures are anticipation, delight in another's misfortune, gift giving, humour, possibility, pride in an accomplishment, purification, surprise, thrill, triumph over adversity and wonder. I believe that they are of a different quality from those mentioned above because they are at a finer level of granularity, and could be present in all game types at different points but are not characteristics of a particular type of game.

Järvinen (2009) presents an analysis of five categories of pleasure, originally from Kubovy (1999), that are manifest in different types of digital game. The categories, definitions and examples are summarised in Table 9.2 below.

Lazzaro (2004, 2008) presents four types of fun. She describes 'hard fun' as overcoming meaningful challenges, strategies and puzzles, creating a sense of fiero (triumph over adversity); Papert (2002) uses the same term to highlight that something is fun because it is hard, not in spite of it being so. Second, 'easy fun' is described as stimulating exploration, discovery and curiosity. The third dimension of fun, 'the people factor', is described as creating opportunities for collaboration, competition and interaction with other people, while the final factor, 'serious fun', is about relaxation, for example through repetition, rhythm, completion and collection. Gajadhar and colleagues (2008) also draw on the people-centric element of fun and link the presence of others in computer game play (co-located players in cooperative play) to significantly higher levels of enjoyment in comparison with solo game play.

TABLE 9.2 Categories of pleasure in video games (from Järvinen, 2009).

Pleasure	Description	Example
Curiosity	Learning something previously unknown.	Exploration of unknown game environments in *Halo* (a first-person shooter).
Virtuosity	Doing something well.	Showing motor and auditory skills in *Guitar Hero* (where the interface is a 'real' guitar that can be played).
Nurture	Taking care of living things.	Nurturing characters in *Animal Crossing* (where the player takes care of a virtual village of small animals).
Sociability	Belonging to a social group.	Guilds in *World of Warcraft* (a massively multiplayer online role-playing game).
Suffering	Negative pleasures arising from 'mundane' psychological pains, such as shame or guilt, or 'existential' pains, such as fear of death.	Creating empathy with refugees, and the associated guilt and unease, in *Darfur is Dying* (a simulation game).

As well as creating ambiguity about the nature of fun, theorists also disagree as to what can create fun. Koster (2005) argues that fun arises from mastery, comprehension and solving puzzles, while Lee and Hoadley (2005) argue that the exploration of possible selves in the virtual game world, and the exploration and consolidation of identity as a result, create fun. Dormann and Biddle (2009) discuss the role of humour in game play, suggesting that "using humor can make games richer, more engaging, as well as fun" (p. 803). They present three main theories of humour: first, that it relates to superiority, such as laughing about the misfortunes of others; second, that it provides a sense of relief, a release of nervous energy; and third, that it is caused by a sense of incongruity, where things are unexpected or surprising. Poris (2005) presents ten dimensions of fun from a marketing perspective, with a focus primarily on children, which highlight the range of different ways in which fun can be engendered. She says that fun can be friend-oriented, empowering through learning and discovery, creative, silly, sports-oriented, competitive, family-oriented and related to social responsibility, surprising and adventurous, relaxing and rebellious through risk-taking. Some of these dimensions of fun are more relevant to learning than others: in particular, the social and friend-oriented aspects that link to ideas of social constructivism; learning and discovery are related to concepts such as enquiry-based learning; and creativity underpins problem-solving, imagination and innovation.

However, fun is not seen as a good thing by all game designers. Rogers (2010) argues that fun is a useless term because it is completely subjective and there is no guarantee that a game idea will be fun in practice, or will be fun for all people. To counter that, he describes what he calls the 'theory of un-fun', which states that once a game designer starts with a fun idea, he or she needs to "find something in the game that is not fun (or un-fun) then remove it. When you have removed all of the un-fun, then all that should be left is the fun". While this seems to make sense, it does not address the issue of different people finding different types of things fun, and sometimes fun in games is fun simply because of its juxtaposition to something boring (or un-fun).

Fun and Emotion

Digital games are increasingly able to engage players emotionally in the gaming experience, through narrative elements and characters in which players can feel an emotional investment, coupled with the use of advanced visual rendering and increased levels of realism (Ferrara, 2012). Emotion enhances memories (LaBar & Cabeza, 2006) and is a key motivator for driving learning, thinking and problem-solving: we store information more deeply when it has an emotional charge; emotions help us to focus our attention more effectively and can provide a more holistic approach to making value judgements, beyond what is simply 'rational' (Gee, 2008). Of course, too much emotion can have the opposite effect, focusing attention away from learning and creating mental blocks.

TABLE 9.3 Types of emotion in games (from Järvinen, 2009, based on Ortony et al., 1990)

Type	Description	Example
Prospect-based	Emotions associated with events.	Curiosity to find out what happens in story-driven games.
Fortunes-of-others	Positive or negative emotions associated with the achievements of others.	Empathy with other players in multiplayer games.
Attribution	Emotional reactions to other agents, such as people or the game itself.	Frustration with a game that is too hard. Pride in personal achievements.
Attraction	Emotions evoked by objects, such as game settings, graphics, soundtrack, visual appearance.	Fear in horror games.
Well-being	Basic emotions that relate to desirable or undesirable events; the intensity is proportionate to the degree to which the event is desirable or undesirable, or in the case of a loss, how unexpected it is.	Happiness at completing a level. Grief at the death of a much-loved character.

Koster (2005) describes a variety of emotions and signals that occur during game play; he highlights that "almost all of them are signals of either pushing someone else down, or pushing yourself up, on the social ladder" (p. 92). These include: schadenfreude – taking pleasure in the failure of a rival; fiero – an expression of triumph upon achieving a significant task; naches – the feeling of pleasure when a protégé succeeds; kvell – the emotion generated when bragging about a mentee; grooming behaviours and feeding other people, which indicate intimacy and status.

Järvinen (2009) draws on the work of Ortony, Clore, & Collins (1990) to link categories of emotion to game play, and highlight elements that affect the intensity of emotion. They describe five types of emotion, with examples of how they are implemented in games, which are summarised in Table 9.3.

Järvinen (2009) discusses different variables that affect the intensity of emotions in games, highlighting the difference between local variables that affect a group, and global variables that have effects across groups. Global variables include the degree of reality, i.e. immersion or engagement in the game, proximity in psychological space to the situation, the unexpectedness of the situation and the degree of physiological and cognitive arousal. Local variables include likelihood, degree of effort, degree of desirability, degree of undesirability and intensity of hope or fear that something will happen.

Fun and Learning

While fun may have social, mental and emotional benefits, there is debate about whether it is appropriate in relation to learning, particularly in formal educational settings. There are two separate issues to be considered here: first, whether fun actually supports or hinders the learning process; and second, whether learners' perceptions of the appropriateness of fun are positive or detrimental. Prensky (2005) argues that those who maintain that learning should not be fun do so because they see fun as being the opposite of hard work, but that in reality fun and hard work are not mutually exclusive.

It has been argued that fun, particularly in the context of play, is crucial for learning and development in children. Hromek and Roffey (2009) say that "playing games and having fun are crucial to development and highly motivating to children" (p. 630). They draw on Fredrickson and Joiner (2002) in claiming that fun and positive emotions enhance optimistic thinking and problem-solving abilities, reduce stress and increase emotional and physical resilience, are a bonding experience and increase group belonging. Bisson and Luckner (1996) suggest that fun can have a positive effect on learning by being an intrinsic motivator for some learners, allowing the suspension of social inhibitions, reducing stress and creating a state of relaxed alertness.

Humour is commonly used in education as a way of building rapport between learners and teachers. Baid and Lambert (2010) suggest that humour can support learning by reducing anxiety, focusing attention, diffusing anger, creating a positive attitude towards the teacher and, in moderation, it can increase attention and interest, although one limitation is a false sense of satisfaction among learners when little of educational value has been achieved. However, they stress that "pedagogical humour with an underpinning educational purpose should ... be differentiated from irrelevant comedy" (Baid & Lambert, 2010, p. 548). Fun also helps to produce a safe environment in which to practise and make mistakes. Koster (2005) highlights this point, saying that fun is contextual and it is all about practice, not 'doing it for real', in an environment where there is no pressure. Hromek and Roffey (2009) suggest that this psychological safety is key to fun, saying "positive feelings are generated by friendship, engagement, safety, inclusion, and having fun" (p. 636).

While fun may have an impact on learning itself, this will be limited by the perceptions of learners as to the appropriateness of fun in an educational context. Some learners, particularly older learners and those in tertiary education, may feel that fun and games are not appropriate in formal learning, particularly if they are seen as being frivolous or a 'waste of time' (Whitton, 2007a). However, others argue that frivolity is positive because it decreases the personal value of failing (Guynup & Demmers, 2005). Prensky (2007) highlights that fun has both positive (enjoyment, pleasure) and negative (amusement, ridicule) connotations, and says this dichotomy is at the root of resistance to new learning approaches based on fun. Issues also arise with learners' perceptions of learning and fun in relation to educational games. Okan (2003) argues that edutainment leads to inflated expectation in learners that learning should always be colourful and fun, and that they can acquire information without work. However, the paper presents little evidence for this assertion, and the emphasis on the acquisition of information suggests a focus predominantly on games that address lower-level learning outcomes. Guynup and Demmers (2005) suggest that the key to fun is transforming educational challenges into the challenges of play, but describe educational games as 'fake fun' because of the lack of enjoyment found in educational games.

Fun, of course, is not unique to games. In the learning context, learning environments themselves can be fun, if there is sufficient control and self-determination for the user (Grosshandler & Grosshandler, 2000). In a recent research study (see Bird, Forsyth, & Whitton, 2012, appendix 5) I interviewed 39 students to look at a range of issues including whether they felt that learning should be fun, and what fun learning is. The vast majority of students interviewed felt that learning at university should be fun, but fun meant different things to different people. Four key elements of fun emerged:

1. Lecturer attitude, enthusiasm and relationship with students.
2. Active, novel and experiential learning.
3. Social and collaborative aspects of learning.
4. A pressure-free learning environment.

While none of these aspects is unique to games, it does look as though games provide one way of bringing fun into learning. An important point for me in relation to the potential of games as vehicles to create fun is that games are not 'serious'. The playful aspect of games is one that is often overlooked or wilfully ignored because learning, particularly for adults, is not meant to be fun, or playful. However, while I recognise the need for terminology that makes games acceptable as a learning tool for adults, I believe that, terms such as 'serious games' actually undermine the true value of games; games are not serious and nor should they be. The value of playful games needs to be lauded and promoted. I hope that this chapter has gone some way to highlighting the importance, much neglected in the literature, of playfulness in game-based learning and the intrinsic value that play can bring to learning.

10

GAMES AS EXPERIMENTAL SPACES

Early computer games were very rigid in structure, giving players a limited experience of what they could do within the game. Modern computer games give players much more control, or at least a feeling of more control, through vastly increased choices of action and opportunities to extend or augment game environments themselves. For example, 'sandbox' games are now increasingly common, which rather than having a set sequence for players to follow allow players to explore and undertake activities in any order or way that they choose, potentially also building or creating artefacts within the game environment itself. This provides an environment for learning through exploration and discovery and by creation and development. In this chapter I explore these ideas in more detail, starting by looking at the importance of freedom and control for learning, before moving on to discuss two areas of learning that are particularly facilitated by the freedom that is inherent in play: exploration and creativity.

Freedom, Control and Agency

One of the fundamental benefits of play is that it provides a safe 'training' space in which players are essentially free (to a greater or lesser extent) to make their own choices and learn from their mistakes. Klopfer, Osterweil, and Salen (2009) describe five axes on which freedom can be exercised (they talk about these freedoms in the context of children but I believe them to be more widely applicable).

1. *Freedom to fail.* To undertake enterprises that are ultimately doomed (for example the sandcastle that gets washed away) or activities that are not successful in the first instance without fear of reprisal or repercussions.

In digital games, failure is an accepted and normal part of play; players do not expect to be able to complete the game easily on the first try, for that would be boring. Failure, repetition and practice are a natural cycle in the context of video games.

2. *Freedom to experiment.* This is closely tied to freedom to fail and provides the space to create and invent things, develop ideas and experiment in a context where it is okay for these inventions, discoveries and ideas to fail.

3. *Freedom to fashion identities.* Trying different roles and experiencing the world from different perspectives in order to discover alternative ways of being.

4. *Freedom of effort.* Being able to decide how much attention and energy to devote to play at any given time. For example, playing fully with enthusiasm for a while, then taking a back seat in order to watch and reflect; this is within the control of the player.

5. *Freedom of interpretation.* Learning about the game at the same time as learning with the game, and interpreting the cultural and social meanings of actions and activity within the game space.

At the heart of game-based learning, I believe, is the ability of games to transform experience and create safe spaces for play, where mistake-making is accepted and embraced, unlike in the traditional classroom setting where failure is seen as a negative evaluative experience rather than a positive learning experience. Gee (2003) argues that video games create a psychosocial moratorium (a term coined by psychologist Erik Erikson), that is a "learning space in which the learner can take risks where real-world consequences are lowered" (p. 62). Juul (2013) highlights the importance of freedom for learning, in particular freedom to fail, suggesting "the freedom found in regular games can only be preserved if we are given room to experiment and the freedom to fail, at least temporarily, such that a single poor performance will not be used against us" (p. 122). Jones (1998), however, argues that despite the playful nature of games, hidden damage can still be caused to participants because of actions being taken in the game space having implications in the real world. He says that "in theory, a debriefing is supposed to remove any damage that occurred. In practice, the facilitator rarely realizes that damage has occurred and has no concepts that can explain the cause or identify the situation" (p. 170). In this case, it is assumed that games are face-to-face and have a facilitator, but the same point can be made for any digital game in which human interaction takes place (in fact, for any activity in which human interaction takes place there is potential for damage to be caused through that interaction). What may be different about games is that it is assumed that they are safe and therefore little thought is given to the potential hazards. This highlights that the safe spaces of play are not always as 'safe' as they might be construed to be and this has implications for game design and their use in education. For example, if a game is assessed and that assessment matters then the safety of play may be lost from that gaming experience.

Freedom can support fun by removing barriers and helping to create a safe play-space without consequences in the real world; however, Schell (2008) argues that, while a free environment may be fun for some people, others find a controlled environment more conducive to creating a fun experience. He suggests that it is not freedom that is actually engaging but the 'feeling of freedom' where the player believes that he or she has freedom of action but is in effect constrained to a limited set of choices. He argues that this is possible through 'indirect control' of the player through various subtle means, and describes six of the most common methods used in games:

- *Constraints* – limiting the number of potential choices available.
- *Goals* – use of the game goals to direct players' actions in desired directions.
- *Interface* – implicitly limiting the players' options and guiding their choices through the limitations and affordances of the physical and virtual game interface.
- *Visual design* – manipulating action by visual effects such as highlighting attention or suggestion of activity paths.
- *Characters* – creating computer-controlled characters that players are interested in and want to protect, obey, help or destroy, for example.
- *Music* – creating suggestions of activity and mood through the music in the game.

Central to a feeling of freedom in games is a feeling of being in control (perceived or real). Malone and Lepper (1987) present this sense of control as being one of the motivations for learning in games. They highlight the following three aspects of control:

- *Contingency* – outcomes are dependent upon actions. Interactions are logical and a certain action might reasonably be expected to achieve a certain result, so that the environment is perceived as being responsive to the player.
- *Choice* – providing the player with different options. However, when there is too much choice (more than, say, five to seven alternatives) the notion of choice will be devalued and the player may become frustrated or overwhelmed rather than feeling in control.
- *Power* – actions that have large and noticeable effects increase the feeling of control.

As well as limiting the number of choices with which a player is presented (either to nudge the player in a certain direction or to increase the feeling of control) there are also different types of choices available to the player. Salen and Zimmerman (2004) differentiate between micro choice (or tactics) and macro choices (strategy). They describe 'failure states' in the game, such as the player feeling that it does not matter what decision he or she makes, not knowing what to do next, losing but not knowing why or not knowing whether an action had an outcome. These failure states are demotivating in a game context, but particularly unhelpful in the context of learning, where a feeling of agency, ability to plan actions and receive and reflect on feedback are all crucial parts of the learning process.

Self-determination theory (Ryan & Deci, 2000) stresses the importance of control for intrinsic motivation, self-regulation and well-being, and describes three innate psychological needs: a perceived feeling of competence; a sense of autonomy; and feelings of relatedness (the need to have a sense of belonging and connections to others). There is evidence that in-game competence and autonomy are related to game enjoyment, preference and well-being (Ryan, Rigby, & Przybylski, 2006). In my own research on motivation and games (Whitton, 2007a), I also found that the two universally motivating factors in games were 'being able to see swift and steady improvement' and 'a perception of being good', whereas 'getting stuck' was a primary de-motivator, which ties in with these first two needs. Most computer games are designed to support competence and autonomy by creating spaces that support players as they progress, providing swift and regular achievements and giving the player at least the illusion of control. Many computer games also facilitate relatedness, if not during the game itself, through player communities and support networks. Calleja (2011) highlights the importance of agency in a game, described as "the ability to perform actions that affect the game world and its inhabitants" (p. 56). This has two dimensions in games: first there is agency in the sense of having the capability of having an impact, for example, being able to pick up and use an object in the game world; and second, there is agency in the sense of knowing how to perform the action, i.e. knowing how to translate actions on the game controller into actions in the game world. In a sense, this can be viewed as the difference between functionality (being able to do something) and usability (knowing how to do something) within a game.

In contrast, Csíkszentmihályi (1992) highlights what he calls the 'paradox of control'. He describes one aspect of the flow experience (discussed in more detail in Chapter 6) as not just a feeling of being in control but "lacking the sense of worry about losing control" (p. 59). He also discusses the fact that when activities that create flow are so enjoyable that they make it difficult to attend to anything else (in the case of addiction, for example) then the perception of control in the activity has actually led to a loss of control and the freedom of whether or not to continue to take part in the activity.

Exploration, Experimentation and Discovery

The freedom to explore environments in an open-ended way, and discover their secrets and potential, is a very powerful tool for motivation and learning. Different games provide different amounts of potential for free exploration; some provide a linear sequence of events with little or no variation while others "leave the player to his own devices and let him find his own way around" (Thompson et al., 2007, p. 32). Open ended (or 'sandbox') games give players ultimate freedom to do what they want, but linear games provide more structure and focus attention on the relevant parts. Squire (2008) describes the possibilities of these open-ended games as 'possibility spaces', which are "spaces in which we can live, experiment, and play for different reasons and with different outcomes" (p. 178). While there is great learning potential in the exploration model, there are also potential issues if the activity undertaken by the learner does not match what it is intended that he or she should learn.

Learning through self-directed exploration, also called discovery learning (Bruner, 1961), is a form of constructivist learning that focuses on problem-solving where students are not provided with 'correct' answers but have to discover the answers for themselves, and has much in common with problem-based learning, as discussed in Chapter 3. While open-ended explorative games and simulations provide the potential for rich experiential learning, without sufficient guidance and time for reflection, a learner may not be able to recognise explicitly what he or she has learned, or see the value and applicability to other learning contexts (Rieber, Tzeng, & Tribble, 2004). Discovery learning has received criticism for the lack of guidance provided to support learners (Kirschner, Sweller, & Clark, 2010) but there is evidence that, while unassisted discovery does not benefit learning, provision of feedback, explanations, worked examples and scaffolding does (Alfieri, Brooks, Aldrich, & Tenenbaum, 2011). As well as providing the environment to explore, digital games are also adept at creating these support structures, which guide learning as well as game play.

The ability to explore a virtual environment, and discover the places, people and challenges that lie within is a way in which to stimulate curiosity. Malone and Lepper (1987) argue that curiosity is one of the core motivational aspects of computer games, and that it takes two forms: sensory and cognitive. Sensory curiosity involves the use of light, sound or other sensory stimuli, and cognitive curiosity involves completing an individual's mental map of the world and ensuring that understanding is comprehensive and consistent. Digital games can appeal to sensory curiosity through audio and visual (and lately haptic) stimuli, which can be merely decoration, designed to enhance the fantasy world of the game, explicitly a reward, or a representation system for concepts that are more easily explained in forms other than words (Malone, 1980). Cognitive curiosity can be stimulated through structural anomalies, where information is incomplete or inconsistent, and people are motivated to make sense of the anomaly (this is not dissimilar to the theory of cognitive dissonance (Festinger, 1962), which argues that the discomfort that arises by the contradiction of conflicting ideas or beliefs is a motivation for resolving this conflict), or by spreading interest, where it is assumed that people are interested in new topics related to areas in which they are already interested (Malone & Lepper, 1987). Kashdan, Rose, and Fincham (2004) hypothesise that curiosity comprises exploration (striving for novelty and challenge) and absorption (full engagement in activities), while Litman (2005) views curiosity as a feeling of being deprived plus a feeling of interest, the idea that

> curiosity could be aroused when individuals feel as though they are deprived of information, and wish to reduce or eliminate their ignorance, as well as when they do not feel particularly deficient of information, but would nevertheless enjoy learning something new.
>
> *(p. 799)*

Creativity and Design

As well as playing games, there are several different ways in which players can become more creatively involved in gaming activities. Table 10.1 provides an overview of different types of creative activity associated with games.

There is growing research and interest (e.g. Al-bow et al., 2009; Korte, Anderson, Good, & Pain, 2007; Robertson & Howells, 2008) in the idea of moving beyond game-based learning to game creation for learning, so that the learner moves from the 'passive' role of game player to the more 'active' role of game designer. This is what Kafai (2006) describes as the difference between an 'instructionist' and 'constructionist' approach to game studies, where "rather than embedding 'lessons' directly in games, their goal has been to provide students with greater opportunities to construct their own games—and to construct new relationships with knowledge in the process" (p. 38). Giving learners agency to design and build their own games presents a paradigmatic shift from teacher (or game) as holder of knowledge to facilitator of learning, which may be problematic for the teacher.

TABLE 10.1 Creative gaming activities

Type	Description	Examples
Maker games	Games that involve building or creation activities as one of their key components.	*Minecraft*
Level development	Games that allow the creation and sharing of additional game levels within the game environment.	*LittleBigPlanet*
Modding	Games that allow the development of game modifications or expansions, usually through an additional game-design engine.	*Neverwinter Nights*
Artefact creation	Games that allow the external creation and sharing of in-game artefacts and objects.	*The Sims*
Game-building	Creation of entire games, often using specific game design and development software.	*GameMaker*

There is evidence that game building can lead to greater intrinsic motivation and deep strategy use (Vos, van der Meijden, & Denessen, 2011), foster creativity (Eow, Ali, Mahmud, & Baki, 2009) and imagination (Kangas, 2010), improve literacy (Owston, Wideman, Ronda, & Brown, 2009), critical thinking and academic achievement (Yang & Chang, 2013), storytelling and visual design skills (Robertson, 2012) and help students become active participants in problem-solving and collaborative activities (Baytak & Land, 2010).

At the present time, possibly because of the ease of curriculum fit or the increased acceptability, the use of game-building for learning is most common in computer science contexts (e.g. Becker & Canada, 2001; Cheng, 2009; Clark & Sheridan, 2010; Hoganson, 2010; Korte et al., 2007). Much of the value of game-building is, however, in the collaborative aspects, particularly for the development of skills such as creativity, lateral thinking, teamwork and problem-solving.

Hayes and Games (2008) suggest that there are four different ways in which game-building is applied to learning:

1. Game-making as a context for learning computer programming.
2. Game-making to interest girls in computing.
3. Game-making as a route to learning in other academic areas.
4. Game-making as a way of teaching design concepts.

Game creation can be long and complex, requiring a variety of technical and design skills. Prensky (2008) argues that there is a fundamental difference between 'mini-games', which are simple, focused and take less than an hour to play, and 'complex games', which are the typical large-scale commercial games, rich and multi-faceted, with many hours of game play. He says that mini-games are more appropriate for education games, particularly those developed by learners because the "design of mini-games is relatively simple, and is often easily borrowed from other mini-games. Game construction takes a couple of months at most, and testing is relatively easy" (p. 1006). While this approach provides a realistic option for development by learners, and may be valuable for supporting learning-by-development, these games tend to be based around knowledge acquisition and other low-level learning outcomes thus perpetuating the behaviourist view of game-based learning among learners. There is no reason why game-building for learning should involve the creation of educational games and, in fact, this seems to only add an unnecessary layer of complexity. Game design for learning has been used effectively, although Lim (2008) argues that using game-based learning or students as game designers within traditional institutional frameworks will be ineffective because

> computer games challenge the prevailing culture of schools where exter-
> nally determined knowledge is packed clearly for teachers to dispense to

their students. If bringing games into schools merely reproduce these power relations or knowledge transmission, there is unlikely to be any significant increase in learning engagement among students.

(p. 1002)

Lim (2008) suggests that fundamental changes such as redesign of the curriculum to focus on key questions, re-structure of timetables, and a focus on assessment for learning (rather than assessment for evaluation) are necessary before game development can truly support learning.

There are also potential issues of gender and game-building that should be considered. Denner, Werner, Bean, and Campe (2013) describe the Girls Creating Games (GCG) programme, which aimed to use game-building as a way of lowering barriers to girls' participation in information technology. The programme used four strategies to encourage the students to play an active role in the design and development of games: game design and production, pair programming, challenging stereotypes and identity-forming activities. In their research into interactive story-building, Carbonaro and colleagues (2008) found no gender differences in quality of output, regardless of prior programming knowledge, while Robertson (2012) found that girls achieved slightly higher than boys.

As well as simply making games, there is an increased interest in the creation of digital artefacts and game objects, which takes game activity outside of the original scope of the game itself. Salen and Zimmerman (2004) highlight that "when players become producers, their activities as players fall outside the magic circle and largely take place in spaces external to the game" (p. 540). They describe a hierarchy of player-oriented design tools (originally described by Will Wright, creator of *The Sims*), from tool-makers who make game creation tools (the smallest number), object-makers who use the design tools to create game artefacts, webmasters who host, share and disseminate the game artefacts and players, who use the objects and artefacts in their game play (the largest number).

There is a variety of different ways in which learners can engage in games that are more creative than simply playing them or engaging in pre-set problems and puzzles. The ability to be more creative in games is increasing, with games that allow players to create and share levels, to customise and personalise characters and levels and to take part in creative collaborative challenges, but these are still the exception in game design rather than the rule. Creativity in games is one of the less explored areas, but one that I believe has possibly the most potential in years to come for providing a relatively low-cost pedagogic framework, which is adaptable and can be used to teach a wide variety of subjects.

In this chapter, I have explored the value of games as spaces that can be explored, where learners can experiment, interrogate the world, generate hypotheses and test solutions in a safe environment. Discovery through games, with appropriate structures and support, can both stimulate curiosity and open up new horizons. I think it is also important, however, in any discussion of games and learning, to think beyond the paradigm of 'learner as player' to start to investigate the rich potential for creativity that can be generated through game design. I believe that the area of game-building for learning, given its relatively inexpensive nature, will be one in which there is a large increase in research and practice in years to come, signifying a move from learners as game consumers to learners as game creators.

11

GAMES AS OTHER WORLDS

Computer games have the power to take players from the real world and immerse them in a world of fantasy and imagination, where identity and accepted behaviours differ from reality. This is one of the most powerful aspects of games for learning, the way in which players can easily suspend disbelief and engage themselves in the game world. In this chapter I shall be discussing three aspects of this transformation to other worlds: first, the concept of the magic circle and its role in gaming; second, the nature of fantasy; and third, the use of narrative in games will be discussed and explored.

Entering the Magic Circle

The 'magic circle' is a metaphor for the common creation of a specific social situation, in which participants cross a virtual boundary into a secondary world or 'playspace'. Salen and Zimmerman (2004) describe the construct of the 'magic circle' (inspired by Huizinga, 1955), as a boundary between real life and the reality of the game, which creates safety, and is responsible for the internal mechanisms and experiences of the game in play. It allows players to enter an 'other world' with different rules and codes of practice, moral and ethical structures and ways of behaving. This magic circle of play is important for learning with games because it provides a safe space in which mistake-making is not only accepted, but is customary.

> The fact that the magic circle is just that – a circle – is an important feature of this concept. As a closed circle, the space it circumscribes is enclosed and separate from the real world. As a marker of time, the magic

circle is like a clock; it simultaneously represents a path with a beginning and end, but one without beginning and end. The magic circle inscribes a space that is repeatable, a space both limited and limitless. In short, a finite space with infinite possibility.

(Salen & Zimmerman, 2004, p. 95)

Montola and colleagues (2009) view the magic circle as a "ritualistic and contractual boundary, which is most often based on a somewhat implicit agreement" (p. 10). The rules of the game form the contract of play, but even though they create a new reality, games cannot be entirely free (at least, the authors argue, in contemporary society) because of societal rules, such as on the use of extreme violence, that are unbreakable. The magic circle that is created during the play of some games (and, for example, during religious rituals) can be considered to be a liminal space. Such spaces are "a step outside mundane reality, yet exist in continuity with it, and have the capacity to facilitate significant social and cognitive changes, such as life transitions and the transmission of secret knowledge" (Harviainen, 2012, p. 508). Harviainen (2012) differentiates between the engrossment of, for example, a chess match and the liminal state created by a game that takes players to a new reality. He argues that it is the continual boundary control of these liminal games that is essential to preserve the game reality. The boundary between the game world and the real world is a crucial space in understanding the motivations and behaviours of players in a game. Crucial to the creation of play states is the meta-communication that occurs between the participants to signify 'this is play' (Bateson, 1972). While the 'rules' of both the real world and game world are to a major degree fixed and explicit, it is in this boundary zone that anomalies arise, owing to different constructions of rules at the limits of the game, notions of acceptability and appropriateness and the existence of inexplicit and tacit knowledge and understanding. The magic circle can be viewed as a 'fuzzy' boundary between the game world and the real world (Remmele & Whitton, 2014).

The idea of the magic circle is one that is, however, somewhat controversial. For example, Consalvo (2009) argues that it is not the case that normal rules do not apply when playing games, but that they do apply but in conjunction with, or in opposition to, additional rules imposed by the game frame. Malaby (2007) argues that the idea of the safe space of the magic circle does not hold true because games cannot be separated from everyday experiences, and whatever happens in the game will inevitably have ramifications in the real world. Moving on from the idea of the magic circle, which they describe as 'questionable', Arsenault and Perron (2009) explore what they call a 'magic cycle' based around the continuous loop of input and output, action and outcome, that happens in computer games. They present a model of game-play that consists of "three interconnected spirals that represent the cycles the gamer will have to go through in order to answer game-play, narrative, and interpretative questions" (p. 115). The first spiral depicts the game-play and it expands with an increasing circumference to represent the fact that video games typically become more complex and difficult as play progresses. The second spiral, situated within the cycle of game-play, is the spiral of narrative, which represents the characters in the game and events that unfold as the game is played. Finally, at the centre of the model is the hermeneutic spiral, the way in which the player interprets and makes sense of the game. The authors make it clear that this third spiral is central, not because it is central to the game, but because it is not obligatory, describing the relationship of the spirals as one of inclusion, where "the gameplay leads to the unfolding of the narrative, and together the gameplay and the narrative can make possible some sort of interpretation" (p. 118).

One of the most powerful features of games that support learning is their ability to move players from one way of seeing the world to another, to enable players to take on the role of another person or being, be it an elven mage in a role-playing game or a detective in an adventure game, with their own goals, aims and ways of behaving in the world. Games allow people to try out possibilities, test theories and, most importantly, to make mistakes and learn from them in an environment where mistake-making is the norm. In education, failure is typically constructed as a bad thing, while in gaming it is seen as an accepted and inevitable part of the gaming process, and fundamental to learning within games. Juul (2013) highlights the importance of mistake-making in games, discussing what he calls the 'paradox of failure' in that people generally aim to avoid failure, but failure is an inevitable part of game playing, yet people seek out to play games, thus choosing to experience something that they would otherwise avoid.

> My argument is that the paradox of failure is unique in that when you fail in a game, it really means that you were in some way inadequate. Such a feeling of inadequacy is unpleasant for us, and it is odd that we choose to subject ourselves to it. However, while games uniquely induce such feelings of being inadequate, they also motivate us to play more in order to escape the same inadequacy, and the feeling of escaping failure (often by improving our skills) is central to the enjoyment of games. Games promise us a fair chance of redeeming ourselves. This distinguishes game failure from failure in our regular lives: (good) games are designed such that they give us a fair chance, whereas the regular world makes no such promises.
>
> *(Juul, 2013, p. 7)*

It is the ability of the magic circle to temporarily transform people, places and activities that provides massive learning potential. There is, however, always the question of how 'safe' game spaces are because they cannot be completely removed from real life (Jones, 1998; Malaby, 2007) and this is especially true in the context of learning, particularly when external factors such as assessment enter the equation. One way of easing the entry to and exit from the magic circle of play in an educational context is through structured briefing and debriefing activities.

The learning that happens while playing games with others is not restricted to what actually happens during the game, and of particular importance are the discursive activities that happen around it. Crookall (2011) recently highlighted a decreased focus on these activities, saying that "one thing that is not being done as much as it should is proper debriefing – that is, the occasion and activity for the reflection on and the sharing of the game experience to turn it into learning" (p. 907). Thiagarajan (1993) is a strong advocate for debriefing, arguing that "people only learn from experience if they take the time to reflect on that experience, derive useful lessons from it, and identify ways to transfer and apply these lessons" (p. 47). He suggests a variety of ways in which debriefing can be facilitated (his work is focused on face-to-face gaming) but the suggestions here apply to digital games too (see Table 11.1 below).

The idea of the magic circle, while it may be contested in some respects, I believe helps to clarify the way in which games help players travel to other

TABLE 11.1 Types of debriefing activity (from Thiagarajan, 1993)

Debriefing activity	Description
Unguided debriefing	Setting aside time and space for the participants to conduct their own free-floating discussion of the game experience and the learning from it.
Guided debriefing	A facilitator initiating and moderating a discussion of the experience.
Mediated debriefing	An external artefact (such as audio, video or computer software) systematically guiding the discussion by identifying guidelines, issues and topics.
Video-supported debriefing	Videotaping critical sections of game play and replaying them during the discussion session as a stimulant for discussion on certain issues.
Debriefing games	The use of games that structure the discussion of the earlier experience.
Journal writing	Asking participants to maintain a journal (or nowadays a blog) to record personal experiences, reflections and analyses.
Individualised debriefing	Participants independently completing a questionnaire about their experiences in the simulation game.
Panel discussion	A talk-show format in which selected participants respond to questions from a moderator and from the members of the audience.
Debriefing dialogue	Participants discussing their experiences in a one-on-one format to enhance their mutual understanding.

real, virtual or imagined worlds. The use of fantasy and narrative are two aspects of games that support the transformation within the magic circle.

Fantasy in Games

In his discussion of motivating factors in educational games, Malone (1980) highlighted fantasy as a motivational element. Fantasy is the notion of a storyline or imaginary scenario in which a game is situated, and can be intrinsic to learning where the fantasy is closely interwoven with and fundamental to the structure of the game (e. g. an adventure game set on a spaceship), or extrinsic, where the fantasy is unrelated to the game structure (e. g. a card game with space-themed playing cards). Malone argues, albeit without solid evidence, that intrinsic fantasies are more interesting and purposeful in an educational context because they relate the learned skills more directly to the real world, saying that "when the fantasy in a game is intimately related to the material being learned, the players are able to exploit analogies between their existing knowledge about the fantasy world and the unfamiliar things they are learning" (p. 164). There is, however, more recent sound research evidence that intrinsic fantasies are better for learning than extrinsic (Habgood, Ainsworth, & Benford, 2005).

By the term 'fantasy' here I do not simply mean a stereotypical fantasy environment involving dwarfs, dragons and wizards, but the element of make-believe that underlies all games, even those where the fantasy is abstract, including the creation of a fictional gaming environment – the narrative that holds together the action and the characters that inhabit the game world. It is used here to describe simply that which is not real. So a fantasy environment could, for example, be a real location in which the element of fantasy is left to the players' imaginations, or it could be an immersive virtual world containing a host of mythical characters. It is the fantasy elements (the locations, characters, story and dialogue) that provide colour and background to a game.

There have been attempts to deconstruct the nature of fantasy in games. Choi, Huang, Jeffrey, & Baek (2013) argue that fantasy is a crucial motivational element for digital games and is a key factor for immersion. They present a four-factor model of fantasy, suggesting that fantasy is about: (1) identification with the game world, through the ability to control and relate to the characters and environment; (2) imagination through the presentation of novel experiences that do not exist in real life, creating a sense of analogy in the relationships between the game and real life and allowing the players to experience satisfaction; (3) fulfilment; and (4) enjoyment from the game experience.

Fantasy, however, is one element of games that may be met with the most resistance, particularly in the context of adults learners, because it is seen as frivolous or inappropriate. However, imaginary and simulated scenarios and cases are commonly used in many aspects of adult education – business and medicine, to name but two. In this context, the realism of the scenario is important as this will impact both on students' willingness to engage with it and on the transferability of learning to the real world. Thompson and colleagues (2007) highlight the importance of consistency, verisimilitude (the realness of the game's internal logic) and fairness within the fantasy game world.

Telling Stories in Games

Telling stories is fundamental to the design of many types of digital game, such as adventure and role-playing games, where the characters and plot drive much of the action and puzzles. Narrative encompasses the idea of a story, which can be true or fictional (and is most likely to contain at least some elements of fiction) and the way in which games are used to tell that story. Carr (2006a) describes narrative as consisting of more than simply the story (the 'what') but also the way in which it is presented or represented (the 'how'), for example the perspective of the character telling the story. Krawczyk and Novak (2006) make a similar distinction between 'story' and 'plot', suggesting that a story is a causal sequence of events and it is the plot that serves to reveal the story so that "the plot is the structure on which you hang the story" (p. 73). However, a story is more than any sequence of events, because a story involves the idea of progression or change (or in some cases trying to avoid an inevitable change to keep things the same). It has a beginning, a middle and an end; typically journeying with a character as he or she overcomes obstacles and becomes a different person as a result of the experiences. A story is set in a consistent narrative world, based around a situation in an environment, with characters experiencing events and interacting through dialogue. Game narrative, which also uses game play to engage the player, has the luxury of being able to employ more simple narrative forms than a pure story, such as the search for an object (or a person), and the description of narrative given here can be seen as being at the sophisticated end of the scale in gaming terms.

   A long-running debate in video games theory is one that opposes narratology and ludology, i.e. the relative importance of story or game play. Juul (2005) provides an overview of the debate, suggesting several reasons why games can be considered as narratives: narratives describe everything that humans do (therefore games are, ipso facto, narratives); most games feature narrative introductions and backstory; and most games share characteristics with narratives, such as reversals (something missing being restored, or vice versa), quest structures and protagonists. However, he also highlights the ways in which games differ from narratives: that games are not part of the narrative media ecology formed by movies, novels and theatre, the 'story' of a game cannot be re-told in another medium; that time in games is different from that in narratives because interactivity and narration cannot exist at the same time; and that the relationship between player and story in a game world is different from that of viewer and story in a narrative, for example readers of stories need characters that they can identify with, whereas many popular games have non-anthropomorphic actors (e.g. *Tetris*). In a reasoned contribution to the narratology/ludology debate, Jenkins (2003) highlights points of agreement, arguing that not all games tell stories, although many games do have narrative aspirations, narrative analysis need not be prescriptive and the experience of a game cannot be reduced to the experience of a story, as games tell stories in different ways from narrative.

Time in digital game narrative is worthy of further consideration. Juul (2005) describes three types of time in traditional narratives and relates them to narratives in games: story time, the events of the story in chronological order; discourse time, the time of the telling of events; and reading time, the time at which the narrative is viewed by the reader. He argues that games construct these three times as synchronous, in the sense that what is happening is happening *now* and what comes next is not yet determined. As well as these senses of time, there is also the retelling time, which incorporates the narratives after the game has been played recounting the game experience. This can be done by players to recount a dramatic victory, share a series of story events, share strategic information or simply to celebrate the pleasure of play (Salen & Zimmerman, 2004).

Schell (2008) refers to the conflict between the narrative and ludic structures of games as a story/game duality and argues that it is not the game or story that is of interest, but the experience, and both game-play and stories can enhance that experience. Both game-play and narrative have a role to play in games but what is important is that narrative is not seen as being at the expense of game-play, or vice versa, but that the two can work together, drawing on the strengths of each form. Games teach experientially, while stories teach vicariously; games are good at objectification, stories are good at creating empathy; games quantify and reduce, stories blur and deepen; games are external because they are about actions, while stories are internal because they are about emotions and thoughts (Koster, 2005). Dansky (2007) suggests that game narrative has three functions: the provision of context for game events; providing a sense of identification and kinship with the central character; and creating a rationale for action, stating that "at its best narrative pulls the player forward through the experience, creating the desire to achieve the hero's goals and, more importantly, see what happens next" (p. 5).

I believe that there are three key differences between video game narratives and stories in linear media such as books and films: interaction, agency and immersion. Traditional stories generally follow a grand-narrative, but within this there may be many sub-plots, and while those reading (or watching) the story may be able to guess what is coming up next, they will not be able to influence it in any way. The ability for the game player to interact with the narrative and shape how the story develops and its outcomes is a very powerful feature of computer games. Players are no longer observers of the story, but are actors within it, able to control actions and events. Some games achieve this by making the player the embodiment of a character, and are often viewed in first person through the eyes of that character. Others do so by expecting players to empathise with a character who is separate from them and is typically shown in third-person view.

It is this interaction and agency to engage with and direct the story (or at least have a perception of directing the story) that leads to greater immersion in the narrative and game environment, and association with the characters. However, real narrative agency in games is rare as there is normally a set of fixed routes that the player can follow, even if the order can change or certain tasks or scenes are optional – giving the player the feeling of choice and control can be more important than complete agency. Schell (2008) argues compellingly that readers of non-interactive stories are not passive, saying that "the idea that the mechanics of traditional storytelling, which are innate to the human ability to communicate, are somehow nullified by interactivity are absurd . . . while interactive storytelling is more challenging than traditional storytelling, by no means is it fundamentally different" (pp. 263–264).

Salen and Zimmerman (2004) distinguish between two different types of narrative components in games: where a game narrative is a crafted story told interactively (e.g. adventure games); or where the narrative emerges as a result of game play (e.g. role playing). Montola and colleagues (2009) have a slightly different angle, distinguishing between 'games of progression' where the narrative is embedded in the game, and 'games of emergence' where the narrative evolves (similar to Jenkins' (2003) ideas of embedded and emergent narratives), arguing that "this distinction critically influences the replayability of the game" (p. 149) where a game of progression can only be completed once, but games of emergence can be played over and over again.

In an adventure game, players typically solve a series of problems or puzzles in order to resolve an overarching mystery; the story provides a rationale for action and a context for problem-solving. Role-playing games, including multi-user role-playing games, are also strongly narrative-driven, so that players undertake a series of quests (alone or as part of a group) in order to achieve the narrative goal of the game. The original interactive fiction (text adventure games) of the 1970s and 1980s is another good example of games where narrative is critical. Interactive fiction now uses a computer program that can input and generate text, produce narrative, simulate an environment and present a structure of rules (Montfort, 2005).

> If you want to tell a story you need to make sure it's either compulsive enough to keep the player involved from beginning to end (as seen in the best adventures), or that it has enough freedom to allow players to go off and do their own thing (offered by the best RPGs). Games will always have plots, but they should never interfere with the entertainment, only enhance it.
>
> *(McCarthy, Curran, & Byron, 2005, p. 58)*

While the narratives that exist in digital games will inevitably differ from the types of narrative told in traditional media, they do present new possibilities. An element

TABLE 11.2 Story types in games (from Brathwaite & Schreiber, 2009)

Story type	Description
Linear	Story progresses from A to B to C in a linear fashion, with occasional or frequent side quests.
Branching	Players are presented with multiple routes through the story, with many different possible endings. To make this manageable it may take the form of key moments joined by parallel paths.
Open-ended	Players start at a single point but then can progress in many different directions, each of which affects the outcome of play. Open-ended stories offer more possible actions and outcomes than branching stories.
Instances	A form common in massively multiplayer online games, where players select instances in a story thread, such as quests, that can be viewed as self-contained mini-stories.
Emergent	Stories that are created from the player experience of the game rather than by the game designers. Common in open simulation games such as *The Sims*.
Thematic	An opening cut scene to set the mood and tone of the game, with no further story components once the game has begun.
Algorithmic	Stories that are constructed by computer AI and respond to the inputs of the player to determine the direction of the story.

unique to digital narrative is the cut scene, where the game pauses and a short video or game animation is played. Cut scenes serve several purposes: they can be used for surveillance and planning; to show movement from one context to another; to set the scene and mood of a game segment; to show the consequences of choices; to provide rhythm and pacing; and as a visually stimulating reward for the player (Salen & Zimmerman, 2004). Brathwaite and Schreiber (2009) describe the different types of stories that appear in games, which are summarised in Table 11.2.

A narrative arc is the way in which a series of events is presented, not as one event simply taking place after another, but incorporating elements like conflict, tension and pace. Events are purposeful in narrative, rather than just being *things that happen*, they lead in a certain direction, and influence how characters change and grow. Every event has a reason for taking place, be it to move the plot forward, or simply to show another side of a character. *The Hero's Journey* (Campbell, 2008) provides an archetypical narrative arc, on which stories throughout history, such as myths and legends, fairy tales, epic novels and films have been based. Vogler (2007) further developed this narrative structure into a practical framework of 12 steps and shows how classic stories, such as *The Wizard of Oz* and *Star Wars*, adhere to this format. This need not be strictly adhered to, but provides a very good starting point for designing a narrative arc. The 12 steps of *The Hero's Journey* narrative arc are as follows:

1. *The ordinary world.* The hero in his or her normal setting (this is used to contrast with the extraordinary world of the main story).
2. *Call to adventure.* The hero is presented with a challenge or problem that takes him or her out of the comfort of the ordinary world (into the extraordinary world).
3. *Refusal of the call.* The hero is reluctant to take the call; an event such as a change in circumstances, or the influence of a mentor, changes his or her mind.
4. *Meeting the mentor.* The idea of a guide, support or mentor is common to many stories; it is the function of the mentor to prepare the hero for his or her adventure.
5. *Crossing the first threshold.* This is the point of no return in which the hero makes a decision to act and the adventure truly begins.
6. *Tests, allies and enemies.* The hero encounters a series of tests and begins to understand the rules of the extraordinary world. He or she makes allies, and enemies are introduced.
7. *Approach to the inmost cave.* The hero prepares and approaches the most dangerous place in the extraordinary world.
8. *The ordeal.* A crisis for the hero in which he or she directly faces the greatest fear and the possibility of death (actual or metaphorical).
9. *Reward.* Having survived 'death', the hero receives a reward, such as an object or knowledge; there is cause for celebration.
10. *The road back.* The hero deals with the consequences of the ordeal and decides to return to the ordinary world, pursued by enemies.
11. *Resurrection.* A final ordeal or second life-or-death moment during which the hero is transformed.
12. *Return with the elixir.* The hero returns to the ordinary world with some sort of treasure or lesson learned.

Dickey (2006) describes how the model of *The Hero's Journey* can be used as a structure for educational adventure games, arguing that "there is great unexplored potential in investigating how to create compelling narratives to support different types of learning" (p. 261). Krawczyk and Novak (2006) suggest three other plot devices or techniques for engaging the game player in the narrative: red herrings, reversals and line of action. Red herrings are story elements that are used to throw the reader off track towards a misleading conclusion. Reversals occur when the story suddenly goes in the opposite direction to that which is expected, for example a shift in perspective such as discovering that a male character is actually female. Line of action involves building the plot around events in which the character can take action or make a choice, rather than the direct causal sequence of events; Krawczyk and Novak argue that forcing the action in this way leads to a build-up of dramatic tension.

Characters are also key to the action in many digital games. Egenfeldt-Neilson and colleagues (2008) suggest that game characters can be stage characters, simply there to set the scene, functional characters who have a general function but are not unique, cast characters who have a particular role in the story related to the narrative and player characters. They suggest that game characters can be constructed in several ways: through what the characters look like, which can be symbolic (using symbols to represent meaning, such as red is diabolic), naturalistic (using natural or stereotypical characteristics to represent meaning, such as bad people are ugly) or use real people as models; through their actions within the game; through their relationship to space, so that their outcomes are directly linked to the fictional world (e.g. in *Donkey Kong* the gorilla falls when Mario breaks his platform); through other characters' views and reactions and through a meaningful name (e.g. *Max Payne*, *Gabriel Knight*). Character development is a key intrinsic motivational aspect in role-playing games (Dickey, 2007) and Paiva and colleagues (2005) argue that creating empathy for game characters is a crucial aspect of the affective experience, and therefore learning, and that this can be achieved most effectively by designing characters that players perceive to be similar to themselves in some way, such as sex, race or shared personal experience.

Whether games are narratives in themselves, or whether they simply incorporate aspects of narrative, this dimension allows them to harness a powerful learning tool, as game stories provide motivation, allow players to empathise and journey with a character and learn through the experiences of others. In all, this chapter has looked at the ways in which games can be viewed as other worlds, which transport players into different realities through the use of fantasy and narrative. These can be very powerful tools for learning, but need to be used with caution as learners can have predetermined ideas about the appropriateness of these sorts of techniques in education, with or without the context of games.

PART V

Games as Learning Technologies

12

GAMES AS INTERACTIVE SYSTEMS

Computer games can be viewed as rich interactive systems, which respond swiftly to a player's actions and provide relevant feedback. In this section I will explore some of the unique aspects of digital games, as opposed to traditional or non-digital games, that support learning. Technology-enhanced learning and digital media offer many benefits to the learner, such as the ability of a computer to provide fast automated responses, to model complex environments accurately, to adapt to the learning patterns of the users and to provide rich interactivity. They enable learners to stay connected at a distance, and interact with the environment in new and engaging ways.

Hollins (2011) argues that digital games need to be recognised as complex cybernetic systems, integrating the game, player, technology and game-play. Activity theory (Engeström, 1987) provides a framework for describing and analysing a system (see Figure 12.1) and it has been argued that it provides a useful alternative tool to help user-experience designers understand the relationships between activity and consciousness (Nardi, 1993).

In the framework of Figure 12.1, there are six components of analysis: the object of the activity system – the motive or purpose; the subject, or people who are part of the system; the tools that mediate interaction between the subject and object, i.e. that allow the people to achieve their goals; the rules that operate within the system; the communities that operate within the system; and the systems that exist for dividing effort through division of labour. Activity theory can be used as an analysis tool for understanding the ways in which computer games operate as human activity systems, for example, Paraskeva, Mysirlaki, and Papagianni (2010) focus on educational multiplayer games as an activity system.

In this chapter I discuss a number of areas in which the digital nature of computer games can impact upon their learning potential. First to be considered is

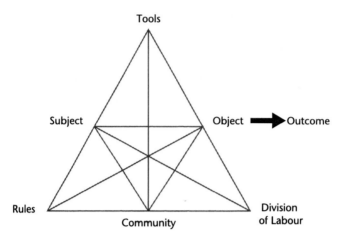

FIGURE 12.1 Structure of a human activity system (from Engeström, 1987)

the role of simulations, and their relationship to games. Second, the potential of adaptivity in game-based learning is explored. Next, the areas of feedback and interactivity are addressed, and finally I discuss key areas of user-experience design, including usability, playability and learnability in digital games.

Simulations and Games

Computer simulations are closely related to digital games, although they are not the same, and provide a way in which to create a digitally authentic learning environment because the simulation accurately mirrors reality. Games, by contrast, use reality as a starting point, adapting it to make the game more fun, making it less like reality but more engaging. Simulations try to model an environment with accuracy and realism, and show genuine cause and effect between elements of the system being simulated. They are often used in learning situations when there is some reason why the actual system cannot be experienced, such as cost, danger, inaccessibility or time (Rieber, 1996). Simulations can be explored and interrogated by the user, providing an environment in which to play and experiment but, unlike games, they do not always have explicit goals, nor are they necessarily approached in a playful manner. Digital simulations are commonly used in scientific disciplines, such as engineering, chemistry or mathematics, where the models that underpin relationships are well understood and can be presented in a meaningful way that enhances learning. They provide dynamic representations of systems where variables can be manipulated so that learners can see the outcomes of various changes. While simulations are, in themselves, not necessarily games there is a huge overlap between the two areas, and the term simulation-game is typically used to describe a simulation that has game characteristics (for example, a flight simulator with explicit goals and scoring) or games that are themselves simulations (for example, *SimCity* or *The Sims*). The use of simulation games for learning is particularly prevalent in the business domain (e.g. Chang, Lee, Ng, & Moon, 2003; Chua, 2005) where economic or financial systems lend themselves easily to modelling.

Dormans (2011) argues that it is the role of a pure simulation to be as realistic a representation of reality as possible, but that this is not the function of games, which necessarily employ simplifications and enhancements to improve playability. Salen and Zimmerman (2004) suggest that simulation games can never be accurately represented at real-life detail, because they are numerical, based on a formal, numerical structure, and are therefore necessarily limited because they cannot ever be complete representations of reality. Instead, they suggest that simulation games should focus on those elements that are necessary for the creation of a fun and playable game. This highlights the question of whether the levels of fidelity and realism of games that attempt to model aspects of real life are important for learning, and in particular, transfer. This issue of necessary and sufficient levels of fidelity and realism in simulations and games is discussed in more detail in Chapter 14.

Adaptivity in Educational Games

Computer games have the ability to adapt dynamically to the skill levels of the players, so that the levels of challenge are neither too hard nor too easy, and practice remains an engaging activity. In theory, this allows personalisation of the gaming and learning experience in order to better meet the needs of the learner. Areas of adaptivity in computer games include the game world and objects, gameplay mechanics, the artificial intelligence of non-player characters, game narratives and the game scenarios and quests (Lopes & Bidarra, 2011).

From a review of educational computer games, Vargas (2012) suggests three commonly used ways in which difficulty can be adjusted: adaptive difficulty, where the game difficulty changes based on the player's performance; incremental difficulty, where the difficulty changes on the basis of a factor unrelated to performance, such as time; and static difficulty, where difficulty does not alter throughout the game, but tasks can be presented in a random order to be less predictable. Difficulty levels can also be user-selected, where the difficulty is chosen in advance by the player, or set by the computer. There is a difference between forward-only progression, where the game gets increasingly more difficult, and forward–backward progression, which allows the game to become easier if it becomes too challenging for the player. There is evidence that this two-way progression leads to greater player immersion in the game (Qin, Rau, & Salvendy, 2010). Adaptivity is also possible through interaction with non-player characters who can act as 'tutors' within the game and provide help and support as required (Prensky, 2006).

Alexander, Sear, and Oikonomou (2013) provide evidence of the relationship between adaptive game difficulty and enjoyment, highlighting that enjoyment is greater when the difficulty matches the experience that a player wants to take away from the game (i.e. whether they are a casual or experienced player) rather than when it matches ability. They suggest that adaptive games should suggest a difficulty based upon play style, provide feedback to players on how well they are doing, ensure that the learning curve matches that of the target audience and that the games challenge meets the learning needs of the player rather than his or her ability. Sampayo-Vargas, Cope, He, and Byrne (2013) also found evidence that games with adaptivity can lead to significantly higher learning outcomes.

As well as adaptivity of game difficulty, there is evidence that adaptive feedback can facilitate positive attitude and immersion (Kickmeir-Rust, Marte, Linek, Lalonde, & Albert, 2008), although other studies have found that adaptive feedback makes no significant difference to student learning (Conati & Manske, 2009). In the section that follows, other aspects of feedback are considered.

Feedback and Interactivity

One of the key ways in which computers can benefit learning is through provision of automated customised feedback. Feedback and interactivity are at the heart of the digital game-based learning experience, and provide something that could not exist without other players or the use of a computer. Performance feedback is essential for both learning and sustained motivation, and is more effective for encouraging intrinsic motivation when it is frequent, clear, constructive and encouraging (Malone & Lepper, 1987). At the heart of every computer game is a mechanism for providing feedback to the player; the player takes an action and sees a reaction from the computer within the game; the player then evaluates the consequences of that reaction and makes another action. Sometimes this is a thoughtful process, such as working out how to solve a puzzle in an adventure game, and at other times processing and reacting to feedback almost happens unconsciously, for example trying to escape from opponents in an action game. In both cases, however, there is a cycle of action and reaction, success or failure and further action, which allows players to progress through the game. This iterative feedback cycle is essential to the process of learning and the fact that a game can make this implicit within the virtual gaming world, situating feedback seamlessly within the game, makes it an incredibly powerful learning tool. This interactivity through feedback is fundamental to the learning process in digital games, be it learning the game itself or an external learning outcome. Oxland (2004) describes several different types of feedback that computer games can facilitate. These include: visual feedback, sounds, action (where explicit feedback is provided after a player's action has occurred); feedback from non-player-controlled characters; accumulative feedback, providing an indication of relative progression through the game; emotional feedback through, for example, empathising with a character; fulfilment such as the feeling of achievement from having solved a puzzle; and informative feedback.

The type of feedback provided in games is almost always formative (as opposed to summative), in that it provides timely information to the players that is intended to modify their behaviours or performance. Formative feedback can take the form of verification or elaboration. Verification is an indication of the correctness of an action and can be explicit (e.g. a text box saying 'the door does not open') or implicit (e.g. being unable to actually open a door). Elaboration feedback is more varied and can provide further information about: the general topic; the learner response, addressing any specific errors made; provision of worked examples; or gentle guidance (Shute, 2008). While entertainment games commonly offer verification feedback, elaboration feedback is less usual, apart from in the form of clues or hints, because of the non-educational intention of these types of games. In educational games, the challenge remains of balancing the fun of the game with the educational content provided through elaboration feedback. Dunwell, de Freitas, and Jarvis (2011) provide examples of various explicit feedback types in serious games, and how they might be implemented (building on Rogers, 1951), which is summarised here:

- Evaluative feedback, for example 'you got a score of 120 out of 200'.
- Interpretive feedback, for example 'you got a score of 120 out of 200, because you failed to respond quickly enough'.
- Supportive feedback, for example 'you got a score of 120 out of 200, and need to improve your response times to challenges'.
- Probing feedback, for example 'you got a score of 120 out of 200, because your response times were too low. Was this because the user interface was too complex, or due to the game being too hard, or something else?'
- Understanding feedback, for example 'you got a score of 120 out of 200, because you found the user interface too complex, and as a result you responded too slowly to the challenges. You should complete the tutorial on the user interface'.

Dunwell and colleagues (2011) highlight that "while the inherent scoring mechanisms common to many entertainment games make their use as a feedback mechanism for serious games an obvious avenue, such usage is grounded more in practicality than learner consideration" (p. 51) and that using facilitative feedback develops a more learner-centred approach. As well as the five types of explicit feedback within the game environment, a further, implicit, type of feedback is described, which they call evolutionary feedback. This is described as feedback where "the learner acts and the world evolves in response providing feedback indirectly" (Dunwell et al., 2011, p. 54). They highlight that, from a critical perspective, this might be seen as 'no feedback' as the interpretation is left to the learner, but counter this by focusing on the emotive power and immersion of high-fidelity virtual spaces and the ability of these spaces to mirror experience in real life and support the transfer of learning. While this might be a valid argument it would seem to imply that implicit or evolutionary feedback is inappropriate or impossible within low-fidelity game environments, a viewpoint with which I disagree. While there may be less feeling of 'presence' or 'being there' with lower-fidelity environments (although this too is debatable and discussed in Chapter 14), a high level of emotional engagement and immersion is possible (one can become emotionally engaged reading a book and immersed playing a game of *Tetris*). While I would agree that implicit feedback needs to be easily interpretable, I would question the need for this to essentially take place within a high-fidelity environment.

The timing and amount of feedback provided is another issue to be considered with educational games. Jarvis and de Frietas (2009) found evidence that when using a game to teach a simple procedural task (in this case an eight-step triage procedure) feedback that was reduced in complexity and delay was more effective for learning; they posit that this may support the novice learner, but that increased delays in feedback may be preferable later when the student is close to mastering the procedure. Shute (2008) provides guidelines, based on an extensive literature review, on the timing issues associated with the provision of feedback, which are summarised below, and could be assumed to apply to educational games.

1. Design timing of feedback to align with desired outcome. Immediate feedback can address errors in real time, producing greater immediate gains and more efficient learning, but delayed feedback has been associated with better transfer of learning.
2. For difficult tasks, use immediate feedback. When learners attempt a new task, that is 'difficult' relative to their existing skills, immediate feedback (at least initially) will help to provide a safety net.
3. For relatively simple tasks, use delayed feedback. It is better to delay feedback to prevent feelings of feedback intrusion and possibly annoyance if the task is easily solvable by the learner.
4. For retention of procedural or conceptual knowledge, use immediate feedback. There is general acceptance that immediate feedback promotes learning and performance on verbal and procedural tasks, and those requiring motor skills.

In digital games, feedback is sometimes immediate (e.g. press a button and a door opens) or delayed (e.g. score at the end of a level) so that there are opportunities for designing educational games that support feedback best attuned to learning. Werbach and Hunter (2012) suggest that quick and regular feedback is necessary but not sufficient. They argue that it should also be unexpected, as informational feedback increases autonomy and intrinsic motivation and people appreciate being surprised by achievements and rewards that they did not expect. Continuous reinforcement feedback on progress should be provided, such as a graph of performance over time. They also highlight that users will regulate their own behaviours based on the metrics and information provided.

It is also worth a brief consideration of the difference between positive and negative feedback, where positive feedback is that which reinforces a player's behaviour ('I chopped down a tree and received a load of gold so I'm going to do it again') while negative feedback encourages the player to alter behaviour ('I chopped down that tree and it fell on me and I lost loads of experience points, so I'm not going to do that again'). Salen and Zimmerman (2004) describe a presentation by Marc LeBlanc at the Game Developers' Conference 1999 (LeBlanc, 1999), in which he presents a series of design rules for feedback in games. He argues that negative feedback stabilises the game as it leads to players trying new possibilities; positive feedback destabilises it as it leads to repeated action. Negative feedback can prolong the game, positive feedback can end it, because it can lead to a win condition quickly. Positive feedback magnifies early successes; negative feedback magnifies late ones. In education, we typically think of positive feedback as being something that is necessary for student learning, but in games it is important to balance the positive and negative to ensure that the game is a playable system (there is more detail about the use of rewards in relation to positive feedback in Chapter 8).

Computer games are good at providing feedback because they are automated environments, which enables computer-generated interactivity. Lucas (1992) suggests that there are three types of interactivity within educational computer systems: reactive, interactive and proactive. Reactive interactivity follows a behaviourist model of providing a response to a stimulus, for example in drill-and-practice games, while proactive interactivity involves the learners constructing their own learning pathways, seeking out knowledge as they need it, for example in an open-ended virtual world. In the middle is what is termed 'interactive interactivity', which allows the learner to branch through a course of instruction based on their responses. Salen and Zimmerman (2004) give examples for four modes of interactivity that occur in games (they also refer to them as levels of engagement). These are described as 'cognitive interactivity', the psychological, emotional and intellectual participation in the game; 'functional interactivity', the actual controls that the player uses to interact with the game; 'explicit interactivity' whereby the player makes choices and responds to events in the game; and 'beyond-the-object interactivity', which relates to interaction outside of the single experience of the game. It has also been argued that there are five different variables of interactivity that affect the degree to which the user feels immersed in a virtual environment: the range of user input allowed, the customisability of the experience, the amount of change possible in each aspect of the environment, the degree of correspondence between the type of input and the response and the speed of response (Lombard, Ditton, & Media, 1997).

In modern networked computer games, interaction is not limited to that which occurs between the player and the system. Manninen (2001) presents a detailed taxonomy of interaction types in virtual worlds, including interaction with the system through object manipulation, world building and movement, and interaction with other people through avatar appearance, gestures, body language and language-based communication.

Games and the User Experience

In the past, the discipline of user-experience design in computer systems was developed to create experiences that help people meet needs in the real world, while the discipline of game design is all about creating an experience for its own sake. Historically, these two areas have been separate but in recent years the two fields have been more closely linked as practitioners discover learning opportunities in each other's fields, and are likely to become more closely intertwined in future (Ferrara, 2012). Considering digital games from a user-experience perspective is particularly important in the context of learning because the usability of the game system can affect motivation, acceptability and its effectiveness as a tool for learning. However, games are different from task-oriented software in that the goals of games are usually defined and motivated within the game world, they actively encourage a variety of experiences rather than consistency, they impose constraints rather than removing them, they use sounds and graphics to convey aesthetics as well as functionality and have a greater degree of innovation (Barr, Noble, & Biddle, 2007). The user interface is the only way for the player to interact with the game system, so its usability is of prime importance to the gaming, and learning, experience. Jørgensen (2012) argues that game interfaces do not disrupt involvement in the game and game-play and that players will accept any user interface that promotes game-play and supports functionality in a consistent manner; however, "making the game interface elegant and appropriate to the environment is paramount" (p. 161).

Usability refers to how easy gaming software is to learn, interact with and navigate, how easy it is to get started and play the game and how forgiving it is if the player makes a mistake. It is about the way in which a digital tool (in this case a game) mediates the experience of play. Benyon, Turner, and Turner (2005) describe a computer system that has a high level of usability as being one that is efficient and requires an appropriate amount of effort, effective in that it has appropriate functionality and information organised appropriately, is easy to learn, safe to operate and has a high level of utility. The usability of games for learning must consider issues such as how effective interaction is, how easy the game is to use, how flexible modes of interaction are and how acceptable it is to students.

Central to the idea of usability is the notion of affordances, originally described as 'action possibilities' (Gibson, 1979), and described in the context of interface design as "the perceived and actual properties of the *thing*, primarily those fundamental properties that determine just how the thing could possibly be used" (Norman, 2002, p. 9). That is, the affordances of an object are the actions that a user perceives to be possible so, for example, a button might afford pressing or a path might afford walking. In the context of games, Brathwaite and Schreiber (2009) note that affordances are not simply inherent in a digital object but depend on the past experiences, culture and the abilities of the player. For example, to a typist the keys ASWD on a keyboard afford the creation of words, to a retro gamer they afford two-dimensional movement. Clear and unambiguous affordances make a game interface easier to master, as does sticking to established gaming conventions (although this might limit creativity to a certain extent).

In my own doctoral research (Whitton, 2007a), I presented six usability design criteria for effective educational games, which emerged from an analysis of entertainment games coupled with a literature review.

1. *Flexible interaction* – interaction is purposeful with a range of interaction methods available, feedback is timely and meaningful, controls are logical and consistent and performance indicators are built in.
2. *Support for player community* – with integrated communication tools, support for use of avatars and personal representations, with the functionality for self-regulation of the community.
3. *Transparent navigation* – navigation is clear and consistent, alternative methods of navigation are provided and it is possible to see an overview of the user's position in the environment; help functions are obvious.
4. *User control* – functionality is appropriate and obvious, tasks can be undertaken in any sequence, pace and level are adjustable and there is a range of customisation options; instructions are obvious and clear.
5. *Robustness* – the game is responsive to a range of inputs and provides for and recovers from errors; provision of context-sensitive help and hints and the ability to save progress.
6. *Appropriate visual design* – a game that is simple, uncluttered and aesthetically pleasing, presenting information in accessible chunks, with consistent placement of controls between screens, purposeful graphics and multimedia, legible text and pleasing colour scheme.

Usability in game design is of particular importance when considering games for non-traditional groups such as older adults, young children and disabled users, and a well-designed game will be accessible to players of all abilities and backgrounds.

> The ultimate goal of the designer is to infuse every responsive element of the game with a perceptible affordance that is internally consistent. These affordances must be evaluated against various levels of player 'game literacy' and some reasonable effort should be made to reveal through tutorial training any that are determined to be hidden.
>
> *(McBride-Charpentier, 2011)*

Korhonen and Koivisto (2006) present a set of heuristics for the usability of games. They look specifically at mobile games, so one of their constructs, mobility, is of less value out of that context, but they also describe two other constructs: usability and game-play. In relation to good practice in visual design, they suggest that it is important to ensure that audiovisual representation supports the game, screen layout is efficient and visually pleasing, status indicators are visible and navigation is consistent, logical and minimalist. González Sánchez, Padilla Zea, and Gutiérrez (2009) present a number of desirable attributes of playability in games that go beyond usability. These are: effectiveness, learnability, satisfaction, immersion, motivation, emotion and socialisation. They argue that usability alone is not sufficient to creating the best user experience, but that playability also has to be taken into account, and propose a model for analysing playability with seven attributes, including: user satisfaction, learnability, effectiveness of the game as a whole, levels of immersion experienced by the player, player motivation, emotion, and the social dimensions of the experience. Järvinen, Heliö, and Mäyrä (2002) distinguish between functional playability (the usability of the game interface), structural playability (the core game mechanisms and dynamics), audiovisual playability (the style and appearance of the game), and social playability (cultures and contexts of play).

An important aspect of the user experience is learnability, both of the interface and of the game itself. When a game is used for learning, there are three aspects of learning that need to be considered: first, learning the user interface; second, learning to play the game; and third, learning from game-play. In order for games to be as effective as possible, the first two steps need to be quick and painless. One of the very interesting ways in which digital games support learning is the ways in which they provide a seamless entry into game-play, where the player does not need to pick up a manual or read a detailed set of instructions, but can be immediately immersed in the centre of the game. Ferrara (2012) advocates the use of minimal just-in-time instructions:

> Ask yourself, 'What's the smallest amount of information the player needs to make the first move?' Then provide nothing more than that; you can get to the second move when the time comes. Play is learning. If people are interested in the game, they'll be motivated to fill in the blanks themselves by playing it.
>
> *(Ferrara, 2012, p. 61)*

Computer games also provide several commonly used ways of supporting players as they learn to play the game, understand the functionality of the interface and navigate the virtual game world, both while initially learning to play the game and also ongoing as they progress. The use of training levels is widespread in digital games, either explicit as training levels or self-contained areas of a game-world, or simply by the introduction of simplified elements that systematically show the full potential of the game in a safe and supported entry space. Often training levels will involve tutorial guidance, with information provided about interface functionality or the mechanics of the game. Support can be provided as part of the gaming interface rather than in the game itself, for example using pop-up information boxes, or within the game world, for example by a non-player character explaining and demonstrating how to use an axe to chop wood. In some cases players will be stopped before they make mistakes and in others the consequences of mistakes will be decreased while they are learning. The training levels can be thought of as like the 'stabilisers' on a bicycle: they stop the player suffering major setbacks while they learn the basics of the game.

While in-built game learning systems can provide the scaffolding to take players from novices in a game to experts, they may not necessarily address the issue of game literacy, which is built up over long periods of interaction with a particular genre. Game literacy involves an understanding of the conventions and histories within a genre, as well as the unwritten codes of practice and in-jokes. The impact of game literacies (or lack of them) should be considered in the context of games and learning, as it may have an impact on the equity of the gaming experience. Buckingham and Burn (2007) also highlight the importance of critical game literacy, which goes beyond understanding the conventions of the game to an "understanding of the wider cultural and social meanings surrounding them and the circumstances of their production and consumption" (pp. 337–338).

In this chapter, I have examined digital games from the perspective of user-experience design, highlighting the benefits and drawback of the intrinsic computer-based nature of the medium. For me, the idea of gaming literacy is a particularly important one, as discourses such as those around 'digital natives' lead to assumptions around the types of games that different types of people play. In the context of games for learning, we cannot afford to make these assumptions but must strive to create accessible and inclusive digital learning experiences for all.

13

GAMES AS DIGITAL HABITATS

The growth of the Internet has enabled the creation of massive online spaces in which people can communicate, work and play together. This allows people to interact with each other in virtual worlds in new ways, creating new experiences and playing with identities online. Essentially, two types of virtual world exist: those with no specific rules or purpose, where people can meet, communicate and carry out activities to suit themselves, such as *Second Life*; and worlds that have purpose and goals, such as massively multiplayer online games like *World of Warcraft*. In the former, activities are more freeform and emergent and, in a sense, they can be viewed as a place in which to play, explore and experiment rather than as a game with goals, rules and outcomes. Much of the literature in the first two sections of this chapter is taken from research undertaken in virtual worlds, as these are much more prevalent in formal education, and are extremely relevant to the context of online games as digital habitats.

In the education literature the focus on virtual worlds is typically on their use as a social learning environment rather than as cultural habitats, the difference between "belonging *in* the culture of the [virtual world] . . . to the sense of belonging *to* a social group that meets within that environment" (White & Le Cornu, 2010, p. 185). In this chapter I have aimed to look at the research and theory pertaining to both views, taking a holistic approach. Childs (2010) presents a conceptual framework, the mediated environments reference model, which draws on activity theory (Engeström, 1999) and the communities of practice model (Wenger, 1998) as well as other literatures and his personal research. This framework describes the elements of a mediated online environment, including virtual worlds and multiplayer role-playing games, and has eight components, described below.

- *Presence*: the experience of 'being there' in the environment.
- *Tools and instruments*: the environment itself.

- *Object*: the task that is the focus of the activity.
- *Division of labour*: the roles that participants take, or are assigned, in the activity.
- *Rules*: constraints and conventions that inform interaction in the environment.
- *Subject*: the participants in the activity.
- *Identity*: the individual's conceptualisations of self.
- *Community*: the community that takes part in the activity.

This is presented as an analysis framework to help to structure our understandings of learners' experiences in mediated environments, and I include it here to give an overview of the elements to consider when viewing a game as a digital habitat. Of particular interest in this context are ideas of identity and presence, and in this chapter I will first look at the formation of identities in digital spaces, in particular the use of avatars as a way of people representing themselves in games, and the ways in which people perceive themselves as being in these virtual worlds. Second, I will consider ideas of immersion and presence, the sense of actually being there, that can take place as participants become engrossed in these digital spaces, looking at the different experiences that participants have in these worlds. The chapter concludes by considering the value of digital habitats as learning environments and exploring types of informal learning that take place in these shared spaces, with a particular focus on massively multiplayer online role-playing games.

Digital Identity and Avatars

Computer games and virtual worlds provide spaces in which players can feel that they 'belong' to the environment and can experiment with their identities within the alternate world of the game, for example exploring different roles, genders and appearances. Gee (2003) argues that "video games recruit identities and encourage identity work and reflection on identities in clear and powerful ways" (p. 51). He suggests that during game-play, specifically in role playing or games where the player takes on a virtual character, there are three separate identities at play. First, there is the real identity, the actual person playing the game. Second, there is the virtual identity, the character within the game world. Third, there is the projected identity, a definition that plays on two definitions of the word 'project'. The first sense is a projection of the player's real identity onto that of the virtual character, so that the player empathises and engages with the character to a degree to which the player's real identity becomes interwoven with that of the character. Second, there is the sense of 'project' where the virtual identity is seen as a project in the making, set along a certain trajectory that is formed by the goals and aspirations of the real identity. This has an important implication for learning, described as the 'identity principle', which states that learning involves adopting and playing with identities so that the learner has real choices in creating the new identity and opportunities to mediate between the real and the virtual (Gee, 2003).

Hand and Moore (2006) describe three approaches to the consideration of the question of identity in games, namely social identity, reflexive self-identity and virtual identity. Social identity highlights the idea that identity is socially defined, is negotiable and can be contested, so identities are formed through beliefs about who we are, and who others think we are. Hence, in the context of games we could consider identities such as being a 'gamer' or a 'girl gamer', as well as the ways in which gamer culture and communities shape player identities. Reflexive self-identity is a person's own understanding of his or her biography, for example the ways in which digital gamers self-consciously develop their identities through their play. Virtual identity reflects how digital technologies enable players to go beyond the wider social, political and economic contexts of gaming so that they do not simply *enact* their identity, but are able to *re-write* it; identities are not static but are "always in process, being formed through ongoing interaction with others and with material artefacts" (Hand & Moore, 2006, p. 177). Traditional identities, such as those constrained by age, sex, class or ethnicity, can be renegotiated in the virtual world, and players can construct their own multiple identities and representations of themselves through player-characters. In-game identities are likely to be an amalgamation of all three identities described above, so a game identity may be fashioned through a player's physical world identity, coupled with a desire to create an alternative identity in the game within the limitations for identity construction offered by the affordances of the game. People are typically fluid in which identity they employ during their interactions, switching easily between their real-world identity and in-game character.

In many games, these characters are represented by avatars, virtual representations of the player characters. The avatar is an important representation of identity and it is "by means of the avatar that the player becomes embodied in the game, and performs the role of protagonist" (Burn, 2006, p. 72). These dual roles of avatar as a fictional character within the game, and as an embodiment of the player, are interdependent and affect each other. Burn (2006) argues that the fictional protagonist role of the avatar is mostly 'read' by the player while the embodiment role is mostly 'played' and that there is an ambiguity in the gaming experience in that the player is, and is not, the avatar, which is central to the experience of the game. Rehak (2003) likens this duality to the 'mirror stage' in psychoanalytic theory where human infants first encounter a reflection of themselves, which "initiates a lifelong split between self-as-observer and self-as-observed" (p. 123) and argues that our relationship with the world is already split between participation and spectatorship, and that "avatars enable players to think through questions of agency and existence, exploring in fantasy form aspects of their own materiality" (p. 123). In relation to embodiment, Gregersen and Grodal (2009) note the difference between a sense of ownership of action, or agency, and a sense of body ownership, which in the real world are one and the same, but which become differentiated in computer games. Agency is the sense that a player feels able to do something, for example the sense of agency a player feels to perform an action will depend on the functionality afforded that character and the player's ability to perform that action via the game interface. In contrast, body ownership is the sense that the virtual body of the character becomes an extension of the physical body of the player so that action on the game interface seamlessly translates to action in the game. Mimetic interface devices, such as the Nintendo Wii or Xbox Kinect where actions in real life (such as jumping or swinging a tennis racquet) are identical to those undertaken in the game, serve to bridge the gap between the sense of ownership of the body and the action (Calleja, 2011).

In some cases, avatars can be highly customised in terms of appearance and names, and this affects how the player and other players in the game see the character (for example in massively multiplayer online role-playing games). Status can also be communicated by the level of sophistication with which appearance is constructed, and in-game achievements can be signified through the display of artefacts or specific items of clothing that are acquired as a result of a successful activity. This gives players the opportunity to represent themselves in different ways, taking on different genders, ethnicities, ages, physical appearance and even species.

> In a virtual world, people can reinvent themselves to become better, worse, or altogether different from their real-world identities. A normally shy player can become someone with a more attractive physique or a more confident personality. Alternatively, a player can choose to have an ugly physique or to adopt a brash, obnoxious personality. He or she may even change gender, age, or ethnicity, or take the opportunity to investigate seemingly impossible options; for example, a disabled person may have an avatar that can walk or fly.
>
> *(Lee & Hoadley, 2005)*

Choice of avatar is important to users of virtual worlds, and lack of choice can create frustration since it denies users the opportunity to show other players who they are or aspire to be (Childs, 2010). Annetta, Klesath, and Holmes (2008) found that students who were given more control over how they represented themselves online had greater feelings of social presence (in the sense of players' abilities to project themselves socially and emotionally) than those with a more restricted choice. However, the ways in which participants represent themselves in learning environments can be controversial, with non-human or outlandish avatars potentially being seen as inappropriate in educational contexts in virtual worlds such as *Second Life*. This is potentially less of an issue in MMORPGs, which have an over-arching layer of fantasy anyway, so fantasy characters are less incongruous in that context. Also, traditional biases and stereotypes can continue to exist in the online environments, for example Lee and Hoadley (2005) found discrimination and preferential treatment still taking place, but based on perceived qualities rather than real ones, such as 'cool' avatars being more popular than unattractive ones.

In other cases the avatars cannot be personalised and take on a given role in the game (for example characters in adventure games). Avatars can be viewed from the first or third person perspective, depending sometimes on the game itself and sometimes on the preferences of the player. First-person perspective shows the game world through the eyes of the avatar, while third-person shows the world through the eyes of someone looking at the avatar, so in first-person perspectives the character can typically not see themselves (unless they look down at their body) but in third-person they can often view the character from all angles. The relationship between the real identity and the virtual, as embodied in the avatar, is complex and may change over time. Warburton (2008) suggests a five-stage process of avatar relationship development in multi-user virtual environments (MUVEs) (see Figure 13.1 below).

In this model, five critical stages are highlighted. First, the user has to overcome any initial technical and competency barriers (1) before passing the threshold where the user begins to feel empathy for and care about the character (2). When the virtual environment is used in a 'professional' context, such as for learning or work, the avatar exists as an extension of the real-world activity. At the next stage (3), tension exists between the professional mode of being and the playful modes, where the avatar develops an identity in its own right and may participate in in-world subcultures. After this, the avatar swings between professional and playful modes of existence (4) until, to stabilise the tension between work and play, a second avatar may be created to take on a different role (5).

While this model applies to avatar development in virtual worlds that are not specifically for game-play (hence the tension between the professional and playful personae), it is still relevant to a gaming context, for example, massively multiplayer online role-playing games where people play for a variety of different reasons at different times. For example, there may be conflicting achievement, exploration and social aims, such as a desire to complete quests allocated by the game environment, or undertake open exploration of the environment, engage

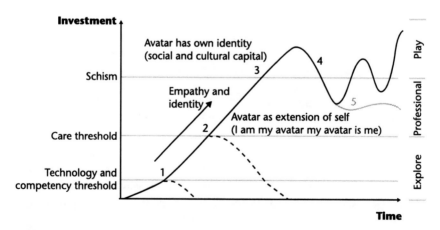

FIGURE 13.1 Development of avatar identity and empathy in MUVEs (Warburton, 2008)

in player vs. player competitions or have social interaction with other players. There may be tensions between the aims of different avatars or characters and also conflicts between the aims of different players at different times, as those interested in social interaction may cross paths with those who are purely aiming at levelling up their characters through competition. This model is also useful for highlighting that the relationship between a player and an avatar is not a static one, but may change over time, and that identification with, and emotional attachment to, a virtual character may be significant.

Presence and Immersion

Presence and immersion in games are connected to the feeling of place, which is a combination of the physical characteristics of the environment, the emotional associations, the possibilities for action and the social interactions associated with the place (Turner & Turner, 2006). The terms 'presence' and 'immersion' are used in a variety of ways in the literature, sometimes interchangeably. Alexander and Brunyé (2005) highlight the difference between what they describe as diegetic immersion, which is the act of being absorbed in a game, and situated immersion, which is described as the illusion of being actually present in the game space, synonymous with presence. This is a similar distinction to Lombard and colleagues' (1997) description of the differences between psychological immersion and perceptual immersion and Calleja's (2011) discussion of 'immersion as absorption' and 'immersion as transportation'. It is the dimension of immersion as 'being there' that I am focusing on in this section, while immersion in the sense of 'being absorbed' has been explored in relation to engagement in Chapter 6. Although immersion can be seen as these distinct concepts, there is evidence that the two experiences of immersion are correlated (Faiola, Newlon, Pfaff, & Smyslova, 2013, using the terms 'flow' and 'telepresence'). While immersion (as absorption) might be felt in a wide variety of contexts, Calleja (2011) argues that presence is a term that is specific to digital environments, saying that

> the scientific community initially coined the term *presence* because a new technology enabled a qualitatively different form of experience than had been possible before its inception . . . extending the term to cover imagined presence in works of literature, film or free-roaming imagination sidelines the core concern: the description and exploration of a phenomenon enabled by a specific technology.
>
> *(p. 22)*

Three-dimensional realistic video games and virtual worlds have the power to create strong feelings of immersion and this sense of actually 'being there', described as presence. The idea of presence in virtual environments is derived from the word 'telepresence' (Steuer, 1992), which was originally used to describe

TABLE 13.1 Types of presence (from Childs, 2010)

Type of presence	Definition
Mediated presence	The feeling of 'being there' in any mediated environment.
Telepresence	The feeling of 'being there' in a telematic environment specifically.
Virtual presence	The feeling of 'being there' in a virtual environment specifically.
Proximal presence	Actually being there in a physical environment.

the feeling of presence when the individual was remote from the activity, for example scientists working remotely on satellites in space (Minsky, 1980). Childs (2010) highlights the ambiguity of the terms surrounding 'presence' in the literature, and suggests the taxonomy shown in Table 13.1, purposefully avoiding the use of the term 'presence' on its own.

Childs (2010) also distinguishes between 'co-presence', a sense of being *with* another person in a remote physical or online environment, and 'social presence', which is the ability of a participant to project him or herself socially and emotionally within that environment. Lombard and colleagues (1997) describe 'presence' as the ability to provide "media users with an illusion that a mediated experience is not mediated" (p. 1) and describe six conceptions of presence from the literature. McMahan (2003) builds on these conceptions to detail six aspects of presence that impact on learning.

1. *Quality of social interaction* – a sense of being present with other people, of intimacy and togetherness. In three-dimensional environments this centres on the use of avatars and means of communication.
2. *Realism* – the degree to which the virtual environment accurately represents objects, events and people. This is divided into social realism (interaction with people) and perceptual realism (interaction with objects, environments and events).
3. *Telepresence, teleoperation, teleportation* – placing the user in a remote or inaccessible location, operating tools remotely, and teleportation instantly from one place to another, as happens in games, for example through the use of portals or maps.
4. *Perceptual or psychological immersion* – blocking sense to the outside world so that only the virtual world is perceived (for example, by goggles or headphones) and complete mental absorption in the world (such as being in a state of flow).
5. *The use of a social actor in the medium* – the use of synthetic social actors such as virtual guides or pets, which can be pre-programmed or interactive.
6. *Intelligent environment* – where users respond to the computer itself as an intelligent social agent, such as showing politeness or gender stereotyping of the computer itself.

Many factors have been cited that potentially contribute to a sense of presence, typically the older literature focusing on technological agents, with greater focus on psychological agents in the more recent literature. Factors include number and consistency of sensory outputs, image quality, image size and viewing distance, motion and colour, dimensionality, camera techniques, degree of interactivity, number of people involved, obtrusiveness of the medium, social realism, nature of the activity, as well as the experience of the user and his or her willingness to suspend disbelief (Lombard et al., 1997). Witmer and Singer (1998) hypothesised four areas that contribute to presence: the amount of control the user feels; sensory factors; levels of distraction; and amount of realism, including visual and functional. However, Childs (2010) found that the technology had a much smaller impact on presence than willingness or ability of the participant to engage with the technology, with aspects such as ease of navigation and previous exposure to technology having no relationship to presence. He identified that a lack of social cues, not knowing who other people 'really are' and insecurity were three key factors that reduced the sense of presence.

The assumption is often made that a sense of presence arises from the fidelity of the experience, that is, how like real life it is. However, this does not give enough significance to the roles of interpretation and agency in creating a sense of presence (Calleja, 2011). Salen and Zimmerman (2004) argue that the belief that the pleasure of a media experience is its ability to recreate a sensory illusory reality is flawed (they call this the immersive fallacy) because it does not take into account that players are always aware of the frame of the game and that engagement in the game is absorption in a sensory world coupled with a personally constructed nature of the game reality. Scoresby and Shelton (2010) found that aspects such as content, emotion, motivation and engagement had more influence on the sense of presence than whether the perspective of the player was first or third person, while Schuurink and Toet (2010) provide evidence that third-person perspective gives the user a greater sense of control and conveys a more distinct impression of the environment.

The impact of user enthusiasm and attitudes towards the environment implies that presence is not something that always occurs naturally and that it is not completely in the hands of the designer of the virtual environment. This is particularly the case in the context of virtual worlds for learning, and acclimatisation and enculturation may need to be a managed process in the context of education. Childs (2010) describes a seven-stage model for acclimatising learners to virtual worlds and developing a sense of presence, shown in Figure 13.2 below.

In this model, the preparatory stage is about helping learners access the world and providing them with the minimum technical requirements they need to get started. During the development of conscious technical skills, learners are focused on learning the skills to engage with the environment itself and are not concerned with the curriculum content. In the acclimatisation stage, which is often overlooked, learners just want to play, which allows them to make the move

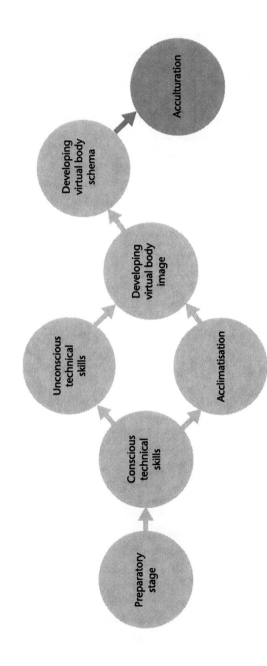

FIGURE 13.2 The stages of learners' participation in virtual worlds (from Childs, 2010)

from conscious to unconscious competency with the technical skills required to navigate and communicate, begin to learn the communication skills and social conventions of the environment, and let the novelty of the virtual world wear off. At the stage of unconscious technical skills, learners are not distracted by the virtual environment and can focus on learning tasks within it. In developing a virtual body image, learners become aware of social presence in the world and recognise the need to customise their avatars to show their places in, and relationship to, the world. This progresses to the development of a body schema, in which they gain the "ability to experience proprioception of their extended body, being able to judge the position of their avatar and how they inhabit the space" (Childs, 2010, p. 250) and players are no longer aware of a separation of themselves and their avatar body. The final stage, acculturation, requires a level of participation in the virtual society and a deep understanding of the social conventions that operate within it. This final stage requires a long period of contact with the virtual world and, in the context of formal learning within accredited mandatory courses, it may not be appropriate to expect learners to engage to that degree. However, it is quite possible that, if the learners are self-selecting, many will already have experienced this degree of participation in-world of their own accord, and in informal learning contexts where players participate through choice this stage may easily be reached.

Informal Learning in Online Worlds

In addition to the learning that takes place in formal educational settings, there is a growing body of evidence of the learning that takes place during the informal use of games, particularly around the massively multiplayer online role playing game *World of Warcraft*. Studies of massively multi-user online role-playing games (MMORGs) have found evidence that participation is similar to participation in communities of practice (Oliver & Carr, 2009). In addition, they support development of social skills such as the etiquette of meeting people, managing a small group, how to coordinate and cooperate with others and how to be sociable (Ducheneaut & Moore, 2005), group cohesion and development (Bluemink et al., 2010) and leadership (Jang & Ryu, 2011). In a study of learner perceptions, Turkay and Adinolf (2012) found that players felt that they learned from the game mechanics, the narratives and from one another, as well as the game subject matter sparking interest outside of the game. These massive virtual worlds immediately embed the players in the full game, not some simplified version, undertaking focused activity with skilled others at the edges of their competences, with information taking a secondary role; initial progress is fast and obvious, supported by immediate feedback from the game and other players; failure functions as feedback, with minimal risks; and there is a "socially-sanctioned precociousness and wonder, that simple secular instinct that provides motivation for scientific inquiry" (Steinkuehler, 2004, p. 526).

MacCallum-Stewart (2011) argues that commercial MMORGs promote what she terms 'stealth learning' as an aspect of game-play, which she describes as "how players absorb information unintentionally within games" (p. 111). I am not personally a fan of the term 'stealth learning'. Learning happens all the time; we all learn things that we do not intend to, and things that we do. The concept of 'stealth learning' (or perhaps 'stealth teaching' is more correct) implies something that is underhand, taking control away from the learners and sneaking in learning. I prefer the term 'informal learning' or even simply 'learning' for, after all, we are learning all the time whether we intend to or not.

There is much evidence to support the notion that MMORG games present rich social learning environments. Hoyle and Moseley (2012) suggest a variety of skills and attributes that can be developed using what they call 'communal games' (but which in fact refer predominantly to massively multiplayer online role-playing games) and the techniques that are employed in games to support this. Their key points are summarised in Table 13.2 below.

In a study into the nature of apprenticeship in massively multiplayer online games, Steinkuehler and Oh (2012) identified three features of apprenticeship:

- apprenticeship is a social interaction and work is necessary at the outset of each pedagogic exchange to establish the roles of master and apprentice, the purpose of the dialogue as pedagogical and the nature of the topic;
- apprenticeship is embedded in practice, with immediate engagement by the novice in the full complexity of the game, supported by scaffolding and modelling from the master;
- and apprenticeship is about sharing of values, "enculturation in its richest sense" (p. 178).

While much of the research that has been undertaken around learning and multiplayer games has focused on the informal use of these games, there are some studies that look at their use within a formal educational setting. In her study of *World of Warcraft* in a university game design class, Dickey (2007) found evidence of peer mentoring and leader/follower role-reversal within the game but that these activities were not translated into the classroom. However, the fostering of collegiality and collaboration in the game, as well as other more negative classroom dynamics (the perception of a player being untrustworthy in the game) did translate back to the classroom environment. Hou (2012) carried out an observational study of an educational MMORPG, *Talking Island*, to explore the behavioural patterns of learners. The game was designed to teach English vocabulary and conversational skills to primary school learners, and although it was designed to incorporate situated learning scenarios and problem-solving quests, (non-violent) battle was the behaviour that most frequently triggered learning, and was most frequently used by players. This serves to highlight the importance of reflection, discussion and debriefing as part of the learning process, which is discussed in more detail in Chapters 4 and 11.

TABLE 13.2 Communal game techniques for developing skills and attributes (adapted from Hoyle & Moseley, 2012)

Skill/Attribute	Game techniques
Cooperative skills	Problems that require skills beyond the individual, such as variety or combinations of specialist skills, or large amounts of distributed effort over time or distance, such as cracking complex codes.
Critical thinking	Player performance metrics. Built-in comparison mechanisms for items and/or players. Support for 'add-ons' or 'mods' to collect and present data. Complex game mechanics. Game item information readily accessible. Third-party knowledge aggregation and discussion sites allowed.
Digital literacy	Screenshot/movie capture built in. Personal artwork use permitted. Visually appealing environments. Tasks that involve the use of social or other media.
Motivation	Completive elements such as leader boards, levels and prizes (at an appropriate level for the player). Involvement in a story or narrative. Delivery of regular new challenges.
Peer mentoring	Equipment and player characteristics inspection possible. Very large knowledge domain. Shared encounter perspective.
Persistence	'Grinding' quests to do something repeatedly. Multiple attempts but at a cost in time and resources. Existence of ongoing groups to which members feel an allegiance. Dying due to inadequate planning or poor performance. Hints when learning new skills. Complex, lengthy tasks broken into chunks.
Shared experience	Group achievement tracking. Group communication channels. Shared 'kill' or experience encounters where whole group credited for work by any member(s). Ability to name and customise groups with logos and slogans.

Games of all sorts allow us to play with reality and identity, but the possibilities are particularly marked in digital games that transport players to other worlds, with different cultures and ways of being and understanding the nature of the game reality. The ability to play with who we are, and what others perceive us to be, in digital worlds can also have a profound impact on an individual's sense of self and what it means to be a learner in the context of digital games.

14

GAMES AS MULTI-SENSORY EXPERIENCES

Most modern digital games employ an array of media types, including visual elements, animations, cut scenes and video, text, speech, sound effects and music. This can create an immersive multi-sensory experience, but can also be overwhelming. In addition to the audio and video elements of games, which have been common for many years, more recently, haptic interface devices have introduced user-feedback cues such as touch, vibration and gesture control to the gaming experience. In this chapter I consider digital games as multi-sensory experiences, exploring the different sensory elements that exist in games. There is very little research on the impact of rich multiple media in games for learning specifically, so in this chapter I present a range of multimedia learning theories and discuss their relevance to computer games for learning.

Before I describe the main theories of multimedia learning, I will touch briefly on learning styles theory. There is a wide variety of ways in which student learning styles have been considered, some more robust than others, looking at learning preferences, attitudes, cognitive styles, approaches to studying and so on. Of particular relevance to multi-sensory learning is the theory of visual-auditory-kinaesthetic learning styles (or VAK, as it is generally called). This hypothesises that people have distinct sensory learning preferences, with every person having a dominant input through either the visual, auditory or kinaesthetic sense. However, while this might make intuitive sense, as a theory it is problematic for a variety of reasons, including the weak evidential base, the robustness of the model on which it is built, the lack of rigorous methods of measurement of preferences and even a lack of clarity about the origin of the VAK learning preferences model itself. Sharp, Bowker, and Byrne (2008) provide an excellent critique of the VAK model of learning, highlighting the fundamental problem that, despite its widespread use and acceptance, in their study "no one we spoke to seemed to have any idea about where the VAK they were familiar with came from" (p. 301).

I highlight the idea of visual, auditory and kinaesthetic learning preferences here because, despite the limitations of the VAK model, ideas of sensory learning preferences are widespread in schools and universities, and the general idea that different individuals prefer to receive information from different sensory inputs, process them and learn from them in different ways is not implausible. It is also backed up in other models of learning, such as Gardner's (1993) theory of multiple intelligences, which identifies different musical, verbal, visual and kinaesthetic intelligences (among others), although it is debatable as to whether these are true intelligences or simply abilities. Despite this, I believe it is worth considering games from a multi-sensory perspective, looking at the relevant theories of multimedia, visual, auditory and kinaesthetic learning.

Computer games have the potential to flood players' senses with audio, visual and haptic information simultaneously, but they are primarily designed for entertainment rather than for learning. Since the majority of multimedia learning theory comes from work carried out with software designed for learning rather than for fun, some of it may be of limited relevance in the context of digital games, and I have tried to take a critical look at the theories presented in this respect. First I provide a brief review of multimedia learning theory, which looks at the impact of rich media as a whole on learning, before moving on to look in more detail at each sense in turn, exploring what learning theories exist and the relevance to games for learning.

Multimedia Learning

Modern computer games make use of a wide range of media such as sound effects, voice, music, video, interactive graphics and animations; they often have rich visual and auditory interfaces that present a wide variety of information simultaneously. Digital games are, by their very nature, multi-sensory learning experiences so it is useful to consider the relevance of theories associated with multimedia learning in order to assess their application to computer game-based learning.

Dual coding theory (Clark & Paivio, 1991) is at the heart of cognitive theories of multimedia learning. These theories suggest that in the human brain there are two separate parallel cognitive subsystems: one that specialises in the processing of non-verbal information, such as graphical or visual information, and the other that deals with language. Dual coding theory therefore suggests that presenting information simultaneously in both visual and verbal forms (for example by showing graphics with an audio commentary) should improve learning, as both channels are receiving and processing information at once. While dual coding theory is widely accepted, some researchers (e.g. Clark & Craig, 1992) argue that there is not enough evidence to support it. Similarly, Baddeley (1992) proposes a model of working memory that separates processing of visual and textual information.

The cognitive theory of multimedia learning (Mayer, 2001) presupposes that dual coding exists, assuming that humans possess separate information-processing channels for verbal and visual material, that there is a limited amount of processing capacity available in both of these processing channels and that learning requires a high level of cognitive processing in both the verbal and visual channels (Mayer & Moreno, 2003). Multimedia learning, described by Mayer (2005) as occurring when "people build mental representations from words (such as spoken text or printed text) and pictures (such as illustrations, photos, animations or video)" (p. 2), emerged in the context of educational multimedia applications designed with the express purpose of supporting or guiding student learning. It might therefore be considered to be of limited application to computer games, particularly those designed for pure entertainment, which is not always about making information easy to access and remember. However, these principles still provide a useful analytic tool for considering the appropriateness of digital games for learning contexts. Mayer (2001) originally described seven principles of multimedia learning, basing his work in the field of educational multimedia, and these were later (Mayer, 2009) expanded to 12, described below, noting the relevance of each to the study of digital games for learning.

The first five principles relate to the reduction of unnecessary cognitive processing:

1. *Coherence principle* – people learn better when extraneous words, pictures and sounds are excluded. This is somewhat at odds with the nature of a video game, where media used might be extraneous for learning but essential for creating the gaming experience.
2. *Signalling principle* – people learn better with pointers that highlight essential information. This is a common strategy in games for drawing the players' attention to, for example, important status information, but also in some contexts, such as adventure games, discovery is part of the fun of the game, so again the duel motivations of entertainment and learning may be at odds.
3. *Redundancy principle* – people learn better from graphics and narration than from graphics, narration and on-screen text. In games, a variety of combinations is used, depending on the game genre, but it is usual for these to be customisable by the user.
4. *Spatial contiguity principle* – people learn better when corresponding words and pictures are presented close to each other. This is possibly relevant to the design of usable and learnable game interfaces, but of less relevance to game design where learning is not the primary objective.
5. *Temporal contiguity principle* – people learn better when corresponding words and pictures are presented simultaneously rather than one after the other. Again, this may be relevant to interface design, but relevance to a game will depend very much on the design of a specific game.

The second three principles are designed to support the management of essential cognitive processes:

6. *Segmenting principle* – people learn better when a lesson is presented in self-paced segments rather than as a continuous unit. Casual games display this characteristic but it is related to convenience rather than to learning.
7. *Pre-training principle* – people learn better when they are familiar with the names and main characteristics presented in the lesson. This is also true of gaming literacy, where a game can be accessed much more simply by the player if he or she is familiar with the conventions of the genre.
8. *Modality principle* – people learn better from animation and narration than from animation and on-screen text. As in the redundancy principle, options are usually provided in games that allow players to tailor their gaming experiences, so a range of combinations is possible.

The final four principles support what is termed 'generative process under-utilisation', which means not using all the available cognitive capacity for the learning task at hand:

9. *Multimedia principle* – people learn better from words and pictures than from pictures alone. Games typically combine visuals with audio or text, and it is uncommon for a game to be solely graphical.
10. *Personalisation principle* – people learn better when words are in a conversational rather than a formal style. It is very uncommon for games to use a formal style, unless it is specifically for effect.
11. *Voice principle* – people learn better when narration is delivered by a friendly human voice rather than one generated by a machine. Again, both techniques are used in games, as appropriate to the individual game.
12. *Image principle* – adding an image of the speaker to narration does not necessarily aid learning. In games, a speaker's image is often shown, but this is related to the play experience rather than to the design of the game to enhance learning.

As can be seen from this list, there is a tension between designing a game for optimum player experience and design for learning. It is also worth noting that Mayer's (2001, 2009) research is based upon materials designed for learning, and so may be entirely inapplicable to games, and that it relies on a cognitive model of learning, which can be viewed as reductionist and lacking a critical understanding of the complexities of different learning contexts and learners involved. There is also contradictory research, for example Sankey, Birch, and Gardiner (2011) found that multiple representations of content did not lead to any significant gains in comprehension, but students were very favourably disposed to the multimedia elements and perceived that they had been helpful in learning.

In addition to the 12 principles described above, various other principles have been suggested by theorists and researchers. Ayres and Sweller (2005) describe the split-attention principle of multimedia, suggesting that it is important not to create learning situations where cognitive load is increased, for example where the learner has to divide his or her attention between disparate sources of information. Game-play, particularly in complex games where many variables are involved, may also involve assimilating information over various screens and other information channels. While the split-attention principle may have some relevance for the design of learning materials, the reality is that analysing and synthesising information from a variety of sources is now a key real-world information literacy skill. Plass, Homer, and Hayward (2009) draw on the existing literature and original research to present additional design factors for educationally effective simulations and animations, including that learning is enhanced when: graphical icons are used rather than text to represent information; colour is used to highlight key features; and visual representations used in several different lessons or contexts are related to one another. In the context of games, the use of colour is the norm, as is the use of icons, but again these are related to gaming literacies and typically icons will have been tested with users to ensure that their meanings are clear and unambiguous.

The final point on different visual representations is an interesting one for games, as there is little consistency in the way in which different visual elements are represented between games of the same genre, or even games in the same series. However, this does not seem to be an issue among game players and it is perhaps again due to the fundamental difference in purpose of entertainment games and digital learning activities. There is very little evidence about the effects of game multimedia on learning, but in an analysis of students using commercial video games, Sharrit (2010) found evidence that presentation of visual and audio media encouraged learning, as did specific visualisations such as the animation of in-game objects.

Another theory worthy of mention in relation to games and learning is the theory of external cognition (Scaife & Rogers, 1996, 2005), which highlights the importance of learners constructing their own external representations, such as diagrams, highlights and notes, as a way of organising, re-structuring and understanding what they are learning. While suggestions about these types of representations are not explicit in games, it is not uncommon for players to draw maps, take extensive notes, or plan activities through diagrams while game playing. The use of external representations in game playing for learning is an area that is little researched, but one that I believe would be worthy of further study.

One of the negative aspects of using simultaneous multiple media, as is common in digital games, is the danger of cognitive overload (Mayer & Moreno, 2003) where "the processing demands evoked by the learning task may exceed the processing capacity of the cognitive system" (p. 45). In games, this may lead to players becoming overwhelmed by the interface or game-play (although good games will lead players in gradually to avoid this problem) and opt out. In the context of games for learning, it is detrimental for a student to feel challenged by the demands of the game itself rather than from the learning within the game. Using games for learning is, in effect, adding another cognitive overhead, as the learner has to learn the game interface and conventions as well as the intended learning outcomes. In a study of the cognitive loads of massively multiplayer online role playing games, Ang, Zaphiris, and Mahmood (2007) found that a variety of different types of cognitive overloads occurred, including overloads from multiple game interactions, social interactions, the user interface and identity construction. While these overloads did cause problems, even to expert players, strategies were typically developed by players to overcome them.

It is also worth noting that multimedia effects differ depending on the characteristics of learners. In his earlier work, Mayer (2001) describes the individual differences principle, which highlights that the multimedia effects described are stronger for learners who start with lower levels of knowledge and for learners with high spatial abilities. Najjar (1998) also found evidence that educational multimedia is more effective with learners with low prior knowledge and low aptitude, and that multimedia makes learning more effective for older learners. These effects may be even stronger in computer games for learning when additional factors such as confidence and gaming literacy are taken into account.

Visual Learning in Games

Of all of our senses, sight is dominant for most people in gaining understanding about the world. The way in which people use and produce visual information is crucial, not just within the context of computer games, and central to this is the idea of 'visual literacy'. There is little consistency in how different disciplines define visual literacy, although the key elements that emerge across definitions are that the concept refers to the use of visuals (seen either with the eyes or in the mind) for communication, thinking, learning, constructing meaning, creative expression and aesthetic enjoyment (Avgerinou & Ericson, 1997).

The visual design of games, and learning materials in general, can influence how usable, acceptable and motivational they are to students. Good visual design can also support learning by reducing cognitive overhead, influencing efficient workflow, and providing cues as attractors and indicators (Kirsh, 2005). Graphics can support learning in a variety of ways, such as drawing attention, helping learners create new mental models from established ones, simplifying presentation, enhancing transfer to real life and increasing motivation (Clark & Lyons, 2004). Visual metaphors help learners transfer learning from one domain to another (Benyon et al., 2005).

The field of visual design is complex and I am not going to go into great detail here. It includes aspects such as layout and composition, grouping and ordering techniques, aesthetic and informational design, and image-processing techniques (Vanderdonckt, 2003). For much of the field there is little or no research evidence on the impact of specific elements on learning, and while individual elements could be considered in relation to learning, it is unlikely that changes in a single aspect of visual design would have a measurable effect on learning (although they might have an effect on the usability or visual appeal of the game).

In games, visual design elements include the game style (for example whether it is photo-realistic or cartoon), the colour palettes used, the perspective taken (for example, first- or third-person), whether the game is shown in two or three dimensions, the degree of professionalism of design and levels of realism. Realism is particularly relevant to learning. Thompson and colleagues (2007) distinguish between three different approaches to realism used in games: first, those that are *models of reality* (for example in a flight simulator); second, those that rely on *visual realism*, including the use of cinematic techniques such as cut scenes; and those that use *simulated realism*, with an emphasis on the real-time game mechanics that aim to mimic reality rather than the game graphics. Alexander and Brunyé (2005) distinguish between: physical fidelity – how much a virtual environment looks, sounds and feels like the real world; functional fidelity – how much it acts like the real world; and psychological fidelity – the degree to which players believe that they are within the real world. In a study with adolescents on video game realism, Malliet (2006) identified five different perceptions of realism in games: factuality and credibility, authenticity, character empathy and involvement, realism of interaction and choice, and perceptual realism.

A recurring debate is around the relative importance of high-fidelity visual design and visual realism in educational games. It has been argued that games with lower graphical quality are seen as boring because they do not use state-of-the-art visual effects (Bellotti, Berta, Gloria, & Primavera, 2009), that educational designers should attempt to emulate the aesthetics, art and design skills of the entertainment industry in order to create material that appeals to students (Squire, 2011), and that higher visual design quality of web sites is linked to higher perceived credibility (Robins & Holmes, 2008). I, on the other hand, believe that high levels of visual realism are only important in the context of simulations that need to accurately represent reality (such as flight simulators); in other contexts, I think that as long as the game meets a certain level of aesthetic acceptability, the game-play is far more significant than the graphical quality. Van Vugt and colleagues (2007) found that the visual realism of game characters had no effect on engagement, but that the presence of the character, the perceived aesthetics and the relevance to the learning task all had an effect on engagement. Similarly, in an evaluation of three different fidelity versions of a mobile game, Sim, Cassidy, and Read (2013) found very little difference between the user experience of the three prototypes.

Zapata-Rivera and Bauer (2012) highlight the negative effects of environments with high levels of visual realism, arguing that "games that make use of rich, immersive graphical environments can impose great visual, motor, auditory, and other demands on the player to just be able to interact in the environment (e.g., sophisticated navigation controls)" but point out that "creating environments that do not make use of some of these technological advances (e.g., a 3D immersive environment) may negatively affect student engagement, especially for students who are used to interacting with these types of games" (p. 152). This establishes two important points, the first about student preferences and the second regarding individual differences. While it might be assumed that students want to learn with the same type of games they play at home, there is little hard evidence for this and, in fact, students play a wide variety of games outside of the classroom, including lower visual quality casual games and games produced and shared by amateurs. The second point is that learners are all different, with diverse game preferences and learning styles, and it cannot be assumed that all students will react to a game in a uniform manner; for any game some learners may find it appropriate and stimulating, while others will feel that it is boring and a waste of time.

Egenfeldt-Nielsen and colleagues (2008) argue that visual effects "add to the atmosphere, provide a sense of realism and generally make the world seem alive" (p. 105). Visual design quality can also affect confidence (Ruecker, Sinclair, & Radzikowska, 2007) and users may choose not to play a particular game simply because the look and feel does not appeal to them (Taylor & Baskett, 2009). Rieber (2001) undertook a study with children where they critiqued games designed by other children and found that "although they like the high-quality graphics and sound of commercial video games, the amateur-like quality of these children-designed games was not a problem nor an important factor in their critiques" (p. 8). On the other hand, Elliott, Adams, & Bruckman (2002) were disappointed with the evaluation of their three-dimensional graphical learning environment for maths exploration, stating that "student expectations for the software were high due to the production values seen in commercial video games" (p. 1).

In recent years there has also been growth in a variety of gaming genres and platforms where sophisticated graphics and graphical realism are not crucial to the game play. For example, the emergence of platforms such as the Nintendo Wii and DS, where the emphasis is on novel forms of interaction rather than visually stunning graphics, which have been used successfully in educational contexts (Miller & Robertson, 2010). Genres such as alternate- and mixed-reality games that take place both online and in the real world have also been used in a variety of contexts (Moseley, Whitton, Culver, & Piatt, 2009), and casual games that focus on the ability to engage with play quickly and in chunks have grown steadily in popularity in recent years. Clearly it is possible for games with lower quality graphics to be engaging and appealing, for entertainment and learning, but there is limited research on the suitability of these types of games in an educational context.

Auditory Learning in Games

Very little research has been carried out in the area of game sound and learning, or on the use of sound in learning in general. Some games are designed specifically to make use of sound, such as children's phonics games and musical games, and others require auditory input from the player, but there is very little research on these in an educational context. There have been some attempts to create audio-learning experiences, such as the use of a handheld device to generate context-specific sounds in a woodland environment (Randell, Price, Rogers, Harris, and Fitzpatrick, 2004) but these are few and far between. Therefore, in this short section I shall simply highlight the types of audio that exist in video games and briefly discuss ways that have been used to classify them, drawing on what research exists throughout. Game audio has the duel function of aiding usability, through the provision of auditory cues and alerts, and providing a sense of mood and presence, although the relative importance of each of these functions will vary depending on the game genre (Jørgensen, 2008). The use of audio in soundscapes (auditory landscapes) is also effective for creating a strong sense of place (Turner, McGregor, Turner, & Carroll, 2003).

Game audio, like that of film, can be described by its position in the overall soundtrack, signifying the amount of direct attention demanded by the player, as foreground, mid-ground or background, as well as being either diegetic sound that emanates from inside the game world, such as footsteps, thunderstorms, engines or revving, or non-diegetic sound that emanates from outside the game world, such as feedback elements or status alerts (Jørgensen, 2010). Rogers (2010) notes the difference between local sound effects, which play only when the player is close to the source (such as a ticking clock or a ringing phone), distant sound effects that can be heard from far away (such as the howl of a wolf or the revving of an engine) and priority sound effects that play irrespective of location and provide the player with information about the game status and feedback on the game (such as loss of health or a power-up).

Follmann (2004) defines four main categories of sound in video games: vocalisation, sound effects, ambient effects and music. Vocalisation is speech-like sound, such as the voice of a narrator or the dialogue of game characters. In modern video games, this speech is usually pre-recorded by voice-actors and is triggered by events in the game, thus providing the recognisable human voice suggested by Mayer's (2009) voice principle as described earlier in the chapter. Sound effects used in games, for example a creak when a door opens, the slam when it closes, the noise of feet running down a corridor or a gun being fired, play an important part of creating ambience and describing the gaming environment to the player. They provide auditory feedback to the player on the environment and the consequences of their actions, and can help to increase dramatic tension. Ambient effects are the background sounds, such as the hum of traffic or the noises of a crowd, of which a player may not even be consciously aware. In addition to providing atmosphere and heightening emotion, these background effects can be effective in giving the game world a sense of place by conveying background activity. Music is also commonly used in games to set the scene, mood, rhythm and pace of the game, from music with a loud pulsing beat in a game that requires fast reactions, to a gentle background melody in a slower-paced adventure game. In a study of the role of background music in virtual worlds and its relationship to learning, Richards, Fassbender, Bilgin, and Thompson (2008) found that, while there was no evidence that the tempo and pitch of the music was related to learning, having music present had a significant impact on the students' abilities to memorise facts.

Kinaesthetic Learning in Games

As in the previous section, there is very little research in this area, although interesting work is currently being carried out by researchers at Aalto University in Finland, and research is emerging, for example on the use of games for trampoline training (Holsti, Takala, Martikainen, Kajastila, & Hämäläinen, 2013). So my aim in this section is simply to present some of the ways in which kinaesthetic learning in games has been made possible in recent years. However, since there is evidence that exercise boosts brain power (Medina, 2009) this is potentially an area that could lead to multiple learning gains. Devices such as joysticks and game controllers have been used for many years in arcade and home video games to control on-screen characters and to interact with games through touch. Early controllers only allowed one-way communication, responding to the players' movements but providing no tactile feedback, but more recent devices enable players to sense reactions to movements on screen and receive cues from the game in the form of vibrations and pressure, for example steering wheels that allow players to sense the bumps in the road or the car slipping out of control. There is also a wide range of haptic interaction devices available such as musical instruments, dance mats, microphones and sports equipment, which provide new opportunities for interaction in different ways.

Console and games manufacturers are constantly developing new devices that allow players to interact in new ways with games through touch and movement. Motion-controlled devices for game consoles are now standard. They enable players to interact with games through their physical movements, either by locating their position and plotting this in relation to the game environment on screen or by using hand-held interaction devices that are motion-sensitive, and have brought a renewed interest in haptic interaction design. Calleja (2011) discusses the importance of kinaesthetic involvement as part of his player involvement model (discussed in more detail in Chapter 6). He argues that the "most intimate link between a player and even the most unlikely-looking avatar is movement" (p. 61) because it represents the "locus of the player's exertion of agency within the game environment" (p. 61) and this link is created by a kinaesthetic relationship between player and avatar. He explores the differences between symbolic and mimetic interfaces, presented in what he calls a continuum of control. At one end of the continuum lies symbolic control through interfaces such as keyboards or controller buttons with no direct relationship between the action performed on the interaction device and the game movement, while at the other end lies symbiotic control, where actual player actions are closely mapped onto those of the game character, for example through gesture control.

Mimetic interfaces are easy to learn because in addition to drawing on established video game conventions, the large-scale movements are easy to see, so that players can learn from watching others. They shift focus from the game's three-dimensional space back to the real-life player space, similar to traditional games such as card or board games (Juul, 2010). As game technology improves there is a greater shift from symbolic to symbiotic control, which makes gaming more accessible to novice gamers, those with disabilities and players of all ages. In addition to motion-control gaming, touch-screen technology is improving and becoming more responsive and is now commonly used in smart phones, tablets and handheld gaming consoles, which rely on the user's touch as the main mode of interaction. This has given mobile-gaming a haptic dimension and allows users to quickly and accurately interact with games on their phones and handheld devices using a range of touch-based commands. Time, and further research, will tell the impact of these modes of interaction on learning.

In this chapter I have investigated the potential of multimedia theory to gain new insights on digital games in the context of learning. While there is much research on the use of rich media in learning contexts there is little in the realm of games specifically, and questions involving, for example, the level of visual realism that is both necessary and sufficient for learning, are very relevant to the design of educational games. The potential of haptic and movement-based interfaces for learning in particular is certainly an area in which further research would be of great value.

PART VI

Conclusion

15
THE FUTURE OF GAMES AND LEARNING

In this book, I have summarised and synthesised a selection of what I consider to be the most relevant, interesting and insightful theories of, and research in, motivation, play and technology that relate to the sphere of digital games and learning. What I hope this has achieved is to provide a critical summary of the added dimensions that can be gained from a cross-disciplinary analysis of the wider field. To structure the book, I selected four theoretical lenses through which digital games can be considered: games as learning environments, games as motivational tools, games as playgrounds and games as learning technologies. In selecting these four lenses, I am implicitly highlighting the importance of each area in relation to the field of games and learning.

The movement of educational games from adopting a predominantly behaviourist to constructivist model is, for me, a crucial repositioning of the field. While it is undoubtedly true that games can be used as an extrinsic motivational device to support learning of facts and to make practice of skills more palatable, this is only scratching the surface of their potential. Games, at their heart, have the potential to be powerful, problem-based authentic and collaborative learning environments, regardless of any motivational qualities they possess. This is not to say that motivation in games is not important. In the second part of this book, I have explored the value of games as motivational tools, going far beyond the simplistic notion that 'games will motivate learners'. What is important here is the concept of a game as a designed experience, and that a skilled game designer has the ability to manipulate player emotions and motivations in profound ways (not all of them positive). The role of games as playgrounds is perhaps an area that is least considered in terms of the research, but the one that I feel most needs to be explored. The value of play for creating safe spaces for exploration and fostering imagination and innovation should not be underestimated; it has been persuasively argued that creativity and the ability to imagine solutions to problems that do not exist are key skills for future generations, not just for individuals but for society (Robinson, 2011), and I believe that play offers a way to develop these skills in all learners. In the final core part, I have included a discussion on the role of digital games as learning technologies, as I think it is essential to highlight the ways in which the use of computer games differs from the use of more traditional game formats, and the affordances that the medium offers for both game play and learning. The fact that players' experiences are mediated through technology, with related social and cultural implications, can be lost in the broader discussion of digital games and learning, so I bring it to the fore here and examine the many ways in which people relate to and experience the phenomenon of digital games.

In this final chapter I start by considering where the insights from this book might take us. What might a blue skies future look like for games and learning? What would need to happen to make this a reality? I then make the case for games and learning as a discipline in its own right, discuss the challenges facing such a discipline of study and research, and conclude with an exploration of some of the emerging areas of research in digital games, including some insights into what I believe will be the future trends for research in the field.

An Imagined Future

Imagine a place where learners work collaboratively to solve problems that are personally meaningful, which cut across disciplinary boundaries, and where the borders between the 'learning institution' and the 'real world' are blurred to the point where they effectively no longer exist. Learners engage with their wider communities and are encouraged to critically challenge the state of the world and imagine what might be; and are empowered to take action for positive change. The focus of learning has moved from 'memorisation' and 'content' to a development of critical digital and information literacies, so that learners know where to find information, how to evaluate it and how to use it appropriately; the ultimate goal of this education system is in creating learners who can think and learn for themselves. Intrinsic motivation is high because learners have clear and achievable goals that they care about, and choice over what and how they study. Assessment is continuous and entirely integrated with learning; and because failure is presented as a natural and positive part of the learning process on the path to success, stress is low. Students and educators work together with a shared sense of enthusiasm and wonder, driven by curiosity to explore alternatives, imagine possibilities, take risks and create new artefacts and solutions. Technology is seamlessly integrated into all aspects of the learning space, enabling learners and teachers to use any device they choose to be connected with others, find information, create, share and build learning networks; developing a critical literacy of technology is fundamental. Students do not sit in one place, but are encouraged to move about and utilise different learning spaces; the atmosphere is one of noise, vibrancy and energy. Playfulness and fun are at the core of all activity, but are not at odds with the passion, the drive and the willingness to work hard that are apparent in every student.

For me, this is where the principles explored in this book might lead us. I realise there are many political, social, economic and cultural hurdles to achieving this vision, but many of these ideas are already used by innovation projects. For example, the Quest Schools developed by the Institute of Play in New York (Salen, Torres, Wolozin, Rufo-Tepper, & Shapiro, 2011), which are based on a pedagogy of play, build study around 'quests' that are personally relevant to learners to build 21st-century skills, and St Joseph's Primary School in Melbourne bases learning around student-selected 'passion projects' (Trapani & Hinds, 2014). However, these models are far from becoming part of the mainstream.

A movement to anything approaching the educational vision described above would need fundamental changes in the way in which the purpose, values and practices of education are constructed. This would include, at the highest levels, policy support and financial backing for alternative pedagogies. There would need to be funding for research coupled with an acceptance of risk and failure and recognition of the importance and relevance of games and learning as a discipline. Another essential item would be institutional support at all levels from top management, to teaching, support, technical and administrative staff. Parents and students too need to be on board and have confidence in models of learning that embody principles of games and play, a significant challenge given the media rhetoric on computer games, discussed later in this chapter. In order to be successful, this would require a paradigm shift in cultural attitudes towards learning and teaching; this model of learning must be seen, by all stakeholders, as appropriate and cost-effective, with the ability to produce active and empowered learners for the 21st century and beyond.

Games and Learning as a Discipline

A necessary hurdle to be overcome if we are to accomplish the vision described above is that games and learning needs to be considered as a discipline in its own right, and I believe the case for this is a persuasive one. It is an area that is substantively different from, yet overlapping with, areas such as simulation and gaming, game-based learning and serious games. Simulation and gaming, being the most established of these three examples, has its roots in business simulation and the development of non-digital games, while game-based learning, with its focus on learning with games, does not encompass the wider areas discussed in Chapter 1, such as game-inspired learning, learning from games and the study of games as cultural artefacts; there also tends to be a focus on the use of games in formal educational settings. The study of serious games is both wider in scope than games and learning, encompassing all games used with a purpose other than simply entertainment, such as games used in advertising, healthcare, corporate training or the military (which could all be considered to be forms of learning in its widest sense), and also narrower, with its emphasis on the use of games as designed purposeful experiences.

Games and learning draws together a wide variety of fields from sociology and cultural studies, psychology and education, to game design, neuroscience and computer science. This cross-disciplinary scope is both a challenge and an opportunity. Each of these disciplines brings its own set of philosophical and methodological assumptions and practices, and it is only by highlighting and dis-cussing these tensions that a single field can emerge. This does, however, create great potential for trans-disciplinary insights, offering a range of epistemological and ontological standpoints, if we as a research community respect and learn from the perspectives of others. It is by articulating the assumptions that underpin our researches and establishing a common vocabulary that games and learning can become established as a discipline that draws on a wide and varied toolset of thought and practice. Through gathering and generating data in a variety of creative and meaningful ways, and offering robust analyses that withstand scrutiny by a multidisciplinary research community we will start addressing the gap in evidence of efficacy the field currently possesses.

I believe that there are three things that we need to address in order to make progress in games and learning, in addition to the oft-cited calls for an evidence base of more robust, longitudinal research. First, we need to rethink the cost models behind games, and consider whether it is really ethical to produce big-budget learning games and whether they are a cost-effective way of creating effective learning experiences. The evidence regarding the link between high-fidelity in games and motivation, learning and transfer is limited, and I believe that there are other, cheaper ways in which to develop and use games, including going back to the use of traditional non-digital game forms, such as card or board games. The rise in use and availability of casual games is causing a shift in the demo-graphics of the gaming population as well as the expectations about the visaul quality and gaming experience, which offers potential for exploring the benefits of different models of games for learning. I believe that further research is required before the development and use of big-budget educational games can be justified. Second, a related point is that we need a move from the 'content-push' model of game-based learning to a more learner-centred gaming approach, where the game is not seen as a vehicle for transferring knowledge or learning content, but as a way for fostering skills such as creativity and imagination; the growing movement towards game-building for learning is very exciting in this respect. Third, the field of games and learning in practice could be facilitated through a greater focus on the playful elements of games and the benefits that they can bring, encouraging a gradual movement from game-based to play-based learning, where play is no longer seen as an activity for children or the antithesis of work, but as an integral and necessary part of any learning experience. Learning in the future cannot simply be about memorising facts, or even applying those facts, but it has to focus on learning how to learn and strategies for managing the unexpected. Working lives have changed, we can no longer expect to have the same job for the whole of our lives; people often have several careers at different stages in their lives, as well as managing portfolio careers where they do many things simultaneously. In many respects, technology forces the pace of change and is a driver for the jobs that exist now and in the future. We cannot give today's learners the information on how to do a job that will not exist in 20 years, but we can – through play – provide them with the skills, tools and confidence to navigate and manage information in an ever-changing digital world, as well as the imagination to envision possibilities for the future.

In order to achieve these aims, it is essential that we take account of, and embrace, the full scope and multidisciplinary nature of the field. Both in terms of its influences and contributing fields of study, but also in recognising the fragmented nature of the field itself, with sub-disciplines such as 'serious games', 'game-based learning' and 'simulation and gaming' that have emerged from different disciplinary routes but have considerable overlap. We need to best utilise, and draw together, the research that already exists in these areas, in order to create a coherent and meaningful field of study.

Challenges to Games and Learning

There are significant challenges surrounding the use of games and learning and the adoption of playful pedagogies, which I will discuss in the section that follows, including the lack of a robust evidence base, the media discourses around digital games, the acceptability of games for learning, particularly in formal learning contexts and with adults, and the ethics of using big budget games at a time of global financial crisis.

As discussed in Chapter 2, there is a lack of robust research on the potential benefits of games for learning. While the theoretical benefits are clear (e.g. Gee, 2003), they are not consistently backed up by research evidence. This lack of evidence is not, however, unique to the area of games and learning, but common in many areas of learning innovation. The field is also hampered by the cross-disciplinary nature of the use of terms such as 'engagement' that are theorised and measured in many different ways (Iacovides et al., 2011; e.g. Trowler, 2010). There is also something of a *Catch 22* situation where, because of a lack of evidence of efficacy, this affects attitudes of teachers, learners and parents, making a large-scale game-based intervention more difficult to develop, in turn leading to a lack of evidence. To combat this issue of mainstream acceptability, much of the research in the field is carried out with optional gaming activities, or takes place within computing contexts, meaning that participants are often self-selecting game players, producing biased results. The wide variety of practice that takes place around the use of games and learning also makes it difficult to make meaningful comparisons or to draw significant conclusions. In addition, games for learning, while growing more commonplace in education, are by no means normalised so there will always be the novelty effect to take into account in any research studies, be it positive or negative.

The ways in which video games are discussed and stereotyped in the media present a significant problem to the field of games and learning, in particular in relation to violence and sexualised content. While some researchers present evidence supporting the hypothesis that playing violent computer games can lead to aggressive or otherwise negative thoughts and behaviours (Anderson & Bushman, 2001; Barlett, Anderson, & Swing, 2008; Gentile & Gentile, 2007), others have found no evidence for a link between violent games and aggressive behaviours (Ferguson, 2007). In short, research on the impact of violent gaming is 'inconclusive and often contradictory' (Bryce & Rutter, 2006), although arguments about reward for, and repetition of, violence leading to increased violence in real life need to be considered in relation to the arguments for games as learning tools in general. Goldstein (2005) highlights the more specific issues, that "discussions of violent video games are clouded by ambiguous definitions, poorly designed research, and the continued confusion of correlation with causality" (p. 341). Kutner and Olson (2008) argue that the impact of media violence is much more complex than simple cause and effect, saying that "the simplistic belief that exposure to media violence will lead directly to individual violence is clearly wrong" (p. 139) but suggest that the effects are subtle, that some children are at greater risk than others, and that there are a whole host of others factors at play. Gee (2005) makes the same point, saying that

> video games are neither good nor bad all by themselves, they neither lead to violence or peace. They can be and do one thing in one family, social or cultural context, quite another in other such contexts. If you want to lower violence, then worry about those contexts, which all extend well beyond just playing video games.
>
> *(p. 5)*

Whether playing violent games leads to violent behaviours or not, this is tangential to the sphere of games and learning. While there are occasional instances of violent games being used as a stimulus for discussion, for example around media representations of gender, race, class or nationality, the vast majority of games used in education are non-violent. However, the dominant media discourse is one that first assumes that all games are violent, and second allows them to shoulder the blame for society's ills, from illiteracy to obesity.

Games and gender is a second issue worthy of consideration. The common topics in gender research include the ways that females are portrayed in games, and the under-representation of females in gamer culture and the industry. There are few female lead characters in games, and those female heroes that do exist, such as Lara Croft from the *Tomb Raider* series, are designed to fit stereotypical male fantasies. Female characters are typically side-lined and play the role of 'damsel-in-distress' or are merely there for their looks, which leaves girl gamers few female heroes with whom they can identify (Kutner & Olson, 2008). Bryce and Rutter (2005) argue that the problem is more subtle: that gaming is not a male-only activity and that "female gamers do exist but often are 'rendered invisible' by male-dominated gaming communities, the games industry and academic research" (p. 301). The societal perception that gaming is a masculine leisure activity is contradicted by the number of females who play on a regular basis. The gender dynamics of masculine and feminine in computer games are no different from wider societal representations; gender dynamics need to be understood in the context of the playing spaces, and female participation in gaming presents the opportunity to both reinforce and resist traditional discourses of masculinity and femininity (Bryce, Rutter, & Sullivan, 2006). Women are massively under-represented in terms of their involvement in the game creation industry, which suggests to me that female gamers will continue to be poorly served until women take control of the means of production in a meaningful way.

Jenkins and Cassell (2008) suggest that the way in which the games industry caters for female gamers has changed over the past 15 years. Emerging models of gaming, in particular casual games, serious and educational games, and adver-gaming (product placement in games), welcome women as participants and are designed with them in mind. Carr (2006b) suggests that the overall growth in the computer gaming industry means that it can now accommodate diversity, and the old distinctions of 'player' and 'non-player' become replaced with a focus on 'hard-core' and 'casual' players; although she points out that "if fewer women have the time or income to devote to gaming on anything more than a casual basis, the division is likely to reflect a gender divide" (p. 177). Game choice, for both sexes, depends on context and previous experiences with games, but the labels of 'non-player' and 'female' tend to become conflated so that female non-players' relationships with games are attributed to their gender rather than a lack of familiarity with the medium (Carr, 2005). Jenson and de Castell (2010) argue that there are serious methodological issues with research into gaming and gender: that gender is not considered at all but is conflated with sex; that it attempts to find gender generalisations; and that gender is only considered as an issue until it can be shown to be a non-contributory variable.

Dealing with the topic of 'game addiction' is another challenge for the field. Addiction is seen as a good thing among game designers, and is not generally used to describe medically pathological behaviour. Salen and Zimmerman (2004) argue that

> the overwhelming majority of play phenomena are not destructively addictive. This is true even for forms of play most commonly associated with pathological addiction, such as gambling. . . . The existence of addictive play disorders doesn't mean that all play is bad for you. Eating disorders and

addictions abound. But that doesn't mean that you should avoid the pleasure of dining.

(p. 356)

In a review of video game addiction, Griffiths and Davies (2005) conclude that "excessive video game playing can have potentially damaging effects upon a minority of individuals who display compulsive and addictive behaviour, and who will do anything possible to feed their addiction" (p. 366). The recent emergence of free-to-play casual games, which aim to make players invest time and energy in the game to the point where they make real-world purchases in order to enhance their gaming experience, has re-ignited the debate on games and addiction, and certainly has an ethically contentious dimension as the games are designed in such a way as to 'addict' players (Rose, 2013), although it is debatable whether this is true addiction. Kutner and Olsen (2008) define an addiction as a compulsive psychological craving, with increased tolerance over time, and uncomfortable physiological withdrawal symptoms. They argue that it is still not known whether true video game addiction exists, or whether the addictive symptoms could be caused by a compulsion similar to obsessive–compulsive disorder (which has a different underlying mechanism from addiction to a drug) so could simply be a result of responding to the powerful behavioural reinforcements present in games (those very reinforcements that make games so engaging and powerful for learning). Wood (2007) suggests that the real reasons behind assumed 'addiction' are poor time management and a need to escape from underlying problems rather than anything inherent in actual games. Computer games are also a victim of perception; because they are seen as a negative behaviour, a high level of use is more likely to be labelled as addictive than, for example, a high level of reading. As is the case with violent games, the problems of video game addiction are massively over-hyped.

The discourse on the 'digital native, digital immigrant' (Prensky, 2001) is one that I believe to be particularly harmful to the field. This is the idea that those who have grown up with technology learn in significantly different ways than those born before the ubiquitous advent of technology. Research shows the simplistic notion of the generational divide and highlights the complexity of young people's experiences with technology (Bennett, Maton, & Kervin, 2008; Bennett & Maton, 2010; Jones, Ramanau, Cross, & Healing, 2010; Margaryan, Littlejohn, & Vojt, 2011) and that factors such as breadth of use, experience, gender and educational levels also play a large part in defining the competence and confidence with which people use the web (Helsper & Eynon, 2010). Bayne and Ross (2007) argue that the notion of 'native' or 'immigrant' is based on a series of binary oppositions in which the native 'occupies the commanding position' (Derrida, 1981) leading to the "structurally embedded de-privileging of the role of the teacher" (Bayne & Ross, 2007, p. 2). They also highlight the problematic construction of immigrants as 'asylum seekers' in the recent political climate. White and Le Cornu (2011) suggest that the metaphor of 'visitors' and 'residents' might be a more useful description of different ways of experiencing the online environment.

The media portrayal of the negative aspects of computer games is one reason why their acceptability in education may be limited; this decreases their acceptability with teachers (Baek, 2008). Other issues around the acceptability of games include them being viewed as age-inappropriate for adults, or silly and frivolous, and inappropriate for learning. Changing perceptions among teachers, parents and learners themselves, about the value and appropriateness of games for learning, is one of the biggest challenges that the field will face.

The Reality: Emerging Fields of Research and Practice

I wanted to conclude this chapter, and the book, by thinking about some of the emerging directions in the field of games and learning. In reality, I believe that changes in pedagogy and practice will happen in small steps rather than giant leaps. The model described earlier in the chapter many be a long way off but there are three key areas in which I believe interesting practice and research will emerge in the relatively near future. These are; movement from game-playing to game-making; emerging educational game types that adopt lower production values; and a gradual shift in focus away from games for learning to an appreciation of the value of playfulness in learning.

The model of game-based learning that focuses on the provision of learning through a game is one that is dominant in the field. In a way, despite the provision of active learning opportunities, this could be viewed as the didactic model of game-based learning, where learning outcomes are pre-defined and learning is predominantly 'pushed' to the student. When students make their own games, this allows them to design their own learning outcomes as well as to develop creativity and problem-solving skills, and the learning can emerge from play and experimentation, whether in formal or informal contexts. I believe that this move from game-playing to game-making signifies a move from teacher-centred game-based learning to learner-centred gaming and that game design and development as a pedagogic model possesses significant potential for the future, reflecting existing pedagogic models that focus on students as co-creators and collaborators in pedagogical planning.

The emergence of relatively low-budget gaming models such as casual games, mobile games and social network games has helped to change the demographic of gamers, from the stereotype of an adolescent male. More women and older people are playing computer games than ever before (ESA, 2013) creating substantial opportunities in the context of games and learning. For example, these quick, accessible and social game types open up the range of possibilities of games for older adults, going beyond the deficit model presented by brain-training games.

Ferrara (2012) suggests that the five key emerging trends in gaming will be mobile gaming using GPS, social interaction, casual play with short learning curves and short engagements, the use of radical interfaces such as motion control and linking different devices together, and improved emotional engagement through narrative and involvement with realistic characters. Linking to this, I anticipate three emerging trends in game-based learning. First, I believe that the current hype over gamification will die down, as it is shown not to be a motivational panacea, and the market will become saturated with points, badges and leaderboards. However, there may be a gradual shift towards more sophisticated models of gamification, perhaps even 'playification', which employs ideas of exploration and creation, curiosity fulfilment and exploitation of the values of play rather than provision of extrinsic motivators. The second trend is one that I can already see happening, as described in Chapter 10, but I think it will grow in years to come, and that is the movement from 'game consumer' to 'game maker'. While playing games allows us to take part in active, engaging learning experiences, they only give the illusion of control; what players do is still limited by the game and its rules. Activities such as game-making, creation of digital narrative and engagement in gaming communities and contributing to game mythologies, for example by writing fan fiction, fosters creativity, imagination, lateral thinking and critical thinking. More and more commercial games provide add-on 'level builders' and 'modding engines' that allow players to create and share their own game content, and I think this trend will be mirrored in educational gaming. The third trend in games and learning I envision is very much related to the growing use and acceptance of mobile gaming and will involve the playful adaptation of physical and virtual learning spaces, in the contexts of both formal and informal learning, combining the principles of mobile and pervasive gaming in learning contexts, so that learning is genuinely situated in the real world and becomes a part of the magic circle of play.

So what is the future for games and learning? Are the three trends outlined above realistic? Could we really move to a world where my imagined future becomes a reality? I truly hope so, but I suspect it will not be in my lifetime. If digital games are to be accepted as a sound and effective way of learning, then attitudes towards education, fun, play and learning need to change. If we can embrace the playfulness inherent in games, move beyond the media discourses that focus on the negative aspects of games, and make that acceptable to learners of all ages, then this presents opportunities for bringing play into learning, with all the benefits that entails. While 'work' and 'play' are viewed as binaries, this still presents a massive challenge. Games can bring joy and delight to learning, but only if entered into in a spirit of play. We need to make learning playful, and playful learning acceptable for everyone.

REFERENCES

Akkerman, S., Admiraal, W., & Huizenga, J. (2009). Storification in History education: A mobile game in and about medieval Amsterdam. *Computers & Education, 52*(2), 449–459.

Al-bow, M., Austin, D., Edgington, J., Fajardo, R., Fishburn, J., Lara, C., Leutenegger, S., & Meyer, S. (2009). Using game creation for teaching computer programming to high school students and teachers. In *ITiSCE '09* (pp. 104–108). Paris, France.

Alexander, A., & Brunyé, T. (2005). From gaming to training: A review of studies on fidelity, immersion, presence, and buy-in and their effects on transfer in pc-based simulations and games. In *Proceedings of the Interservice/Industry Training, Simulation, and Education Conference (I/ITSEC)* (pp. 1–14).

Alexander, J. T., Sear, J., & Oikonomou, A. (2013). An investigation of the effects of game difficulty on player enjoyment. *Entertainment Computing, 4*(1), 53–62.

Alfieri, L., Brooks, P. J., Aldrich, N. J., & Tenenbaum, H. R. (2011). Does discovery-based instruction enhance learning? *Journal of Educational Psychology, 103*(1), 1–18.

Anderson, C. A., & Bushman, B. J. (2001). Effects of violent video games on aggressive behavior, aggressive cognition, aggressive affect, physiological arousal, and prosocial behavior: A meta-analytic review of the scientific literature. *Psychological Science, 12*(5), 353–359.

Anderson, L., & Krathwohl, D. A. (2001). *Taxonomy for learning, teaching and assessing: A revision of Bloom's taxonomy of educational objectives.* New York, NY: Longman.

Ang, C., Zaphiris, P., & Mahmood, S. (2007). A model of cognitive loads in massively multiplayer online role playing games. *Interacting with Computers, 19*(2), 167–179.

Annetta, L., Klesath, M., & Holmes, S. (2008). V-Learning: How gaming and avatars are engaging online students. *Innovate Journal of Online Education, 4*(3). Retrieved 14 November, 2013 from www.editlib.org/p/104249

Antin, J., & Churchill, E. (2011). Badges in social media: A social psychological perspective. In *CHI 2011.* Vancouver, BC: ACM.

Appleton, J., Christenson, S., Kim, D., & Reschly, A. (2006). Measuring cognitive and psychological engagement: Validation of the Student Engagement Instrument. *Journal of School Psychology, 44*(5), 427–445.

Arsenault, D., & Perron, B. (2009). In the frame of the magic circle: The circle(s) of gameplay. In B. Perron & M. J. P. Wolf (Eds.), *The video game theory reader 2* (pp. 109–132). New York, NY: Routledge.

Atkinson, J. W. (1957). Motivational determinants of risk-taking behavior. *Psychological Review, 64, Part 1*(6), 359–372.

Avgerinou, M., & Ericson, J. (1997). A review of the concept of visual literacy. *British Journal of Educational Technology, 28*(4), 280–291.

Ayres, P., & Sweller, J. (2005). The split-attention principle in multimedia learning. In R. Mayer (Ed.), *The Cambridge handbook of multimedia learning* (pp. 135–146). Cambridge: Cambridge University Press.

Baddeley, A. (1992). Working memory. *Science, 255*(5044), 556–559.

Baek, Y. K. (2008). What hinders teachers in using computer and video games in the classroom? Exploring factors inhibiting the uptake of computer and video games. *Cyberpsychology & Behavior: The Impact of the Internet, Multimedia and Virtual Reality on Behavior and Society, 11*(6), 665–671.

Baid, H., & Lambert, N. (2010). Enjoyable learning: The role of humour, games, and fun activities in nursing and midwifery education. *Nurse Education Today, 30*(6), 548–552.

Bandura, A. (1977). *Social learning theory.* Englewood Cliffs, NJ: Prentice Hall.

Barlett, C. P., Anderson, C. A., & Swing, E. L. (2008). Video game effects – confirmed, suspected, and speculative: A review of the evidence. *Simulation & Gaming, 40*(3), 377–403.

Barr, P., Noble, J., & Biddle, R. (2007). Video game values: Human–computer interaction and games. *Interacting with Computers, 19*(2), 180–195.

Bartle, R. (1996). Hearts, clubs, diamonds, spades: Players who suit MUDs. *Journal of MUD research, 1*(1), 1–24.

Bateson, G. (1972). *Steps to an ecology of mind.* Northvale, NJ: Jason Aronson Inc.

Bayne, S., & Ross, J. (2007). *The "digital native" and "digital immigrant": a dangerous opposition.* Paper presented at the Annual Conference of the Society for Research into Higher Education.

Baytak, A., & Land, S. M. (2010). A case study of educational game design by kids and for kids. *Procedia – Social and Behavioral Sciences, 2*(2), 5242–5246.

Becker, K., & Canada, A. (2001). Teaching with games: The minesweeper and asteroids experience. *Journal of Computing Sciences in Colleges, 17*(2), 23–33.

Begg, M., Dewhurst, D., & Macleod, H. (2004). Game-informed learning: Applying computer game processes to higher education. *Innovate, 1.*

Bellotti, F., Berta, R., Gloria, a. De, & Primavera, L. (2009). Enhancing the educational value of video games. *Computers in Entertainment, 7*(2), 1.

Bennett, S., & Maton, K. (2010). Beyond the "digital natives" debate: Towards a more nuanced understanding of students' technology experiences. *Journal of Computer Assisted Learning, 26*(5), 321–331.

Bennett, S., Maton, K., & Kervin, L. (2008). The "digital natives" debate: A critical review of the evidence. *British Journal of Educational Technology, 39*(5), 775–786.

Benyon, D., Turner, P., & Turner, S. (2005). *Designing interactive systems: People, activities, contexts, technologies* (p. 832). Upper Saddle River, NJ: Pearson Education.

Bird, P., Forsyth, R., & Whitton, N. (2012). *Supporting responsive curricula final evaluation report.* Bristol. Retrieved 14 November, 2013 from www.jisc.ac.uk/media/documents/programmes/curriculumdesign/SRC_Final_Evaluation_Report.pdf

Bisson, C., & Luckner, J. (1996). Fun in learning: The pedagogical role of fun in adventure education. Perspectives. *Journal of Experiential Education, 19*(2), 108–112.

Bloom, B. S. (1956). *Taxonomy of educational objectives, Handbook I: The cognitive domain.* New York: David McKay Co Inc.

Bluemink, J., Hämäläinen, R., Manninen, T., & Järvelä, S. (2010). Group-level analysis on multiplayer game collaboration: How do the individuals shape the group interaction? *Interactive Learning Environments, 18*(4), 365–383.

Bogost, I. (2010). *Persuasive games: The expressive power of videogames.* Cambridge, MA: MIT Press.

Borland, M. (2005). Blurring the line between games and life. *CNET News.* Retrieved 14 November, 2013 from http://news.cnet.com/Blurring-the-line-between-games-and-life/2100-1024_3-5590956.html

Bostan, B. (2009). Player motivations. *Computers in Entertainment, 7*(2), 1.

Bottino, R. M., & Ott, M. (2006). Mind games, reasoning skills, and the primary school curriculum. *Learning, Media and Technology, 31*(4), 359–375.

Boud, D., & Feletti, G. (1998). *The challenge of problem based learning* (p. 356). New York, NY: Routledge.

Boyle, E., Connolly, T., Hainey, T., & Boyle, J. M. (2012). Engagement in digital entertainment games: A systematic review. *Computers in Human Behavior, 28*(3), 771–780.

Brathwaite, B., & Schreiber, I. (2009). *Challenges for game designers: Non-digital exercises for video game designers.* Boston, MA: Delmar Publishing.

Brockmyer, J. H., Fox, C. M., Curtiss, K. A., McBroom, E., Burkhart, K. M., & Pidruzny, J. N. (2009). The development of the Game Engagement Questionnaire: A measure of engagement in video game-playing. *Journal of Experimental Social Psychology, 45*(4), 624–634.

Brookes, S. (2009). Using an alternate reality game to teach enterprise. *Learning and Teaching in HE on WordPress.com.* Retrieved 25 March, 2013, from http://simonbrookes.wordpress.com/2009/11/03/using-an-alternate-reality-game-to-teach-enterprise/

Brookes, S., & Moseley, A. (2012). Authentic contextual games for learning. In N. Whitton & A. Moseley (Eds.), *Using games to enhance teaching and learning: A beginner's guide* (pp. 91–107). New York, NY: Routledge.

Brown, E., & Cairns, P. (2004). A grounded investigation of game immersion. In *Proceedings of CHI 2004* (pp. 1297–1300). New York, NY: ACM.

Brown, J. S., Collins, A., & Duguid, P., (1989). Situated cognition and the culture of learning. *Educational Researcher, 18*(1), 32–42.

Brown, S., & Vaughan, C. (2010). *Play: How it shapes the brain, opens the imagination, and invigorates the soul.* New York, NY: Penguin.

Bruner, J. S. (1961). The act of discovery. *Harvard Educational Review, 31*(1), 21–32.

Bryce, J., & Rutter, J. (2005). Gendered gaming in gendered space. In J. Raessens & J. Goldstein (Eds.), *Handbook of computer game studies* (pp. 301–310). Cambridge, MA: MIT Press.

Bryce, J., & Rutter, J. (2006). Digital games and the violence debate. In J. Rutter & J. Bryce (Eds.), *Understanding digital games* (pp. 205–222). London: Sage.

Bryce, J., Rutter, J., & Sullivan, C. (2006). Digital games and gender. In J. Rutter & J. Bryce (Eds.), *Understanding digital games2* (pp. 185–204). London: Sage.

Buckingham, D., & Burn, A. (2007). Game literacy in theory and practice. *Journal of Educational Multimedia and Hypermedia, 16*(3), 323–349.

Buckingham, D., & Scanlon, M. (2003). Interactivity and pedagogy in 'edu-tainment' software. *Information Technology, Education and Society, 4*(2), 107–126.

Burn, A. (2006). Playing roles. In D. Carr, D. Buckingham, A. Burn, & G. Schott (Eds.), *Computer games: Text, narrative and play* (pp. 72–87). Cambridge: Polity Press.

Burn, A., & Carr, D. (2006). Motivation and online gaming. In D. Carr, D. Buckingham, A. Burn, & G. Schott (Eds.), *Computer games: Text, narrative and play* (pp. 103–118). Cambridge: Polity Press.

Caillois, R. (2001). *Man, play, and games*. Champaign, IL: University of Illinois Press.

Calleja, G. (2007). Digital game involvement: A conceptual model. *Games and Culture, 2*(3), 236–260.

Calleja, G. (2010). Digital games and escapism. *Games and Culture, 5*(4), 335–353.

Calleja, G. (2011). *In-Game: From immersion to incorporation*. Cambridge, MA: MIT Press.

Calvert, S. L. (2005). Cognitive effects of video games. In J. Raessens & J. Goldstein (Eds.), *Handbook of computer game studies* (pp. 125–131). Cambridge, MA: MIT Press.

Campbell, J. (2008). *The hero with a thousand faces* (p. 436). Novato, CA: New World Library.

Carbonaro, M., Cutumisu, M., Duff, H., Gillis, S., Siegel, J., Schaeffer, J., & Schumacher, A. (2008). Interactive story authoring: A viable form of creative expression for the classroom. *Computers & Education, 51*(2), 687–707.

Carr, D. (2005). Contexts, gaming pleasures, and gendered preferences. *Simulation & Gaming, 36*(4), 464–482.

Carr, D. (2006a). Games and narrative. In D. Carr, D. Buckingham, A. Burn, & G. Schott (Eds.), *Computer games: Text, narrative and play* (pp. 30–44). Cambridge: Polity Press.

Carr, D. (2006b). Games and gender. In D. Carr, D. Buckingham, A. Burn, & G. Schott (Eds.), *Computer games: Text, narrative and play* (pp. 162–178). Cambridge: Polity Press.

Carroll, J. M., & Thomas, J. C. (1988). FUN. *SIGCHI Bulletin, 19*(3), 21–24.

Chang, J., Lee, M., Ng, K., & Moon, K.-L. (2003). Business simulation games: The Hong Kong experience. *Simulation & Gaming, 34*(3), 367–376.

Chapman, E. (2003). Alternative approaches to assessing student engagement rates. *Practical Assessment, Research & Evaluation, 8*(13). Retrieved 14 November, 2013 from http://PAREonline.net/getvn.asp?v=8&n=13

Charlier, N., & Clarebout, G. (2009). Game-based assessment: Can games themselves act as assessment mechanisms? A case study. In M. Pivec (Ed.), *Proceedings of the 3rd European Conference on Games Based Learning* (pp. 404–411). Reading, UK: Academic Publishing Limited.

Chen, M., Kolko, B. E., Cuddihy, E., & Medina, E. (2011). Modeling but NOT Measuring Engagement in Computer Games. In *Proceedings of the 7th international conference on Games + Learning + Society* (pp. 55–63).

Chen, M., & Johnson, S. (2004). *Measuring Flow in a computer game simulating a foreign language environment*. Retrieved 14 November, 2013 from www.markdangerchen.net/pubs/flow_in_game_simulating_fle.pdf

Cheng, G. (2009). Using game making pedagogy to facilitate student learning of interactive multimedia. *Australasian Journal of Educational Technology, 25*(2), 204–220.

Childs, M. (2010). *Learners' experience of presence in virtual worlds*. University of Warwick.

Choi, B., Huang, J., Jeffrey, A., & Baek, Y. (2013). Development of a scale for fantasy state in digital games. *Computers in Human Behavior, 29*(5), 1980–1986.

Chua, A. Y. K. (2005). The design and implementation of a simulation game for teaching knowledge management. *Journal of the American Society for Information Science and Technology, 56*(11), 1207–1216.

Clark, J. M., & Paivio, A. (1991). Duel coding theory and education. *Educational Psychology Review, 3*(3), 149–210.

Clark, K., & Sheridan, K. (2010). Game design through mentoring and collaboration. *Journal of Educational Multimedia and Hypermedia, 19*(2), 5–22.

Clark, R. C., & Lyons, C. (2004). *Graphics for learning: Proven guidelines for planning, designing, and evaluating visuals in training materials.* San Franscisco, CA: Pfeiffer.

Clark, R. E., & Craig, T. G. (1992). Research and theory on multi-media learning effects. In M. Giardina (Ed.), *Interactive multimedia learning environments. Human factors and technical considerations on design issues* (pp. 19–30). Heidleberg: Springer.

Colarusso, C. A. (1993). Play in adulthood. A developmental consideration. *The Psychoanalytic Study of the Child, 48,* 225–245.

Coles, C. D., Strickland, D. C., Padgett, L., & Bellmoff, L. (2007). Games that "work": Using computer games to teach alcohol-affected children about fire and street safety. *Research in Developmental Disabilities, 28*(5), 518–30.

Coller, B. D., & Scott, M. J. (2009). Effectiveness of using a video game to teach a course in mechanical engineering. *Computers & Education, 53*(3), 900–912.

Collins, A. (2006). Cognitive apprenticeship. In R. K. Sawyer (Ed.), *The Cambridge handbook of the learning sciences* (pp. 47–60). Cambridge: Cambridge University Press.

Collins, A., Brown, J. S., & Newman, S. E. (1989). Cognitive apprenticeship: Teaching the crafts of reading, writing and mathematics. In L. Resnick (Ed.), *Knowing, learning, and instruction: Essays in honor of Robert Glaser* (p. 512). New York, NY: Routledge.

Conati, C., & Manske, M. (2009). Evaluating adaptive feedback in an educational computer game. In Z. Ruttkay et al., (Eds.), *Intelligent virtual agents: 9th international conference, IVA 2009, Amsterdam, The Netherlands* (pp. 146–158). Heidelberg: Springer Berlin.

Connolly, T., Boyle, E., MacArthur, E., Hainey, T., & Boyle, J. M. (2012). A systematic literature review of empirical evidence on computer games and serious games. *Computers & Education, 59*(2), 661–686.

Connolly, T., Stansfield, M., & Hainey, T. (2007). An application of games-based learning within software engineering. *British Journal of Educational Technology, 38*(3), 416–428.

Connolly, T., Stansfield, M., & Hainey, T. (2008). Development of a general framework for evaluating games-based learning. In T. Connolly & M. Stansfield (Eds.), *Proceedings of the 2nd European Conference on Games Based Learning* (Vol. 1990, pp. 105–114). Reading, UK: Academic Conferences Ltd.

Connolly, T., Stansfield, M., & Hainey, T. (2011). An alternate reality game for language learning: ARGuing for multilingual motivation. *Computers & Education, 57*(1), 1389–1415.

Consalvo, M. (2009). There is no magic circle. *Games and Culture, 4*(4), 408–417.

Cooper, P. A. (1993). Paradigm shifts in designed instruction: From behaviorism to cognitivism to constructivism. *Educational Technology, 61*(3), 12–19.

Cordova, D. I., & Lepper, M. R. (1996). Intrinsic motivation and the process of learning: Beneficial effects of contextualization, personalization, and choice. *Journal of Educational Psychology, 88*(4), 715–730.

Crawford, C. (1984). *The art of computer game design.* New York, NY: McGraw-Hill.

Crookall, D. (2011). Serious games, debriefing, and simulation/gaming as a discipline. *Simulation & Gaming, 41*(6), 898–920.

Csíkszentmihályi, M. (1992). *Flow: The classic work on how to achieve happiness.* London: Random House.

Csíkszentmihályi, M. (1997). *Finding flow: The psychology of engagement with everyday life.* New York, NY: Basic Books.

Dansky, R. (2007). Introduction to game narrative. In C. M. Bateman (Ed.), *Game writing: Narrative skills for videogames.* Boston, MA: Charles River Media.

Davies, C. H. J. (2002). Student engagement with simulations: A case study. *Computers & Education, 39*(3), 271–282.

De Freitas, S. (2007). *Learning in immersive worlds: A review of game-based learning.* Bristol: JISC.

De Freitas, S., & Oliver, M. (2006). How can exploratory learning with games and simulations within the curriculum be most effectively evaluated? *Computers & Education, 46*(3), 249–264.

Denner, J., Werner, L., Bean, S., & Campe, S. (2013). The girls creating games program. *Frontiers: A Journal of Women Studies, 26*(1), 90–98.

Derrida, J. (1981). *Positions.* Chicago, IL: University of Chicago Press.

Dickey, M. (2006). Game design narrative for learning: Appropriating adventure game design narrative devices and techniques for the design of interactive learning environments. *Educational Technology Research and Development, 54*(3), 245–263.

Dickey, M. (2007). Game design and learning: A conjectural analysis of how massively multiple online role-playing games (MMORPGs) foster intrinsic motivation. *Educational Technology Research and Development, 55*(3), 253–273.

Dickey, M. D. (2011). World of Warcraft and the impact of game culture and play in an undergraduate game design course. *Computers & Education, 56*(1), 200–209.

Dolcos, F., LaBar, K. S., & Cabeza, R. (2004). Interaction between the amygdala and the medial temporal lobe memory system predicts better memory for emotional events. *Neuron, 42*(5), 855–863.

Domínguez, A., Saenz-de-Navarrete, J., De-Marcos, L., Fernández-Sanz, L., Pagés, C., & Martínez-Herráiz, J.-J. (2013). Gamifying learning experiences: Practical implications and outcomes. *Computers & Education, 63,* 380–392.

Dormann, C., & Biddle, R. (2009). A review of humor for computer games: Play, laugh and more. *Simulation & Gaming, 40*(6), 802–824.

Dormans, J. (2011). Beyond iconic simulation. *Simulation & Gaming, 42*(5), 610–631.

Downes, S. (2011, May). "Connectivism" and connective knowledge. *Huffington Post.* Retrieved 25 January, 2013, from www.huffingtonpost.com/stephen-downes/connectivism-and-connecti_b_804653.html

Draper, S. (1999). Analysing fun as a candidate software requirement. *Personal and Ubiquitous Computing, 3*(3), 117–122.

Dreyfus, H. L., & Dreyfus, S. E. (1986). *Mind over machine: The power of human intuition and expertise in the era of the computer.* New York, NY: The Free Press.

Ducheneaut, N., & Moore, R. J. (2005). More than just "XP": Learning social skills in massively multiplayer online games. *Interactive Technology and Smart Education, 2*(2), 89–100.

Dumbleton, T., & Kirriemuir, J. (2006). Digital games and education. In J. Rutter & J. Bryce (Eds.), *Understanding Digital Games* (pp. 221–240). London: Sage.

Dunwell, I., de Freitas, S., & Jarvis, S. (2011). Four-dimensional consideration of feedback in serious games. In S. de Freitas & P. Maharg (Eds.), *Digital games and learning* (pp. 42–62). London: Continuum.

Ebner, M., & Holzinger, A. (2006). Successful implementation of user-centered game based learning in higher education: An example from civil engineering. *Computers & Education, 49*(3), 873–890.

Egenfeldt-Nielsen, S., Smith, J. H., & Tosca, S. P. (2008). *Understanding video games: The essential introduction.* New York, NY: Routledge.

Elliott, J., Adams, L., & Bruckman, A. (2002). No magic bullet: 3D video games in education. In *Proceedings of ICLS 2002.* Seattle, WA.

Engeser, S., & Rheinberg, F. (2008). Flow, performance and moderators of challenge-skill balance. *Motivation and Emotion, 32*(3), 158–172.

Engeström, Y. (1987). *Learning by expanding: An activity-theoretical approach to developmental research*. Helsinki: Orienta-Konsultit.

Engeström, Y. (1999). Activity theory and individual and social transformation. In Y. Engeström, R. Miettinen, & R.-L. Punamäki (Eds.), *Perspectives on activity theory* (pp. 19–38). Cambridge: Cambridge University Press.

Eow, Y. L., Ali, W. Z. bte W., Mahmud, R. B., & Baki, R. (2009). Form one students' engagement with computer games and its effect on their academic achievement in a Malaysian secondary school. *Computers & Education, 53*(4), 1082–1091.

Erickson, T. (1997). Social interaction on the Net: Virtual community as participatory genre. *Proceedings of the Thirtieth Hawaii International Conference on System Sciences, 6,* 13–21.

ESA. (2013). Game player data. Retrieved 14 November, 2013 from www.theesa.com/facts/gameplayer.asp

Facer, K., Joiner, R. Ã., Stanton, D. Ã., Reid, J., Hull, R., & Kirk, D. (2004). Savannah: Mobile gaming and learning? *Journal of Computer Assisted Learning, 20,* 399–409.

Facer, K. L., Furlong, V. J., Furlong, R., & Sutherland, R. J. (2003). "Edutainment" Software: A site for cultures in conflict? In R. Sutherland, G. Claxton, & A. Pollard (Eds.), *Learning and teaching where worldviews meet* (Vol. 6, pp. 207–225). Stoke on Trent, UK: Trenthan Books.

Faiola, A., Newlon, C., Pfaff, M., & Smyslova, O. (2013). Correlating the effects of flow and telepresence in virtual worlds: Enhancing our understanding of user behavior in game-based learning. *Computers in Human Behavior, 29,* 1113–1121.

Falchikov, N., & Boud, D. (1989). Student self-assessment in higher education: A meta-analysis. *Review of Educational Research, 59*(4), 395–430.

Felicia, P. (2009). *Digital games in schools: A handbook for teachers*. Brussels: European Schoolnet.

Ferguson, C. J. (2007). The good, the bad and the ugly: A meta-analytic review of positive and negative effects of violent video games. *The Psychiatric Quarterly, 78*(4), 309–16.

Ferguson, C. J., & Garza, A. (2011). Call of (civic) duty: Action games and civic behavior in a large sample of youth. *Computers in Human Behavior, 27*(2), 770–775.

Ferrara, J. (2012). *Playful design: Creating game experiences in everyday interfaces*. New York, NY: Louis Rosenfeld.

Festinger, L. (1962). *A theory of cognitive dissonance*. Stanford, CA: Stanford University Press.

Fisser, P., Voogt, J., & Bom, M. (2012). Word Score: A serious vocabulary game for primary school underachievers. *Education and Information Technologies, 18*(2), 165–178.

Follmann, T. (2004). Dimension of game audio. *Official Blog of Troels Folmann*. Retrieved 14 November, 2013 from http://troelsfolmann.blogspot.co.uk/2004/11/dimensions-of-game-audio.html

Francis, R. (2011). Revolution: Experiential learning through virtual role play. In S. de Freitas & P. Maharg (Eds.), *Digital games and learning* (pp. 83–106). London: Continuum.

Fredrickson, B. L., & Joiner, T. (2002). Positive emotions trigger upward spirals toward emotional well-being. *Psychological science, 13*(2), 172–175.

Fu, F., Su, R., & Yu, S. (2009). EGameFlow: A scale to measure learners' enjoyment of e-learning games. *Computers & Education, 52*(1), 101–112.

Fullerton, T., Swain, C., & Hoffman, S.S. (2008). *Game design workshop: A playcentric approach to creating innovative games*. Burlington, MA: Morgan Kaufmann.

Gagné, R. M. (1965). *The conditions of learning*. New York, NY: Holt, Rinehart & Winston.

Gajadhar, B. J., de Kort, Y. A. W., & IJsselsteijn, W. A. (2008). Shared fun is doubled fun: Player enjoyment as a function of social setting. In *CHI 2008 Proceedings* (pp. 106–117). Florence, Italy: ACM.

Gardner, H. (1993). *Frames of mind: The theory of multiple intelligences.* New York, NY: Basic Books.

Garfield, R. (2000). Metagames. In J. Dietz et al. (Eds.), *Horsemen of the apocalypse: Essays on roleplaying.* London: Jolly Roger Games.

Garris, R., Ahlers, R., & Driskell, J. E. (2002). Games, motivation, and learning: A research and practice model. *Simulation & Gaming, 33*(4), 441–467.

Gee, J. P. (2003). *What video games have to teach us about learning and literacy.* New York, NY: Palgrave Macmillan.

Gee, J. P. (2005). *Why video games are good for your soul.* Milton Keynes, UK: Common Ground Publishing.

Gee, J. P. (2008). Learning and games. In K. Salen (Ed.), *The ecology of games: Connecting youth, games and learning* (pp. 21–40). Boston, MA: MIT Press.

Gee, J. P., & Hayes, E. (2012). Nurturing affinity spaces and game-based learning. In C. Steinkuehler, K. Squire, & S. Barab (Eds.), *Games, learning and society* (pp. 129–153). New York, NY: Cambridge University Press.

Gentile, D. A., & Gentile, J. R. (2007). Violent video games as exemplary teachers: A conceptual analysis. *Journal of Youth and Adolescence, 37*(2), 127–141.

Gibson, J. J. (1979). *The ecological approach to visual perception. Perceiving, acting, and knowing: Toward an ecological psychology.* Hillsdale, NJ: Lawrence Erlbaum.

Girard, C., Ecalle, J., & Magnan, A. (2012). Serious games as new educational tools: How effective are they? A meta-analysis of recent studies. *Journal of Computer Assisted Learning, 29*(3), 207–219.

Glasemann, M., Kanstrup, A. M., & Ryberg, T. (2010). Making chocolate-covered broccoli: Designing a mobile learning game about food for young people with diabetes. In *Proceedings of the 8th ACM Conference on Designing Interactive Systems* (pp. 262–271). New York, NY: ACM.

Goldstein, J. (2005). Violent video games. In J. Raessens & J. Goldstein (Eds.), *Handbook of computer game studies* (pp. 342–357). Cambridge, MA: MIT Press.

González Sánchez, J. L., Padilla Zea, N., & Gutiérrez, F. L. (2009). From usability to playability: Introduction to player-centred video game development process. In M. Kurosu (Ed.), *Human centred design: First International Conference, HCD 2009, Held as Part of HCI International 2009, San Diego, CA, USA, July 19–24, 2009 Proceedings* (pp. 65–74). Berlin: Springer Berlin Heidelberg.

Gregersen, T., & Grodal, T. (2009). Embodiment and interface. In B. Perron & M. J. P. Wolf (Eds.), *The video game theory reader 2* (pp. 65–83). New York, NY: Routledge.

Griffiths, M., & Davies, M. N. O. (2005). Does video game addiction exist? In R. Joost & J. Goldstein (Eds.), *Handbook of computer game studies* (pp. 359–369). Cambridge, MA: MIT Press.

Grosshandler, D., & Grosshandler, E. N. (2000). Constructing fun: Self-determination and learning at an afterschool design lab. *Computers in Human Behavior, 16*(3), 227–240.

Guynup, S., & Demmers, J. (2005). Fake fun: Transforming the challenges of learning to play. In *International Conference on Computer Graphics and Interactive Techniques: ACM SIGGRAPH.* Los Angeles, CA.

Habgood, M. P. J., Ainsworth, S. E., & Benford, S. (2005). Endogenous fantasy and learning in digital games. *Simulation & Gaming, 36*(4), 483–498.

Hainey, T., Connolly, T., Stansfield, M., & Boyle, E. (2011). The differences in motivations of online game players and offline game players: A combined analysis of three studies at higher education level. *Computers & Education, 57*(4), 2197–2211.

Hallford, N., & Hallford, J. (2001). *Swords and circuitry: A designer's guide to computer role-playing games*. Roseville, CA: Cengage Learning.

Hämäläinen, R., Manninen, T., Järvelä, S., & Häkkinen, P. (2006). Learning to collaborate: Designing collaboration in a 3-D game environment. *The Internet and Higher Education, 9*(1), 47–61.

Hämäläinen, R., & Oksanen, K. (2012). Challenge of supporting vocational learning: Empowering collaboration in a scripted 3D game – How does teachers' real-time orchestration make a difference? *Computers & Education, 59*(2), 281–293.

Hand, M., & Moore, K. (2006). Community, identity and digital games. In J. Rutter & J. Bryce (Eds.), *Understanding digital games* (pp. 166–182). London: Sage.

Harviainen, J. T. (2012). Ritualistic games, boundary control, and information uncertainty. *Simulation & Gaming, 43*(4), 506–527.

Harviainen, J. T., Lainema, T. & Saarinen, E. (2012). Player-reported impediments to game-based learning. In *Proceedings of 2012 DiGRA Nordic*, Tampere: University of Tampere.

Hayes, E. R., & Games, I. A. (2008). Making computer games and design thinking: A review of current software and strategies. *Games and Culture, 3*(3–4), 309–332.

Hays, R. T. (2005). *The effectiveness of instructional games: A literature review and discussion.* Orlando, FL: Naval Air Warfare Center Training Systems Division.

Helsper, E. J., & Eynon, R. (2010). Digital natives: Where is the evidence? *British Educational Research Journal, 36*(3), 503–520.

Hirumi, A., Appelman, B., Rieber, L., & Eck, R. Van. (2010). Preparing instructional designers for game-based learning: Part 1. *TechTrends, 54*(3), 27–37.

Hoffman, B., & Nadelson, L. (2010). Motivational engagement and video gaming: A mixed methods study. *Educational Technology Research and Development, 58*(3), 245–270.

Hoganson, K. (2010). Teaching programming concepts with gamemaker. *Journal for Computing Sciences in Colleges, 26*(2), 181–188.

Holden, C. L., & Sykes, J. M. (2011). Leveraging mobile games for place-based language learning. *International Journal of Game-Based Learning, 1*(2), 1–18.

Hollins, P. (2011). Recognition of variety: Considering learning with digital games as cybernetic systems. *International Journal of Technology Enhanced Learning, 3*(5), 456–467.

Holsti, L., Takala, T., Martikainen, A., Kajastila, R. & Hämäläinen, P. (2013). Body-controlled trampoline training games based on computer vision. In *CHI '13 Extended Abstracts*. Paris, France.

Hong, J.-C., Cheng, C.-L., Hwang, M.-Y., Lee, C.-K., & Chang, H.-Y. (2009). Assessing the educational values of digital games. *Journal of Computer Assisted Learning, 25*(5), 423–437.

Horne, C. (2013). QRienteering: Mobilising the M-learner with affordable learning games for campus inductions. In Y. K. Baek & N. Whitton (Eds.), *Cases on digital game-based learning: Methods, models, and strategies* (pp. 97–118). Hershey, PA: IGI Global.

Hou, H.-T. (2012). Exploring the behavioral patterns of learners in an educational massively multiple online role-playing game (MMORPG). *Computers & Education, 58*(4), 1225–1233.

Howard-Jones, P., & Demetriou, S. (2008). Uncertainty and engagement with learning games. *Instructional Science, 37*(6), 519–536.

Howard-Jones, P., Taylor, J., & Sutton, L. (2002). The effect of play on the creativity of young children during subsequent activity. *Early Child Development and Care, 172*(4), 323–328.

Hoyle, M. A., & Moseley, A. (2012). Community: The wisdom of crowds. In *Using games to enhance teaching and learning: a beginner's guide* (pp. 31–44). New York, NY: Routledge.

Hromek, R., & Roffey, S. (2009). Promoting social and emotional learning with games: "It's fun and we learn things". *Simulation & Gaming*, *40*(5), 626–644.

Hughey, L. M. (2002). *A pilot study investigating visual methods of measuring engagement during e-learning*. Report produced by The Learning Lab at the Centre for Applied Research in Educational Technologies (CARET), University of Cambridge.

Huizinga, J. (1955). *Homo ludens: A study of the play element in culture*. Boston, MA: Beacon Press.

Huizenga, J., Admiraal, W., Akkerman, S., & ten Dam, G. (2009). Mobile game-based learning in secondary education: Engagement, motivation and learning in a mobile city game. *Journal of Computer Assisted Learning*, *25*(4), 332–344.

Huizenga, J., Admiraal, W., & ten Dam, G. (2010). Claims about games: A literature review of a decade of research on the effects on learning and motivation. In B. Meyer (Ed.), *Proceedings of the 4th European Conference on Games Based Learning*. Reading, UK: Academic Conferences Ltd.

Hunicke, R., LeBlanc, M., & Zubek, R. (2004). MDA: A formal approach to game design and game research. In *Proceedings of the AAAI-04 Workshop on Challenges in Game AI* (pp. 1–5).

Iacovides, I., Aczel, J., Scanlon, E., Taylor, J., & Woods, W. (2011). Motivation, engagement and learning through digital games. *International Journal of Virtual and Personal Learning Environments*, *2*(2), 1–16.

Infante, C. C., Weitz, J., Reyes, T. T., Nussbaum, M., Gomez, F., Radovic, D., & Gómez, F. (2010). Co-located collaborative learning video game with single display groupware. *Interactive Learning Environments*, *18*(2), 177–195.

Jacques, R., Preece, J., & Carey, T. (1995). Engagement as a design concept for multimedia. *Canadian Journal of Educational Communication*, *24*(I), 49–59.

Jang, Y., & Ryu, S. (2011). Exploring game experiences and game leadership in massively multiplayer online role-playing games. *British Journal of Educational Technology*, *42*(4), 616–623.

Järvinen, A. (2009). Understanding video games as emotional experience. In B. Perron & M. P. J. Wolf (Eds.), *The video game theory reader 2* (pp. 85–108). New York, NY: Routledge.

Järvinen, A., Heliö, S., & Mäyrä, F. (2002). *Communication and community in digital entertainment services*. Tampere, Finland: University of Tampere.

Jarvis, S., & Freitas, S. De. (2009). Evaluation of an immersive learning programme to support triage training. *2009 Conference in Games and Virtual Worlds for Serious Applications*, 117–122.

Jenkins, H. (2003). Game design as narrative architecture. In N. Wardrip-Fruin & P. Harrigan (Eds.), *First person*. Cambridge, MA: MIT Press.

Jenkins, H., & Cassell, J. (2008). From Quake Grrls to Desperate Housewives: A decade of gender and computer games. In Yasmin B. Kafai, C. Heeter, J. Denner, & J. Y. Sun (Eds.), *Beyond Barbie & Mortal Kombat: New Perspectives on gender and gaming* (pp. 5–20). Cambridge, MA: MIT Press.

Jennett, C., Cox, A. L., Cairns, P., Dhoparee, S., Epps, A., Tijs, T., & Walton, A. (2008). Measuring and defining the experience of immersion in games. *International Journal of Human-Computer Studies*, *66*(9), 641–661.

Jenson, J., & de Castell, S. (2010). Gender, simulation, and gaming: Research review and redirections. *Simulation & Gaming*, *41*(1), 51–71.

Johnson, D. W., & Johnson, F. P. (2003). *Joining together: Group theory and group skills* (8th ed.). Boston, MA: Pearson Education.

Johnson, D. W., & Johnson, R. T. (1999). *Learning together and alone: Cooperative, competitive, and individualistic learning.* Boston, MA: Allyn and Bacon.

Jonassen, D., Davidson, M., Campbell, J., & Bannan Haag, B. (1995). Constructivism and computer-mediated communication in distance education. *American Journal of Distance Education, 9*(2), 7–26.

Jones, C., Ramanau, R., Cross, S., & Healing, G. (2010). Net generation or Digital Natives: Is there a distinct new generation entering university? *Computers & Education, 54*(3), 722–732.

Jones, K. (1998). Hidden damage to facilitators and participants. *Simulation & Gaming, 29*(2), 165–172.

Jørgensen, K. (2008). Left in the dark: Playing computer games with the sound turned off. In K. Collins (Ed.), *From Pac-man to pop music: Interactive audio in games and new media* (pp.163–176). Aldershot, UK: Ashgate Publishing Limited.

Jørgensen, K. (2010). Time for a new terminology? Diegetic and non-diegetic sounds in computer games revisited. In M. Grimshaw (Ed.), *Game sound technology and player interaction: Concepts and developments.* Hershey, PA: IGI Global.

Jørgensen, K. (2012). Between the game system and the fictional world: A study of computer game interfaces. *Games and Culture, 7*(2), 142–163.

Juul, J. (2005). Games telling stories? In J. Raessens & J. Goldstein (Eds.), *Handbook of computer game studies* (pp. 219–226). Cambridge, MA: MIT Press.

Juul, J. (2010). *A casual revolution: Reinventing video games and their players.* Cambridge, MA: MIT Press.

Juul, J. (2013). *The art of failure: An essay on the pain of playing video games.* Cambridge, MA: MIT Press.

Kafai, Y. B. (2006). Playing and making games for learning: Instructionist and constructionist perspectives for game studies. *Games and Culture, 1*(1), 36–40.

Kallio, K. P., Mäyrä, F., & Kaipainen, K. (2010). At least nine ways to play: Approaching gamer mentalities. *Games and Culture, 6*(4), 327–353.

Kambouri, M., Thomas, S., & Mellar, H. (2006). Playing the literacy game: A case study in adult education. *Learning, Media and Technology, 31*(4), 395–410.

Kangas, M. (2010). Creative and playful learning: Learning through game co-creation and games in a playful learning environment. *Thinking Skills and Creativity, 5*(1), 1–15.

Kapp, K. M. (2012). *The gamification of learning and instruction: Game-based methods and strategies for training and education.* San Franscisco, CA: Pfeiffer.

Kashdan, T. B., Rose, P., & Fincham, F. D. (2004). Curiosity and exploration: Facilitating positive subjective experiences and personal growth opportunities. *Journal of Personality Assessment, 82*(3), 291–305.

Ke, F. (2009). A qualitative meta-analysis of computer games as learning tools. In R. E. Ferdig (Ed.), *Effective electronic gaming in education (vol. 1)* (pp. 1–32). Hershey, PA: Information Age Publishing.

Ke, F., & Grabowski, B. (2007). Gameplaying for maths learning: Cooperative or not? *British Journal of Educational Technology, 38*(2), 249–259.

Kickmeir-Rust, M. D., Marte, B., Linek, S., Lalonde, T., & Albert, D. (2008). The effects of individualized feedback in digital educational games. In *Proceedings of the 2nd European Conference on Games Based Learning* (pp. 137–236).

Kiili, K. (2005). Digital game-based learning: Towards an experiential gaming model. *The Internet and Higher Education, 8*(1), 13–24.

Kiili, K. (2007). Foundation for problem-based gaming. *British Journal of Educational Technology*, *38*(3), 394–404.

Kiili, K., & Lainema, T. (2008). Foundation for measuring engagement in educational games. *Journal of Interactive Learning Research*, *19*(3), 469–488.

Kim, B., Park, H., & Baek, Y. (2009). Not just fun, but serious strategies: Using meta-cognitive strategies in game-based learning. *Computers & Education*, *52*(4), 800–810.

Kirschner, P. A., Sweller, J., & Clark, R. E. (2010). Why minimal guidance during instruction does not work: An analysis of the failure of constructivist, based teaching work. *Educational Psychologist*, *41*(2), 75–86.

Kirsh, D. (2005). Metacognition, distributed cognition and visual design. In P. Gärdenfors & P. Johansson (Eds.), *Cognition, education, and communication technology* (pp. 147–180). Mahwah, NJ: Lawrence Erlbaum Associates.

Klabbers, J. H. G. (2003). "Interactive learning of what?" In F. Percival, H. Godfrey, P. Laybourn, & S. Murray (Eds.), *The international simulation & gaming yearbook vol 11* (pp. 257–266). Edinburgh: Napier University.

Klabbers, J. (2006). *The magic circle: Principles of gaming & simulation*. Rotterdam: Sense Publishers.

Klopfer, E., Osterweil, S., & Salen, K. (2009). *Moving learning games forward: Obstacles, opportunities & openness*. Cambridge, MA: MIT The Education Arcade.

Kolb, D. A. (1984). *Experiential learning: Experience as the source of learning and development*. Englewood Cliffs, NJ: Prentice Hall.

Korhonen, H., & Koivisto, E. M. I. (2006). Playability heuristics for mobile games. *Proceedings of the 8th conference on Human-computer interaction with mobile devices and services – MobileHCI '06, 9.*

Korte, L., Anderson, S., Good, J., & Pain, H. (2007). Learning by game-building: A novel approach to theoretical computer science education. *SIGCSE Bulletin*, *39*(3), 53–57.

Koster, R. (2005). *Theory of fun for game design*. Scottsdale, AZ: Paraglyph Press.

Krawczyk, M., & Novak, J. (2006). *Game development essentials: Game story & character development*. Clifton Park, NY: Thompson Delmar Learning.

Kubovy, M. (1999). On the pleasures of the mind. In D. Kahneman, E. Diener, & N. Schwarz (Eds.), *Well-being: The foundations of hedonic psychology* (pp. 134–154). New York: Russel Sage Foundation.

Kuh, G. D., Kinzie, J., Schuh, J. H. & Whitt, E. J. (2010). *Student success in college: Creating conditions that matter*. San Franscisco, CA: John Wiley & Sons.

Kutner, L., & Olson, C. K. (2008). *Grand theft childhood*. New York, NY: Simon & Schuster.

LaBar, K. S., & Cabeza, R. (2006). Cognitive neuroscience of emotional memory. *Nature reviews. Neuroscience*, *7*(1), 54–64.

Lafrenière, M.-A. K., Verner-Filion, J., & Vallerand, R. J. (2012). Development and validation of the Gaming Motivation Scale (GAMS). *Personality and Individual Differences*, *53*(7), 827–831.

Lainema, T., & Makkonen, P. (2003). Applying constructivist approach to educational business games: Case REALGAME. *Simulation & Gaming*, *34*(1), 131–149.

Lazzaro, N. (2004). *Why we play games: Four keys to more emotion without story*. Oakland, CA. Retrieved 14 November, 2013 from www.xeodesign.com/xeodesign_whyweplaygames. pdf

Lazzaro, N. (2008). Are boy games even necessary? In Yasmin B. Kafai, C. Heeter, J. Denner, & J. Y. Sun (Eds.), *Beyond Barbie & Mortal Kombat: New perspectives on gender and gaming* (pp. 199–215). Cambridge, MA: MIT Press.

LeBlanc, M. (1999). Feedback systems and the dramatic structure of competition. Retrieved 14 November, 2013 from http://algorithmancy.8kindsoffun.com/cgdc99.ppt

Lee, D., & Larose, R. (2007). A socio-cognitive model of video game usage. *Journal of Broadcasting and Electronic Media, 51*(4), 632–651.

Lee, J. J., & Hoadley, C. M. (2005). Leveraging identity to make learning fun: Possible selves and experiential learning in Massively Multiplayer Online Games (MMOGs). *Innovate Journal of Online Education, 3*(6).

Lepper, M. R., & Malone, T. W. (1987). Intrinsic motivation and instructional effectiveness in computer-based education. In R. E. Snow & M. J. Farr (Eds.), *Aptitude, learning, and instruction: III. Conative and affective process analysis* (pp. 255–286). Hillsdale, NJ: Lawrence Erlbaum.

Lepper, M. R., & Greene, D. (1972). Turning play into work: Effects of adult surveillance and extrinsic rewards on children's intrinsic motivation. *Journal of Personality and Social Psychology, 31*(3), 479–486.

Lewis-Evans, B. (2010). From novice to expert – Skills, rules & knowledge. *Gamasutra*. Retrieved 14 November, 2013 from www.gamasutra.com/blogs/BenLewisEvans/20101210/88567/From_Novice_to_Expert__Skills_Rules__Knowledge.php

Lim, C. P. (2008). Spirit of the game: Empowering students as designers in schools? *British Journal of Educational Technology, 39*(6), 996–1003.

Litman, J. (2005). Curiosity and the pleasures of learning: Wanting and liking new information. *Cognition & Emotion, 19*(6), 793–814.

Lombard, M., Ditton, T., & Media, M. (1997). At the heart of it all: The concept of presence. *Journal of Computer-Mediated Communication, 3*(2), 1–23.

Lopes, R., & Bidarra, R. (2011). Adaptivity challenges in games and simulations: A survey. *IEEE Transactions on Computational Intelligence and AI in Games, 3*(2), 85–99.

Lucas, L. (1992). Interactivity: What Ii it and how do you use it? *Journal of Educational Multimedia and Hypermedia, 1*, 7–10.

Mabe, P. A., & West, S. G. (1982). Validity of self-evaluation of ability: A review and meta-analysis. *Journal of Applied Psychology, 67*(3), 280–296.

MacCallum-Stewart, E. (2011). Stealth learning in online games. In S. de Freitas & P. Maharg (Eds.), *Digital games and learning* (pp. 107–128). London: Continuum.

Maharg, P. (2004). Authenticity in learning: Transactional learning in virtual communities. In *ISAGA/SAGSAGA Bridging the gap: Transforming knowledge into action through gaming and simulation*. Atlanta, GA.

Malaby, T. M. (2007). Beyond play: A new approach to games. *Games and Culture, 2*(2), 95–113.

Malliet, S. (2006). An exploration of adolescents' perceptions of videogame realism. *Learning, Media and Technology, 31*(4), 377.

Malone, T. W. (1980). *What makes things fun to learn? Heuristics for designing instructional computer games. Challenge* (Vol. 162, pp. 162–169). Palo Alto, CA: Xerox Palo Alto Research Center.

Malone, T. W., & Lepper, M. R. (1987). Making learning fun: A taxonomy of intrinsic motivations for learning. In R. Snow & M. Farr (Eds.), *Aptitude, learning and instruction: Volume 3: Conative and affective process analyses* (Vol. 3, pp. 223–253). Hillsdale, NJ: Lawrence Erlbaum.

Manninen, T. (2001). Rich interaction in the context of networked virtual environments – Experiences gained from the multi-player games domain. In A. Blanford, J. Vanderdonckt, & P. Gray (Eds.), *Joint Proceedings of HCI 2001 and IHM 2001 Conference* (pp. 383–398). Berlin: Springer-Verlag.

Margaryan, A., Littlejohn, A., & Vojt, G. (2011). Are digital natives a myth or reality? University students' use of digital technologies. *Computers & Education, 56*(2), 429–440.

Martin, A., Thompson, B., & Chatfield, T. (2006). Alternate reality games white paper. *The New York Times*, 1–82.

Matthew, B., & Sayers, P. (1997). Group exercises – collaboration or competition? In D. Saunders & B. Cox (Eds.), *The international simulation and gaming yearbook: Research into simulations in education* (pp. 22–27). London: Kogan Page.

Mayer, R. (2001). *Multimedia learning.* Cambridge, MA: Cambridge University Press.

Mayer, R. (2005). Introduction to multimedia learning. In *The Cambridge handbook of multimedia learning* (pp. 1–16). Cambridge: Cambridge University Press.

Mayer, R. (2009). *Multimedia learning* (2nd ed.). Cambridge: Cambridge University Press.

Mayer, R., & Moreno, R. (2003). Nine ways to reduce cognitive load in multimedia learning. *Educational Psychologist, 38*(1), 43–52.

McAlpine, M., van der Zanden, L., & Harris, V. (2011). Using games based technology in formal assessment of learning. In *Proceedings of the 4th European Conference on Games Based Learning* (pp. 242–250). Reading, UK: Academic Publishing Limited.

McBride-Charpentier, M. (2011). Affordance design in Half-Life 2. *Gamasutra.* Retrieved 14 November, 2013 from www.gamasutra.com/blogs/MichelMcBrideCharpentier/20110102/88710/Affordance_Design_in_HalfLife_2.php

McCarthy, D., Curran, S., & Byron, S. (2005). *The complete guide to game development art and design.* Lewes, UK: Ilex Press.

McConnell, D. (2006). *E-Learning groups and communities.* Milton Keynes, UK: Open University Press.

McGonigal, J. (2003). 'This is not a game': Immersive aesthetics and collective play. In *Proceedings of Melbourne Digital Arts and Culture.* Melbourne: RMIT University.

McGonigal, J. (2007). Why I love bees: A case study in collective intelligence gaming. In *The ecology of games: Connecting youth, games and learning* (pp. 199–228). Cambridge, MA: The MIT Press.

McGonigal, J. (2011). *Reality is broken: Why games make us better and how they can change the world.* London: Jonathan Cape.

McMahan, A. (2003). Immersion, engagement and presence. In M. J. P. Wolf & B. Perron (Eds.), *The video game theory reader* (pp. 67–86). New York, NY: Routledge.

McMahon, M. (1997). Social constructivism and the World Wide Web – A paradigm for learning. In *Ascilite.* Perth, Australia: ASCILITE. Retrieved 14 November, 2013 from www.ascilite.org.au/conferences/perth97/papers/Mcmahon/Mcmahon.html

Medina, J. (2009). *Brain rules: 12 principles for surviving and thriving at work, home and school.* Seattle, WA: Pear Press.

Michael, D. R., & Chen, S. (2006). *Serious games: Games that educate, train and inform.* Boston, MA: Thomson Course Technology.

Miller, D. J., & Robertson, D. P. (2010). Using a games console in the primary classroom: Effects of "Brain Training" programme on computation and self-esteem. *British Journal of Educational Technology, 41*(2), 242–255.

Minsky, M. (1980). Telepresence. *OMNI, 2*(9), 45–51.

Montfort, N. (2005). *Twisty little passages: An approach to interactive fiction.* Cambridge, MA: MIT Press.

Montola, M., Stenros, J., & Waern, A. (2009). *Pervasive games: Theory and design (Morgan Kaufmann Game Design Books).* CRC Press. Retrieved 14 November, 2013 from www.amazon.com/Pervasive-Games-Theory-Design-Kaufmann/dp/0123748534

Moseley, A. (2008). An alternative reality for higher education? Lessons to be learned from online reality games. In *Paper presented at ALT-C*. Leeds, UK: ALT. Retrieved 14 November, 2013 from http://moerg.files.wordpress.com/2008/10/moseley2008a.pdf

Moseley, A. (2012a). An alternate reality for education? *International Journal of Game-Based Learning, 2*(3), 32–50.

Moseley, A. (2012b). Competition: Playing to win? In N. Whitton & A. Moseley (Eds.), *Using games to enhance teaching and learning: A beginner's guide* (pp. 57–66). New York, NY: Routledge.

Moseley, A. (2012c). Assessment and games. In N. Whitton & A. Moseley (Eds.), *Using games to enhance teaching and learning: a beginner's guide* (pp. 124–138). New York, NY: Routledge.

Moseley, A., Whitton, N., Culver, J., & Piatt, K. (2009). Motivation in alternate reality gaming environments and implications for education. In *Proceedings of the 2nd European Conference on Games Based Learning* (pp. 279–286). Reading, UK: Academic Publishing Limited.

Muehrer, R., Jenson, J., Friedberg, J., & Husain, N. (2012). Challenges and opportunities: Using a science-based video game in secondary school settings. *Cultural Studies of Science Education, 7*(4), 783–805.

Myers, D. (2010). *Play redux: The form of computer games*. Ann Arbor, MI: University of Michigan Press.

Nacke, L., & Lindley, C. A. (2008). Flow and immersion in first-person shooters: Measuring the player's gameplay experience. In *Proceedings of the 2008 Conference on Future Play: Research, Play, Share* (pp. 81–88). New York, NY: ACM.

Najjar, L. J. (1998). Principles of educational multimedia user interface design. *Human Factors: The Journal of the Human Factors and Ergonomics Society, 40*(2), 311–323.

Nardi, B. A. (1993). Activity theory and human–computer interaction. In B. A. Nardi (Ed.), *Context and consciousness: Activity theory and human–computer interaction* (pp. 1–8). Cambridge, MA: The MIT Press.

Ng, F., Zeng, H., & Plass, J. L. (2009). *Research on educational impact of games: A literature review*. New York, NY: Microsoft Research.

Norman, D. A. (2002). *The design of everyday things*. New York, NY: Basic Books.

O'Neil, H. F., Wainess, R., Baker, E. L., & Neil, H. F. O. (2005). Classification of learning outcomes: Evidence from the computer games literature. *Curriculum Journal, 16*(4), 455–474.

Okan, Z. (2003). Edutainment: Is learning at risk? *British Journal of Educational Technology, 34*(3), 255–264.

Oliver, M., & Carr, D. (2009). Learning in virtual worlds: Using communities of practice to explain how people learn from play. *British Journal of Educational Technology, 40*(3), 444–457.

Ortony, A., Clore, G. L., & Collins, A. (1990). *The cognitive structure of emotions*. Cambridge: Cambridge University Press.

Owston, R., Wideman, H., Ronda, N. S., & Brown, C. (2009). Computer game development as a literacy activity. *Computers & Education, 53*(3), 977–989.

Oxland, K. (2004). *Gameplay and design*. Harlow, UK: Pearson Education.

Ozcelik, E., Cagiltay, N. E., & Ozcelik, N. S. (2013). The effect of uncertainty on learning in game-like environments. *Computers & Education, 67*, 12–20.

Paiva, A., Dias, J., Sobral, D., Aylett, R., Woods, S., Hall, L., & Zoll, C. (2005). Learning by feeling: Evoking empathy with synthetic characters. *Applied Artificial Intelligence, 19*(3–4), 235–266.

Pannese, L., Ascolese, A., Prilla, M., & Morosini, D. (2013). Serious games for reflective learning: Experiences from the MIRROR Project. In Y. Baek & N. Whitton (Eds.), *Cases on digital game-based learning: Methods, models, and strategies* (pp. 452–474). Hershey, PA: IGI Global.

Papastergiou, M. (2009a). Digital Game-Based Learning in high school Computer Science education: Impact on educational effectiveness and student motivation. *Computers & Education, 52*(1), 1–12.

Papastergiou, M. (2009b). Exploring the potential of computer and video games for health and physical education: A literature review. *Computers & Education, 53*(3), 603–622.

Papert, Seymour. (2002). Hard fun. *Bangor Daily News*. Bangor, Maine. Retrieved 14 November, 2013 from www.papert.org/articles/HardFun.html

Paraskeva, F., Mysirlaki, S., & Papagianni, A. (2010). Multiplayer online games as educational tools: Facing new challenges in learning. *Computers & Education, 54*(2), 498–505.

Parlett, D. (2005). Rules OK or Hoyle on troubled waters. Retrieved 14 November, 2013 from www.davidparlett.co.uk/gamester/rulesOK.html

Perrotta, C., Featherstone, G., Aston, H., & Houghton, E. (2013). *Game-based learning: Latest evidence and future directions*. Slough, UK: NFER.

Piatt, K. (2009). Using alternate reality games to support first year induction with ELGG. *Campus-Wide Information Systems, 26*(4), 313–322.

Pink, D. H. (2009). *Drive: The surprising truth about what motivates us*. Edinburgh: Canongate Books Ltd.

Plass, J. L., Homer, B. D., & Hayward, E. O. (2009). Design factors for educationally effective animations and simulations. *Journal of Computing in Higher Education, 21*(1), 31–61.

Poels, K., de Kort, Y., & IJsselsteijn. (2007). It is always a lot of fun!: Exploring dimensions of digital game experience using focus group methodology. In *Proceedings of the 2007 Conference on Future Play* (pp. 83–89). Toronto, Canada: ACM.

Poris, M. (2005). Understanding what fun means to today's kids. *Young Consumers: Insight and Ideas for Responsible Marketers, 7*(1), 14–22.

Prensky, M. (2001). Digital natives, Digital immigrants. *On the Horizon, 9*(5), 1–6.

Prensky, M. (2005). Computer games and learning: Digital game-based learning. In J. Raessens & J. Goldstein (Eds.), *Handbook of computer game studies* (pp. 97–121). Cambridge, MA: MIT Press.

Prensky, M. (2006). *"Don't bother me Mom – I'm learning!"* St Paul, MN: Paragon House.

Prensky, M. (2007). *Digital game-based learning*. St Paul, MN: Paragon House Publishers.

Prensky, M. (2008). Students as designers and creators of educational computer games: Who else? *British Journal of Educational Technology, 39*(6), 1004–1019.

Qin, H., Rau, P.-L. P., & Salvendy, G. (2010). Effects of different scenarios of game difficulty on player immersion. *Interacting with Computers, 22*(3), 230–239.

Randell, C., Price, S., Rogers, Y., Harris, E., & Fitzpatrick, G. (2004). The ambient horn: Designing a novel audio-based learning experience. *Personal and Ubiquitous Computing, 8*(3–4), 177–183.

Rasmussen, J. (1983). Skills, rules, and knowledge; Signals, signs, and symbols, and other distinctions in human performance models. *IEEE Transactions on Systems, Man, and Cybernetics, 13*(3), 257–266.

Read, J., MacFarlane, S., & Casey, C. (2002). Endurability, engagement and expectations: Measuring children's fun. In *Proceedings of the Interaction Design and Children* (pp. 189–198). Germany: Shaker Publishing.

Rehak, B. (2003). Playing at being: Psychoanalysis and the avatar. In M. J. P. Wolf & B. Perron (Eds.), *The video game theory reader* (pp. 103–127). New York, NY: Routledge.

Remmele, B., & Whitton, N. (2014). Disrupting the magic circle: The impact of negative social gaming behaviours (pp. 111–126). In T. M. Connolly, L. Boyle, T. Hainey, G. Baxter, & P. Moreno-Ger (Eds.), *Psychology, pedagogy and assessment in serious games*. Hershey, PA: IGI Global.

Rice, J. W. (2007). Assessing higher order thinking in video games. *Journal of Technology and Teacher Education, 15*(1), 87–100.

Richards, D., Fassbender, E., Bilgin, A., & Thompson, W. F. (2008). An investigation of the role of background music in IVWs for learning. *ALT-J: Research in Learning Technology, 16*(3), 231.

Rieber, L. (1996). Seriously considering play: Designing interactive learning environments based on the blending of microworlds, simulations, and games. *Educational Technology Research and Development, 44*(2), 43–58.

Rieber, L. P. (2001). Designing learning environments that excite serious play. In *Proceedings of the Annual Conference of the Australasian Society for Computers in Learning in Tertiary Education*.

Rieber, L. P., Tzeng, S.-C., & Tribble, K. (2004). Discovery learning, representation and explanation within a computer-based simulation: Finding the right mix. *Learning and Instruction, 14*(307–323).

Robertson, J. (2012). Making games in the classroom: Benefits and gender concerns. *Computers & Education, 59*(2), 385–398.

Robertson, J., & Howells, C. (2008). Computer game design: Opportunities for successful learning. *Computers & Education, 50*(2), 559–578.

Robins, D., & Holmes, J. (2008). Aesthetics and credibility in web site design. *Information Processing & Management, 44*(1), 386–399.

Robinson, K. (2011). *Out of our minds: Learning to be creative*. Chichester, UK: John Wiley & Sons.

Rogers, C. (1951). *Client-centred therapy: Its current practice, implications and theory*. London: Constable.

Rogers, S. (2010). *Level up: The guide to great video game design*. Chichester, UK: John Wiley & Sons Ltd.

Rooney, P., & MacNamee, B. (2007). Students @ play: Serious games for learning in higher education. In *INTED 2007, International Technology, Education and Development*. Dublin: Dublin Institute of Technology.

Rose, M. (2013) *Chasing the whale: Examining the ethics of free-to-play games*. Gamasutra. Retrieved 14 Novmber, 2013 from www.gamasutra.com/view/feature/195806/chasing_the_whale_examining_the_.php

Ruecker, S., Sinclair, S., & Radzikowska, M. (2007). Confidence, visual research, and the aesthetic function. *Partnership: The Canadian Journal of Library and Information Practice and Research, 2*(1).

Ryan, R. M., & Deci, E. L. (2000). Self-determination theory and the facilitation of intrinsic motivation, social development, and well-being. *The American Psychologist, 55*(1), 68–78.

Ryan, R. M., Rigby, C. S., & Przybylski, A. (2006). The motivational pull of video games: A self-determination theory approach. *Motivation and Emotion, 30*(4), 344–360.

Salen, K., & Zimmerman, E. (2004). *Rules of play: Game design fundamentals*. Cambridge, MA: MIT Press.

Salen, K., Torres, R., Wolozin, L., Rufo-Tepper, R. & Shapiro, A. (2011). *Quest to learn: Developing the school for digital kids*. Cambridge, MA: MIT Press.

Sampayo-Vargas, S., Cope, C., He, Z., & Byrne, G. (2013). The effectiveness of adaptive difficulty adjustments on students' education and learning in an educational computer game. *Computers & Education, 69*, 452–462.

Sankey, M. D., Birch, D., & Gardiner, M. W. (2011). The impact of multiple representations of content using multimedia on learning outcomes across learning styles and modal preferences. *International Journal of Education and Development using Information and Communication Technology, 7*(3), 18–35.

Savery, J. R., & Duffy, T. M. (1995). Problem-based learning: An instructional model and its constructivist framework. *Educational Technology, 35*(5), 135–150.

Scaife, M., & Rogers, Y. (1996). External cognition: How do graphical representations work? *International Journal of Human-Computer Studies, 45*(2), 185–213.

Scaife, M., & Rogers, Y. (2005). External cognition, innovative technologies and effective learning. In P. Johansson & P. Gardenfors (Eds.), *Cognition, education and communication technology* (pp. 181–202). Mahwah, NJ: Lawrence Erlbaum.

Schell, J. (2008). *The art of game design: A book of lenses.* Boca Raton, FL: CRC Press.

Schmidhuber, J. (2010). Formal theory of creativity, fun, and intrinsic motivation. *IEEE Transactions on Autonomous Mental Development, 2*(3), 230–247.

Schott, G., & Kambouri, M. (2006). Social play and learning. In D. Carr, D. Buckingham, A. Burn, & G. Schott (Eds.), *Computer games: Text, narrative and play* (pp. 119–132). Cambridge: Polity Press.

Schuurink, E. L., & Toet, A. (2010). Effects of third person perspective on affective appraisal and engagement: Findings from SECOND LIFE. *Simulation & Gaming, 41*(5), 724–742.

Scoresby, J., & Shelton, B. E. (2010). Visual perspectives within educational computer games: Effects on presence and flow within virtual immersive learning environments. *Instructional Science, 39*(3), 227–254.

Selinker, M., & Snyder, T. (2013). *Puzzle craft.* New York: Puzzlewright Press.

Shaffer, D. W. (2004a). Epistemic frames and islands of expertise: Learning from infusion experiences. In *International Conference of the Learning Sciences (ICLS)* (pp. 473–480). Santa Monica, CA.

Shaffer, D. W. (2004b). Pedagogical praxis: The professions as models for postindustrial education. *Teachers College Record, 106*(7), 1401–1421.

Shaffer, D. W. (2005). Epistemic games. *Innovate: Journal of Online Education, 1*(6). Retrieved 14 November, 2013 from www.innovateonline.info/pdf/vol1_issue6/Epistemic_Games.pdf

Shaffer, D. W. (2006). Epistemic frames for epistemic games. *Computers & Education, 46*(3), 223–234.

Shaffer, D. W. (2012). Models of situated action: Computer games and the problem of transfer. In C. Steinkuehler, K. Squire, & S. Barab (Eds.), *Games, learning and society* (pp. 403–431). New York, NY: Cambridge University Press.

Sharp, J. G., Bowker, R., & Byrne, J. (2008). VAK or VAK-uous? Towards the trivialisation of learning and the death of scholarship. *Research Papers in Education, 23*(3), 293–314.

Sharritt, M. J. (2010). Designing game affordances to promote learning and engagement. *Cognitive Technology Journal, 1–2*(14–15).

Sheldon, L. (2011). *The multiplayer classroom: Designing coursework as a game.* Boston, MA: Delmar Cengage Learning.

Shute, V. J. (2008). Focus on formative feedback. *Review of Educational Research, 78*(1), 153–189.

Shute, V., & Ventura, M. (2013). *Measuring and supporting learning in games: Stealth assessment.* Cambridge, MA: MIT Press.

Siemens, G. (2006). Connectivism: A learning theory for the digital age. *International Journal of Instructional Technology and Distance Learning, 2*(1). Retrieved 15 November, 2013 from www.elearnspace.org/Articles/connectivism.htm

Sim, G., Cassidy, B., & Read, J. C. (2013). Understanding the fidelity effect when evaluating games with children. *Proceedings of the 12th International Conference on Interaction Design and Children – IDC '13, 193–200.*

Squire, K. (2005). Changing the game: What happens when video games enter the classroom? *Innovate: Journal of Online Education, 1*(6).

Squire, K. (2008). Open-ended video games: A model for developing learning for the interactive age. In K. Salen (Ed.), *The ecology of games: Connecting youth, games, and learning* (pp. 167–198). Cambridge, MA: MIT Press.

Squire, K. (2011). *Video games and learning: Teaching and participatory culture in the digital age.* New York: Teachers College Press.

Squire, K., & Barab, S. (2004). Replaying history: Engaging urban underserved students in learning world history through computer simulation games. In *Proceedings of the 6th International Conference on Learning Sciences* (pp. 505–512).

Steinkuehler, C. A. (2004). Learning in massively multiplayer online games. In Y. B. Kafai, W. A. Sandoval, N. Enyedy, A. S. Nixon, & F. Herrera (Eds.), *Proceedings of the Sixth International Conference of the Learning Sciences* (pp. 521–528). Mahwah, NJ: Lawrence Erlbaum.

Steinkuehler, C., & Oh, Y. (2012). Apprenticeship in massively multiplayer online games. In C. Steinkuehler, K. Squire, & S. Barab (Eds.), *Games, learning and society* (pp. 154–184). New York, NY: Cambridge University Press.

Steuer, J. (1992). Defining virtual reality: Dimensions determining telepresence. *Journal of Communication, 42*(4), 73–93.

Suits, B. (1978). *The grasshopper: Games, life and utopia.* Peterborough, Canada: Broadview Press.

Sung, Y.-T., Chang, K.-E., & Lee, M.-D. (2008). Designing multimedia games for young children's taxonomic concept development. *Computers & Education, 50*(3), 1037–1051.

Sutton-Smith, B. (2001). *The ambiguity of play* (New ed.). Cambridge, MA: Harvard University Press.

Sweetser, P., & Wyeth, P. (2005). GameFlow: A model for evaluating player enjoyment in games. *Computers in Entertainment (CIE) – Theoretical and Practical Computer Applications in Entertainment, 3*(3), 1–24.

Taylor, M. J., & Baskett, M. (2009). The science and art of computer games development for undergraduate students. *Computers in Entertainment, 7*(2), 1.

Thiagarajan, S. (1993). How to maximise transfer from simulation games through systematic debriefing. In S. Lodge, F. Perciva, & D. Saunders (Eds.), *Simulation and gaming yearbook, volume 1: Developing transferable skills in education and training.* London: Kogan Page.

Thomas, G. (2007). *Education and theory: Strangers in paradigms.* Milton Keynes, UK: Open University Press.

Thompson, J., Berbank-Green, B., & Cusworth, N. (2007). *The computer game design course.* London: Thames & Hudson.

Trapani, F. & Hinds, L. (2014) Three boys and a chess set. In A. Moseley & N. Whitton (Eds). *New traditional games for learning* (pp. 34–46). New York, NY: Routledge.

Trowler, V. (2010). *Student engagement literature review*. York, UK: Higher Education Academy.

Turkay, S., & Adinolf, S. (2012). What do players (think they) learn in games? *Procedia – Social and Behavioral Sciences, 46,* 3345–3349.

Turner, P., McGregor, I., Turner, S., & Carroll, F. (2003). Evaluating soundscapes as a means of creating a sense of place. In *Proceedings of the 2003 International Conference on auditory display*. Boston, MA.

Turner, P., & Turner, S. (2006). Place, sense of place and presence. *Presence: Teleoperators and Virtual Environments, 15*(2), 204–217.

Tuzun, H., Yilmazsoylu, M., Karakus, T., Inal, Y., KIzIlkaya, G., Tüzün, H., & YIlmaz-Soylu, M. (2009). The effects of computer games on primary school students' achievement and motivation in geography learning. *Computers & Education, 52*(1), 68–77.

Van der Meij, H., Albers, E., Leemkuil, H., & Meij, H. van der. (2011). Learning from games: Does collaboration help? *British Journal of Educational Technology, 42*(4), 655–664.

Van Eck, R. (2002). The effect of competition and contextualized advisement on the transfer of mathematics skills in a computer-based instructional simulation game. *Educational Technology Research and Development, 50* (3), 23–41.

Van Eck, R. (2007). Six ideas in search of a discipline. In B. E. Shelton & D. Wiley (Eds). *The design and use of simulation computer games in education* (pp. 31–60). Rotterdam: Sense Publishers.

Van Vugt, H. C., Konijn, E. A., Hoorn, J. F., Keur, I. et al. (2007). Realism is not all! User engagement with task-related interface characters. *Interacting with Computers, 19*(2), 267–280.

Vanderdonckt, J. (2003). Visual design methods in interactive applications. In M. J. Albers & M. B. Mazur (Eds.), *Content and complexity: Information design in technical communication* (pp. 171–185). Mahwah, NJ: Lawrence Erlbaum Associates.

Vargas, S. S. (2012). *The effectiveness of adaptive difficulty adjustments in educational computer games*. Bundoora, Victoria: La Trobe.

Virvou, M., Katsionis, G., & Manos, K. (2004). On the motivation and attractiveness scope of the virtual reality user interface of an educational game. In *Paper presented at the 4th International Conference on Computer Science*. Krakow, Poland.

Vogel, J. J., Vogel, D. S., Cannon-Bowers, J., Bowers, C. a., Muse, K., & Wright, M. (2006). Computer gaming and interactive simulations for learning: A meta-analysis. *Journal of Educational Computing Research, 34*(3), 229–243.

Vogler, C. (2007). *The writer's journey: Mythic structure for writers*. Studio City, CA: Michael Wiese Productions.

Vos, N., van der Meijden, H., & Denessen, E. (2011). Effects of constructing versus playing an educational game on student motivation and deep learning strategy use. *Computers & Education, 56*(1), 127–137.

Vygotsky, L. S. (1978). *Mind in society: Development of higher psychological processes* . Cambridge, MA: Harvard University Press.

Warburton, S. (2008). Loving your avatar: Identity, immersion and empathy. *Liquid Learning*. Retrieved 15 November, 2013 from www.warburton.typepad.com/liquidlearning/2008/01/loving-your-ava.html

Wenger, E. (1998). *Communities of practice: Learning, meaning, and identity*. Cambridge: Cambridge University Press.

Wenger, E. (2000). Communities of practice and social learning systems. *Organization, 7*(2), 225–246.

Werbach, K., & Hunter, D. (2012). *For the win: How game thinking can revolutionize your business*. Philadelphia, PA: Wharton Digital Press.

White, D., & Le Cornu, A. (2010). Eventedness and disjuncture in virtual worlds. *Educational Research*, 52(2), 183–196.

White, D., & Le Cornu, A. (2011). Visitors and residents: A new typology for online engagement. *First Monday*, 16(9). Retrieved 15 November, 2013 from http://firstmonday.org/article/view/3171/3049

Whitton, N. (2007a). *An investigation into the potential of collaborative computer game-based learning in Higher Education*. Edinburgh: Edinburgh Napier University.

Whitton, N. (2007b). Motivation and computer game based learning. In *Proceedings of ASCILITE 2007* (pp. 1063–1067). Singapore: ASCLITE.

Whitton, N. (2009). *ARGOSI Evaluation Report*. Bristol. Retrieved 15 November, 2013 from http://argosi.playthinklearn.net/evaluation.pdf

Whitton, N. (2010a). *Learning with digital games*. New York, NY: Routledge.

Whitton, N. (2010b). Game engagement theory and adult learning. *Simulation & Gaming*, 42(5), 596–609.

Whitton, N., & Hynes, N. (2006). Evaluating the effectiveness of an online simulation to teach business skills. *e-Journal of Instructional Science and Technology*, 9(1). Retrieved 15 November, 2013 from www.ascilite.org.au/ajet/e-jist/docs/vol9_no1/papers/current_practice/whitton_hynes.htm

Whitton, N., Jones, R., Wilson, S., & Whitton, P. (2012). Alternate reality games as learning environments for student induction. *Interactive Learning Environments*, iFirst. Retrieved 15 November, 2013 from www.tandfonline.com/doi/abs/10.1080/10494820.2011.641683

Whitton, N., & Moseley, A. (Eds.). (2012). *Using games to enhance learning and teaching: A beginner's guide*. New York, NY: Routledge.

Wideman, H. H., Owston, R. D., Brown, C., Kushniruk, A., Ho, F., & Pitts, K. C. (2007). Unpacking the potential of educational gaming: A new tool for gaming research. *Simulation & Gaming*, 38(1), 10–30.

Wilson, B. G. (1996). Introduction: What is a constructivist learning environment? In B. G. Wilson (Ed.), *Constructivist learning environments: Case studies in instructional designs* (pp. 3–8). Englewood Cliffs, NJ: Educational Technology Publications.

Witmer, B. G., & Singer, M. J. (1998). Measuring presence in virtual environments: A presence questionnaire. *Presence: Teleoperators and Virtual Environments*, 7(3), 225–240.

Wittgenstein, L. (1958). *Philosophical investigations*. Oxford: Basil Blackwell.

Wood, R. T. A. (2007). Problems with the concept of video game "addiction": Some case study examples. *International Journal of Mental Health and Addiction*, 6(2), 169–178.

Wouters, P., Spek, E. D., & Oostendorp, H. (2011). Measuring learning in serious games: A case study with structural assessment. *Educational Technology Research and Development*, 59(6), 741–763.

Wu, W.-H., Chiou, W.-B., Kao, H.-Y., Alex Hu, C.-H., & Huang, S.-H. (2012). Re-exploring game-assisted learning research: The perspective of learning theoretical bases. *Computers & Education*, 59(4), 1153–1161.

Yang, Y.-T. C., & Chang, C.-H. (2013). Empowering students through digital game authorship: Enhancing concentration, critical thinking, and academic achievement. *Computers & Education*, 68, 334–344.

Yee, N. (2006). The labor of fun: How video games blur the boundaries of work and play. *Games and Culture*, 1(1), 68–71.

Yee, N. (2007). Motivations of play in online games. *Journal of CyberPsychology and Behavior, 9*, 772–775.

Zagal, J. P. (2010). Ludoliteracy: Defining, understanding and supporting games education, Pittsburgh, PA: ECT Press.

Zapata-Rivera, D., & Bauer, M. (2012). Exploring the role of games in educational assessment. In M. C. Mayrath (Ed.), *Technology-based assessments for 21st century skills: Theoretical and practical implications from modern research* (pp. 149–172). Charlotte, NC: IAP.

Zaphiris, P., Ang, C. S., & Law, D. (2007). Individualistic versus competitive game-based E-learning. *Advanced Technology for Learning, 4*(4), 206–211.

INDEX